Warrior Cults

Warrior Cults

A HISTORY OF MAGICAL, MYSTICAL AND MURDEROUS ORGANIZATIONS

Paul Elliott

BLANDFORD

A BLANDFORD BOOK

First published in the UK 1995 by Blandford
A Cassell Imprint
Cassell PLC,
Wellington House, 125 Strand,
London WC2R 0BB

Reprinted 1996

Distributed in the United States by Sterling Publishing Co., Inc.
387 Park Avenue South, New York, NY 10016-8810

A Cataloguing-in-Publication Data entry for this title is available from the British
Library

ISBN 0-7137-2531-1

Designed by Kathryn S.A. Booth
Typeset by Litho Link Ltd, Welshpool, Powys, Wales
Printed and bound in Great Britain by Hartnolls

Contents

Introduction

There can be few periods in history that have not witnessed the rise of one cult or another. However, what defines a cult is rarely easy to agree upon. A cult can be said to be a religion, or at least a set of beliefs; to be followed by a small minority; to have practices or teachings that are to some extent secret, and generally to allow only those people who have been initiated to join in its practices. This rough definition covers most of the organizations described in this book, but we can go further. Each cult has a focus, whether it be the gratification of lust, as with the Victorian cult of the Agapemonites, the austere but childlike devotion of the Hare Krishnas or the spiritualism that characterized the Theosophists. There have, in fact, been almost as many different types of cult as there have been cults themselves – cults of love, cults of Christianity and of Islam, Eastern cults of mysticism, occult and magical cults, cults of politics and cults of murder and death.

In this book it is the growth of cults in the ancient world that interests us, and how the forces outside those cults reacted to, and persecuted, them. As in the handy blueprint above, the cults often required initiation of their membership, found themselves in the minority, and had secret beliefs that set them apart from the establishment. These beliefs often concentrated on the furtherance of the particular group's goals through violence and murder, whether that goal was the worship of the goddess Kali or the overthrow of the ruling dynasty of the day. The use of murder and terror almost always requires a great deal of secrecy to conceal these activities from the forces of law and order, so secrecy usually went hand in hand with violence. This separated the Roman legions (who had initiation ceremonies, were a minority sect with established beliefs and customs, and practised the art of war), for example, from the Middle Eastern Assassins. The latter cloaked themselves in secrecy, while the former were an open organization and part of the establishment. The Assassins were a secret cult; the legions were an army. On occasion this distinction has become blurred, as when, in modern times, special units of the armed forces have sometimes taken on the trappings of secrecy in order to carry out covert operations against the enemy. In so doing, these special forces are merely harking back to the warrior cults of the ancient world. They have tapped into a tradition of fighting against their enemies with élite troops using guile, surprise and secrecy, a tradition that has been in existence for thousands of years.

Magic also figured strongly in the cults of the ancient world, but it was not the everyday, extrovert ritual magic of the large religions (worship of such gods as Zeus, Apollo and Ahura-Mazda, for example) that they practised but the private and secret teachings of arcane traditions. Occult groups reached new heights of popularity in Greek and Roman times, and, mixed as they were with mysticism and religion, they formed a personal link between initiates and their deity through the cult's individual practices. All of the organizations discussed in this book were intensely secretive, and to retain their secrets most employed the method of initiating members, cutting them off from the mundane world, placing them in a new one where new rules of behaviour, new standards and new ideas held sway. Such social isolation made initiates utterly dependent on the cult for even the smallest of things, and it is this total dependence that bred such loyalty. Members of the Assassin sect were fanatics, induced as much by fear as by religious fervour – no doubt of the Grand Master and the austere regime over which he presided. Most cults today use fear in this way, and by crushing the individual's ego and forcing him or her to rely on the group, loyalty is guaranteed.

The Children of God cult, which still exists today, forces members to channel their worship through its enigmatic leadership; the head of the cult is both their spiritual link and their physical crutch. When women and children accused the male hierarchy of sexual abuse in the 1970s, they found that they could not leave the cult of their own free will. Some were unable to drive a car and had no idea how to go about getting a job, getting to the local supermarket, etc. Even the concept of turning to the local authorities for justice was alien, since the cult had convinced its members that the world outside was a den of iniquity.

Feelings of fear and isolation must have been far stronger in previous centuries, when the mass media did not exist to provide people with a broader outlook on life. The narrow-minded view of the world that members were fed became practically the *only* view they ever experienced, making the practice of mind control that typifies the majority of cults so much easier. The ubiquity of a magical tradition in past ages goes some way towards explaining the preponderance of occult ceremony within the secret cults of the time, but such is the reliance on magical formulae and ritual that another explanation is equally valid. They helped both to reinforce the idea that the cult was 'special', that it had access to unique and secret traditions, and to bind the initiates into the workings of the organization. Oaths, duties, curses and the fantastic powers of cult adepts kept initiates in line, and perhaps even eager to reach the dizzy heights of illumination themselves.

As with many cults past and present, including such august bodies as the Freemasons, a mechanism of advancement was often employed that kept newly initiated members lacking certain knowledge, and a great (or not-so-great) ladder of secrets underpinned the rank structure within a cult. The initiate stood on the bottom rung of the ladder and the cult leader – Grand Master, Chief Priest or whoever – occupied the very top. Military organizations divide the lowest ranks from the highest by the gulf of responsibility between them, and a traditional religion divides its priesthood from the lay membership by the former's preferential access to God. But cults employ secrets to invisibly separate the hierarchy from the lay cultists. Not all the groups discussed here are organized quite like this, but wherever esoteric magic or a policy of covert violence exists, a layer of secrets will often be in existence to cover it up and cloak it from the world at large.

Warrior Cults looks at some of the most significant violent and arcane cults of ancient history. The intention is not to introduce new arguments as to the nature or origins of these cults, disconnected as they are in time and space, but to study each organization separately, allowing direct comparison. Generally held academic views on the cults are preferred where controversy exists, and there is no attempt to synthesize the history of those included into the grand conspiracy so beloved of the writers of 'para-politics', where cults such as these are held to be the true arbiters of humankind's destiny. The featured groups are (in the main) clandestine fighting forces using magic and mysticism to achieve their goals, but the occult groups that seemed to flourish in early Greece are included because of the heavy emphasis they placed on secrecy, and on their dark and unwholesome rituals. The first chapter also takes a cursory glance at the society of ancient Sparta, geared as it was to war and the forcible suppression of its own farm workers in an attempt (not always successful) to prevent revolution. Sparta's 'warrior cult' did not involve magical ritual but is a fascinating example of a secret society of aristocrats jealous of their position and ever fearful of rebellion.

Other warrior cults at other times existed on the battlefield, glorifying in some élite status or supposed supernatural power. Two such mystical fighting groups were the Viking Berserkers, known to whip themselves into violent frenzy and unleash their unbridled fury upon the enemy, and the Celtic Riastarthae. Members of this latter class of warrior were said to be touched with the 'warp-frenzy', which turned them into twisted and distorted monsters capable of great feats. It is likely that the Riastarthae were thought of as gifted troops capable of 'psyching' themselves up into a state of frenzy, much like the Berserkers. Neither, however, qualify as a secret cult, with the organization that that entails and the secrecy that is the central theme of the groups studied in *Warrior Cults*.

The chronological cut-off point for this study of ancient cults is purely arbitrary, since the rise of industrialized society that effectively brought an end to arcane warrior cults reached some nations later than others. But in general the existence of cult activities is not earnestly charted much past 1900. The Indian thuggee cult had been crushed by then, the ninjas had been reined in by the Meiji Restoration that brought Western civilization to Japan, and the Chinese Triad Society had by then abandoned its guerrilla war against the imperial throne and moved into organized crime.

Other societies have since been reworked and given a new lease of life in the twentieth century, but these 'museum cults' are mere parodies of the earlier groups, re-creating the titles and ceremonies but empty of both belief and meaning. The Order of Bards, Ovates and Druids that was established in 1964 is almost pure fabrication, based as it is on a Druidic organization that flourished before the First World War. By 1911 this previous order numbered some 300,000 and was led by the Archdruid William McAuliffe, but it lacked both authenticity and real meaning, since few of the gentlemen practitioners can have actually *believed* in the rituals that they were performing. The famous Order of the Knights Templar was later reborn in Germany at the start of the twentieth century as the Order of the New Templars, but again the name was chosen more for its mystical connotations than for the existence of any real pedigree.

This is not to say that warrior cults have not existed this century, for sporadic outbursts of violence and magical fervour have shocked the world. From 1952 the British authorities in the crown colony of Kenya were faced with a tribal uprising of serious size and sinister intent. One tribal group, the Kikuyu, were the main protagonists in this unrest, and a Kikuyu secret society, the Mau Mau, began a campaign of murder and mayhem against the British regime and its supporters. The Mau Mau were not simple terrorists but active members of a crude magical cult that used the supernatural as another weapon of fear in its guerrilla war. In their turn, the government used magic as a defence, paying witch doctors to remove the Mau Mau oaths that had been placed on captured cultists. The Kenyan Emergency ended in January 1960, by which time the cult had been effectively suppressed.

One secret society that revels in terror and violence and has been in existence for over a century is the Ku Klux Klan. Originally a racist 'secret army', with its origins in the defeat of the Confederate South in the American Civil War, the Klan has reorientated itself to the modern social climate and now preaches Christian fundamentalism and post-nuclear survivalism. To this end it has ominously invested in paramilitary training camps and secret weapons caches.

Some of the more recently established Western cults have been led by disturbed 'messiahs' offering a dedicated group of followers the true way through violence and bloodshed. The most famous and the most shocking of these have been Charles Manson's 'family'; the gun-toting followers of David Koresh's apocalyptic cult, the Branch Davidians, who perished in the Waco siege of 1993; and the Order of the Solar Temple, which came to a bloody end with the simultaneous death of its members in Switzerland and Quebec in 1994. Other equally desperate and disturbed groups have appeared briefly in the last forty years, to be put down by the authorities, and undoubtedly more will follow. It is plain that the capacity of men and women willingly to isolate themselves from the established society around them and live out some theological fantasy is as great as ever. In addition, it is feared that the opportunities for such cults to perpetrate the kinds of mass murders of their ancestors (such as the Thugs and Assassins) are shockingly ever-present, as the recent use of nerve gas by the Japanese Aum Shinrikyo Cult attests. The need to 'belong' and the need for life to have a purpose are the most pressing causes of cult recruitment among today's disenchanted youth.

Paul Elliott,
Canterbury, Kent

CHAPTER 1
The Greek Cults of Magic

Perhaps the best known of all the cults in the ancient world is the Mystery cult at Eleusis in Greece. However, many students of the period may not have realized that the Mysteries were only one of many covert religious cults in existence at the time. This emphasis on the Eleusian cult is mainly due to the fact that it was neither a criminal organization nor a proscribed religion. It flourished under the patronage of Greece's pre-eminent city state, Athens, and its existence and outward rituals are well known to historians today; only the cult's inner ceremonies were hidden from the uninitiated. Since the religion contained this secret element in its practice, it is almost universally referred to as a 'cult'. The theme of secrecy is one that runs through almost every cult described in this book, and those of ancient Greece were no exception.

Without doubt, the Greeks had a great capacity for superstition and for combining fear with the occult. Although often thought of as supremely rational – as architects, poets, philosophers and scientists – the Greeks were just as obsessed with magic as other ancient peoples. It was the élite class of writers and teachers who tended to oppose such thinking, but to little avail. The politician Nikias, who led Athenian troops in battle, was notoriously pious and a believer in oracles and omens. During the Sicilian expedition that sailed from Greece in 415 BC, he was to lead the defeated Athenian soldiers out of danger but delayed when a sudden eclipse of the moon was taken as a bad omen for a night march. The resulting massacre cost Athens dear and the heeding of the omen by Nikias was one of the main causes of the disastrous outcome of the expedition. Generally, though, the Greeks did not allow the secret cults to play any part in politics or war. For many Greeks, the cults were low-key affairs, remnants of an older kind of worship and, for the most part, innocuous. The Greek practice of witchcraft was just such a cult, a minor religion with mysterious and occult ceremonies practised by a handful of initiates.

Witches and Werewolves
The gods of ancient Greece were thought to touch on every aspect of life and death, and for the witch with her mastery of the physical

13

world through the use of spells and enchantments, this remained true. Every witch in Greece sacrificed to Hecate, goddess of death and sterility, sorcery and the moon. Magicians do not traditionally recognize the power of deities, for, as Sir James Frazer argues strongly in *The Golden Bough*, they consider themselves the initiates of a magical science capable of achieving fantastic things without any need for divine intervention. Throughout history witches and sorcerers have been hounded by the religious establishment, as much for their staunch opposition to organized religion as for their illicit practices. Witchcraft in Greece was not the evil cult that it later became in medieval times, however, for Hecate was a recognized goddess in the Greek pantheon, and both she and her followers had a place in Greek life. But the initiates of Hecate did form a diffuse cult of magicians, cut off from the mainstream of Greek (and Roman) life. There was no organized and hierarchical cult in the sense that there was with Druids, for example, but witches perpetuated a tradition that was despised and frowned upon by their contemporaries. Hecate was the black sheep of the Olympian pantheon, and witches from Thessaly to Crete, from Rome to Ptolemaic Egypt, were her priestesses.

Almost all magical (as opposed to religious) rituals in Greece called on Hecate for help and guidance. She was believed to harness the powers of darkness and to rule the night with her army of living dead. The cult originated in Asia Minor in the worship of a moon goddess, and her early character was in fact quite benevolent. She watched over flocks and navigators; she granted men and, especially, women their desires: wealth, victory and knowledge. The Greeks worked her into their pantheon, but were never in agreement as to her lineage. Some traditions said she was the daughter of the Titans Perses and Asteria, both of whom were deities of light; others gave her parents as Zeus, king of the gods, and Hera, his wife, but explained that she fell out of favour with her mother when she stole rouge from her to give to Europa. The young goddess fled from Olympus to the world of humans, where she hid within a house, and while she hid, a woman living there gave birth, ritually contaminating the goddess. Hecate sought ritual purification and found help among a cult of magicians called the Cabeiri, who immersed her in the enchanted River Acheron that flowed in the Underworld. From that moment on she became a deity of the Underworld and received all of the trappings with which she was later associated.

The Cabeiri are commonly connected with the god of metalworking, Hephaestus, as well as the goddess of the Underworld. They were an order of magical spirits who were recognized throughout the Aegean, and may have been an actual magical cult in early Greek history, associated with fire and metallurgy. There were other legendary orders of magicians that in later times became established religious cults, and may equally have been descended from actual magical colleges. The Dactyls were skilled metalworkers and were supposed to have lived within the forests and caves of Phrygia and Crete, while the cult of the Telchines, also based on the island of Crete, as well as the island of Rhodes, had a more malign character. Not only were the Telchines formidable smiths but they were also able to control the weather, put the evil eye on their enemies and blight both crops and herds with sulphur and the waters of another river of the Underworld, the Styx.

Enchantments and black magic were the true province of Hecate, and she was able to cast such spells because although she dwelt in the Underworld as the Invincible Queen alongside Hades, she also travelled to the world of humans at night. She was called upon during purifications, expiations and all manner of magical rituals. Hecate was often thought of as one aspect of a triple goddess, an aspect that emphasized the goddess's destructive, negative powers. Not only did she reign supreme in the Underworld but as Artemis, the goddess of hunting, she held sway on earth, and she also became Luna, the moon, who commanded the night sky. As these aspects became more firmly established, the Greeks began to elaborate the dark goddess's malign and supernatural character. She also became intricately associated with the goddess Persephone, who was abducted by Hades and ruled as queen of the Underworld, a living symbol of the cycle of the seasons.

The number three played a prominent part in the worship of Hecate, and her character and representations altered according to the moon's three main cycles. With the new moon she was sometimes given a lion's head, with the full moon the head of a dog, and the old moon saw her depicted with the head of a horse. Typical statues of Hecate also show her to be triple-bodied: as a woman with a single head and three bodies, or as three women standing back to back against a pillar. The commonest statues of Hecate were columns with three faces ('triple Hecates') and these were to be found at crossroads throughout Greece. Her magic at these holy places was believed to be very powerful, and offerings were left at the bases of her statues on the eve of a full moon. As a triple-faced deity, Hecate looked in all directions at once, reflecting her strong association with the crossroads. Offerings of food were made at crossroads either to beg Hecate for arcane knowledge or to protect individuals from her nightly visits to earth. Every mortal feared the witch goddess at night, for she was believed to journey across the land clutching two burning torches and accompanied by a pack of hellhounds. A legion of the living dead made up her terrible retinue.

Hecate's favoured places to visit were the scenes of violent crimes and burials and, as already mentioned, crossroads. All things of death – tombs and ghosts, blood and terror, fear and the night – were associated with the goddess, and as she passed by mortals in the darkness, she was believed to remain utterly invisible; only dogs, with their intimate connection to Hecate, could detect her presence.

The Romans also adopted Hecate as their deity of witchcraft and dark magic, and, like the Greeks, they believed that witches who sacrificed to her were capable of real-world effects, such as the destruction of crops, the causing of illness or death, and the bringing of storms, floods and other calamities. These sorcerers were believed to gather together to practise their rituals, often at places that Hecate herself was supposed to frequent at night: crossroads, tombs and the scenes of murders. The Roman writer Lucan, in his work *Pharsalia*, dating from around the time of the Emperor Nero, provides a detailed description of the activities of a witch of Hecate. A Roman general approached the witch to ask her what fate had in store for him, and the woman, named Erichtho, consulted the dead in an attempt to help him. Her powers of communication with the Underworld were heightened by her custom of living in tombs and surrounding herself with items of the macabre and cadaverous: the grave clothes of corpses, the bones and flesh of children's funeral pyres, human skin robbed from corpses, and human eyeballs, tongues and fingernails. To summon the dead to appear before her, Erichtho called upon Hecate and Persephone, as well as the ferryman of Hell, Charon, and Hermes, who was the god who led the newly dead to their final resting place in the Underworld. Among those also invoked were the River Styx and the Kindly Ones, the Furies, the feared demons of retribution who tormented wrongdoers for their crimes.

The River Styx was invariably invoked by all who wished to converse with the dead, by those who wished to harness the dark and mysterious powers of the Underworld and by those who wished to murder by poison. Its waters were so potentially magical that a single drop of Styx water would supposedly kill someone instantly. One authority claimed that the world-conquering Greek general Alexander the Great, who died so suddenly in 323 BC, had been poisoned by Styx water.

When Hecate became recognized in Rome as a divinity of the dead and of the dark terrors of the Underworld, she was renamed 'Trivia' because of her triple-aspected statues, and also perhaps because of her three-part nature: as Selene (the moon), Diana (the huntress) and Hecate (the witch goddess). As Trivia, she was 'Goddess of the Three Ways' and was invoked in Virgil's epic tale of Roman history, *The Aeneid*. A female oracle, the Sibyl, prepares to contact the spirits of the Underworld on behalf of Virgil's hero, Aeneas, and in doing so she calls on Hecate, who originally gave the Sibyl her powers. Hecate is referred to as 'mighty in Heaven and mighty in Hell', and even though, as an oracle, she is a priestess of the god Apollo, she must still call upon Hecate when interacting with the Underworld.

In another of Virgil's works, his *Eighth Eclogue*, a witch spins a thread around the small wax and clay figure of her would-be lover to entwine him in love for her. But the magic of real-world witches was not always so innocent or harmless. A Graeco-Egyptian ritual has been discovered that was supposed to reanimate a grave corpse, and this living-dead zombie was to be sent through the streets to the house of a woman with whom the magician desired sex. At his command the corpse would kidnap the woman and return her to the magician. Love and sex seem almost inseparable from the rituals and rewards of Greek and Roman witchcraft, although Hecate was never associated with such erotic pleasures, only with the power to achieve them.

Intimately bound-up in the stories and rumours of ancient witchcraft was the belief in a breed of seductive demons who preyed upon the sexual energies of men and women. The Empusae, as they were known, were the daughters of Hecate and were ass-haunched and brazen-hoofed. Prowling around at night, they descended upon travellers and terrified them, often transforming themselves into dogs or cows. They were most feared, however, when they took the shape of beautiful and seductive maidens, for in this disguise they were thought to lay with men and suck out the life force from within them. They were greedy and rapacious, hungry and evil, and their name meant 'forcers-in'. Other demonesses called Lamiae were also regarded with equal fear, while the Romans had a tradition of fearful demons called Lemures, who pounced on victims and drank their blood.

These demons never existed, of course, but the belief in them did, and it shaped attitudes towards witches in general until by medieval times the witches of the Sabbat were thought to be living examples of these cannibal vampires. Referred to as 'night-riders', the early medieval witches were feared both for their ability to fly through the night sky to rendezvous with the goddess and for their unearthly desire to suck the warm blood from still-living victims before devouring them. These beliefs were directly descended from the folk-tales of the Greek Empusae and Lamiae, and also the Roman Lemures.

But it was not just Hecate's children who survived the downfall of Graeco-Roman civilization; the goddess herself re-emerged in the early Middle Ages to lead her macabre band of night-riders to their nightly covens. She did not survive unchanged. The post-Roman witch cult elevated the goddess's earthly aspect until the character of Hecate was eclipsed. Now Artemis, under the Roman title of Diana, became the witches' occult mistress. When a demon was exorcized from a young girl in France by St Caesarius during the sixth century, it was specifically named as 'the demon whom the peasants call Diana'. In some instances, too, the goddess became confused with a species of demoness called Dianae, and a number of these were said to have slept with magicians at the court of Pope John XXII when he launched an investigation into scandalous goings-on in 1318. According to Burchard, the eleventh-century Bishop of Worms, Diana was also well known as Herodias. Herodias, wife of Herod Antipas named in the Bible, had been virulently denounced by John the Baptist, since she had previously been the wife of his half-brother. For this sin the princess was personified as a minion of the Devil, another embodiment of Diana. The name of an ancient Teutonic goddess, Holda, was also sometimes connected with the pagan goddess.

Religious men across Europe found the stories of Diana, or Hecate, and her train of seductive, cannibalistic vampire demonesses not just believable but genuinely frightening. Hecate's night-time prowl across the Greek countryside attended by a horde of animated corpses and spectral hounds was transferred, in almost every detail, to the paranoid mind-set of medieval Europe. Women were prime suspects for this kind of activity, since Diana had a long tradition of loyal female followers in Roman and Greek times. That they were said to be able to fly must be put down to the goddess's close association with the night-riders. For the religious authorities, the women accused of witchcraft *became* the ghostly night-riders that flew with Diana each night. Every magical power that had previously been ascribed to the classical demonesses was now attributed to the witches. They flew to arcane meetings by the light of the moon on animals, broomsticks or by the use of magical ointments; they ate babies; they drank human blood; they seduced morally upstanding menfolk; they worshipped the evil she-demon Diana and renounced Christ; they partook of a great feast; and they were rewarded or punished by the goddess as they deserved.

Burchard once quoted a passage from a ninth-century tract called the *Canon Episcopi*, which was often repeated by religious writers. In it the night-time flights were described as fantasies and delusions inspired by the Devil. Other persecutors quoted the passage, although it was eventually ignored by later inquisitors, who considered it a hindrance to successful persecution, torture and execution of the witches. However, blind faith and a belief in the guilt of the accused women was strong, even if not total. Fifteenth-century writers on demonic matters actually recognized that the 'flying ointments' sometimes mentioned by suspected witches could cause the hallucinations described by the *Canon Episcopi*! Recipes for the flying ointment often included the same herbal ingredients, hemlock, hellebore root, belladonna and aconite, all of which are poisonous plants and capable of inducing hallucinogenic experiences. Again, the tradition of a flying ointment was not a medieval creation but has its origins in the witch cult of Hecate. The Roman writer Apuleius wrote in *The Golden Ass* of one witch smearing her body with a type of cream that transformed her into a bird, giving some credence to the view that the medieval witch phenomenon did not exist in a vacuum, and was not a fiction of the Church but an ancient tradition.

Many pagan cults had weathered the arrival of Christianity by transforming their deities into benign saints or local folk-heroes, but only Hecate seems to have seen her worship (or her traditions, for it is not clear how much 'Hecate worship' actually took place after the fall of Rome) persist, to be crushed centuries later. It was Margaret Murray, in her book *The Witch-Cult in Western Europe*, who first postulated the theory that the practice of witchcraft from the Middle Ages onwards was only a survival of the pagan cult of Diana.

In fact, any true lineage from the witch cult of Hecate was not to survive for long. In 1458 the French inquisitor Nicholas Jacquier identified a new cult of witchcraft that differed from the earlier night-riders. This assumption may primarily have served to side-step the comments of delusion and drug-induced fantasy that the earlier *Canon Episcopi* made about the night-riders. From now on, witches were depicted as minions of the Devil, a distinctly male figure, and the Invincible Queen faded from the public consciousness. This new Devil presided over the twisted ceremony of the witches' Sabbat, while at the same time the witch lost all of her obviously magical powers. No longer did she harbour a thirst for blood or have the ability to appear as a beautiful temptress to kill a man by sapping his life energy during sex.

Witches and sorcerers may no longer have been tied to Diana, goddess of the moon, but their mystical relationship with that heavenly body continues up to the present day. The Lunacy Act of 1842 clearly linked the moon's phases with the mental afflictions of the lunatic. The very word 'lunacy' is derived from '*luna*', Roman for the moon, and it was only as recently as the late nineteenth century that the authorities decided the moon was no longer the prime cause of madness. Of course, in modern mythology also the phases of the moon have a profound effect on that familiar supernatural creature the werewolf. From Lon Chaney to Jack Nicholson, the half-man, half-wolf is always depicted by Hollywood as a creature whose life is a slave to the cycles of the moon, with the cursed victim involuntarily becoming a fully fledged wolf during periods of the full moon. But the creatures have a much more ancient lineage than modern cinematic fiction and the folk-legends of Europe suggest.

The ancient Greeks had a cult of werewolves that practised its rituals high up in the mountain wilderness of Arcadia. The legend of its origins recounts how the second king of the Arcadian region, Lycaeon, fathered fifty sons, who went forth to establish Arcadia's towns and cities. He also founded the cult of Lycaeon Zeus ('Zeus of the She-Wolf'), but was unimpressed when the god actually visited his house one day, dressed as a traveller. Zeus declared his divinity to Lycaeon, who decided to test the god by cooking up one of his own sons as a dish! As a punishment for this blasphemous gesture, the king of the gods transformed Lycaeon into a wolf and called down lightning upon his house, destroying it. But, the legend continues, Lycaeon's sons continued the practices of sacrifice and cannibalism in an effort to halt the slaughter of their sheep and cattle by roaming wolves.

To attempt the eradication of the cult a second time, Zeus unleashed a flood upon the world, but many people survived, including the inhabitants of Parnassus. After they were woken from their sleep by the howling of nearby wolves, some of these survivors made their way into Arcadia and revived the werewolf cult yet again. Mount Lycaeus in Arcadia was known as the Sacred Peak because it was held to be the site of the birth and infancy of Zeus, and a precinct for the worship of Lycaeon Zeus was established there. Such was its holiness that any mortal who set foot within the precinct would die within the year. No living creature on the Sacred Peak was supposed to cast a shadow. Lycaeon established several altars on the summit dedicated to Zeus the She-Wolf, and the Arcadians were said to perform secret rites on the mountain of Zeus's birth, even into classical times.

The traveller and writer Pausanias learned that the Arcadians still sacrificed to Lycaeon Zeus. A young boy was killed and his entrails mixed with those of animals in a soup. This concoction was presented to the congregation of shepherds present at the sacrifice and whichever one ate the flesh of the boy became a werewolf. The man howled like a wolf and, after leaving his clothes under an oak tree, swam across the stream that ran beside the crowd to leave civilization behind. As a wolf he ran with other wolves and fed on the prey killed by his pack. Only if the werewolf was able to refrain from eating the flesh of humans for eight years would he be allowed to return to his former life. Pausanias even goes as far as to name such a reformed werewolf, Damarchus the Parrhasian, who went on to win the boxing contest at the Olympic Games after his stint as a werewolf. Such a ritual may have had its origins in the need for a local scapegoat, someone who was chosen as a living sacrifice to the Arcadian wolves. In return the farmers and shepherds of the villages would remain unmolested by the animals.

The cult of Lycaeon Zeus does not seem to have been unique. A tribe of horse-nomads called the Neuri in southern Russia were reported by the respected historian Herodotus to have werewolves of their own. Herodotus travelled extensively, learning about the customs of many different tribes, and discovered that the Neuri believed that every member of the tribe became a werewolf for a few days each year before returning to human form again.

The ancient Romans were also concerned with wolves and wolf-men, making animal sacrifices to wolves as a means of guaranteeing protection from them. A ceremony was held in the Lupercal, a cave near the Porta Romana that was associated with the she-wolf who suckled Romulus and Remus (the twin brothers who were the mythical founders of Rome). The festival that took place in the grotto was actually devoted to Faunus, the god of plants and animals, and was called the Lupercalia. Held on 15 February each year, it was in essence a fertility rite and may have involved the cult initiates taking on the role of wolf-men and carrying out magical rituals which kept the herds and flocks safe from the wolves of the countryside. Traditionally a human victim was led around the cave of the Lupercal and was then sacrificed. In later imperial Rome, these wolf-men became a respected caste of priests called the Luperci, and they dispensed with the human victim altogether, sacrificing dogs and goats instead.

When the Indians of Nootka Sound in North America initiated their young men into the tribe's secret wolf cult, called Tlokoala, the candidate feigned death as werewolves abducted him. These creatures were in fact men dressed up as wolves, with skins and face masks made from the hides of the animals. After being returned to the tribe by the werewolves, the initiate would then be 'reborn' as a wolf-man and adult member of the tribe.

Obviously, none of these werewolves existed in reality, but the persuasive aura of magic that surrounded these ancient ceremonies would have guaranteed that most of the participants believed they did. For example, the account given by Herodotus concerning the Neuri werewolves also mentions that it was not just the local tribesmen who told the werewolf story but also Greeks who lived in the area. It is likely that, as with the Luperci, the wolf-men were just that: men acting out the role of a local wolf deity as an act of propitiation.

A scapegoat for the community's ills (in the examples above, the threat from wolves) was a familiar concept to the ancients. The

Athenian government kept several ne'er-do-wells at its own expense, feeding and clothing them and providing them with shelter. When a disaster befell the city, such as famine or plague, two of these pitiful victims were brought forward, one to represent the men of Athens, the other to represent the women. After being led around the city, they were taken outside the walls and publicly stoned to death, thus expelling the evil from the city and hopefully bringing an end to its woes. According to Sir James Frazer, the Athenians performed this ritual annually, as a matter of course, during the May festival of Thargelia. Other Greek cities also carried out expulsions or the murder of scapegoats – an indication that the enlightenment associated with the classical Greeks went hand in hand with primal terror and a desperate belief in the occult.

The Eleusian Mysteries

Exactly how strong the Athenian fear of the dark and mysterious forces of the occult actually was can be judged by accounts of the disastrous Sicilian expedition in 415 BC. As already noted, one of the Athenian force's two generals was devoutly superstitious, leading the army into disaster after the omen of the lunar eclipse. The other leader of the expedition, Alcibiades, did not make it as far as Sicily, since he faced serious charges of impiety that threatened if not his life, then his career. As a result, Alcibiades jumped war galley as the expedition sailed from Athens to Sicily, and he became both an international adventurer and a political survivor. The charges laid against him were not clearly substantiated, but their grave nature had shocked and disturbed the entire city, much as rumours of a Member of Parliament engaging in a Black Mass would do today.

As the vast Athenian fleet prepared to set sail for Sicily and engage in war with the island's chief city, Syracuse, a great desecration of the city's Hermae took place throughout Athens. Hermae were little phallic statues of the god Hermes that stood at crossroads and other public places as symbols of good fortune, and comprised a quadrangular pillar surmounted by the bearded head of the god. From the pillar's centre an erect phallus protruded. On the eve of the fleet's departure, all the Hermae were mutilated, which would have been a great sacrilege and bad omen at any time, but as the city was poised to send the vast majority of its young men to war, the outrage assumed gigantic proportions. Who could have done such a thing? And why? What could have been hoped for from such a venture? Alcibiades was immediately implicated because of certain rumours that were circulating about his conduct regarding the Eleusian Mysteries. No one could see exactly *why* he would want to carry out such an act, since it could only lower morale and have detrimental effects on the forthcoming expedition, and

Alcibiades was actually responsible for persuading the Athenian voters to launch this war fleet against Syracuse in the first place.

It is likely that he was in fact guilty of the charges, but he was not the initial suspect. An aristocrat called Andokides was arrested on a charge of defacing the statues but could shed no light on the mystery. Alcibiades's association with the mutilation of the Hermae, however, came as a gift to his political opponents, who lost no time in exploiting the rumours. Also implicated was his drinking club (or *symposium*), called the Kakodaimonistai. Athenian *symposia* were aristocratic dining and drinking clubs that came together through friendship, religious ties and politics. It seems that the mutilation had been discussed at a *symposium* several days before and so the affront may have been nothing more than an aristocratic dare, a youthful attempt to defy authority. Whichever secret and political *symposium* was actually responsible for the mutilations, it may have been attempting to prevent the Athenians from sailing, and this thought terrified the citizenry. Both the mutilation and the rumours of blasphemy concerning the Eleusian Mysteries gave rise to a tangible fear that the next step would be the fall of democracy and the rise of an oligarchic tyranny inspired by the totalitarian government of Sparta. There were in existence many oligarchic *symposia*, and the possibility of a conspiracy was ever-present. Whether one of the secret oligarch clubs actually carried out this piece of symbolic vandalism as a prelude to a revolution or not, an oligarchic revolution did actually occur four years later, in 411 BC.

Alcibiades was forced to sail with the Sicilian expedition with the situation unresolved, much to his annoyance. When Athens requested that he return to the city to stand trial for the Hermae incident, he fled to the enemy state of Sparta and became a double-agent. It is clear that the revolutionary *symposia* played an important part in the later coup of 411 BC, but whether they were directly responsible for the mutilation of the sacred statues is not known. Alcibiades had the right kind of temperament for such an elaborate 'joke' and had flouted authority all his life. The city's greatest religious festival, the Mysteries of Eleusis, was parodied by Alcibiades and other members of the Kakodaimonistai. If, as is likely, he participated in, or even orchestrated, the desecration of the Hermae, one could see in that act the undertakings of a devil-may-care rogue in the mould of Sir Francis Dashwood. Unlike Alcibiades, Dashwood was no politician, but much like the Greek aristocrat, he had an infatuation with the occult and a great desire to appal his peers.

Sir Francis Dashwood was owner of West Wycombe Park, near High Wycombe in Buckinghamshire, and some time around 1755 he founded an occult society called the Knights of St Francis. A wealthy man and a dilettante, he became the group's Grand Master, organizing elaborate parodies of Christian rituals at nearby Medmenham Abbey. Like the ancient Greek Kakodaimonistai, the Knights of St Francis earned themselves a terrible reputation, soon becoming known as the Hellfire Club, and their scornful motto was 'Do what you will'. The Hellfire Club had a passion for the arts and was made up of intelligent and well-educated men, but it had an unhealthy fascination with Satanism and the erotic. Both Alcibiades and Dashwood were known to be as much obsessed with men as with women.

It was the blasphemous parodies of the Mysteries that so scandalized the Athenians, but Dashwood's intended 'audience' was less susceptible to such parody. The days of witch-hunts were over and the full force of the Enlightenment and the Industrial Revolution had already humbled established religion. The shock was not quite so great. Every Athenian, on the other hand, saw the Eleusian Mysteries as the very heartbeat of Athenian life. It was politically, socially and spiritually the most important festival of the many that Athens undertook during the year. Quite why Alcibiades chose to parody the Mysteries rather than any other religious occasion, and why the Athenians took such offence, are questions that cannot be answered without a closer look at the Mysteries themselves. For 2,000 years their home, Eleusis was one of the greatest sites of the Greek world and its contribution to the shaping of the Greek mind was significant. The Mysteries were just one aspect of Greek religion; specifically they were the annual celebrations of the elaborate, private ritual of the earth goddess, Demeter.

The religion of ancient Greece was rich and diverse, with a vast array of gods and goddesses, demi-gods and heroes to be worshipped. Each divinity had its own religious cult, with attendant devotees, priests and temples, and in this the cults were very much alike. Only the details differed; the actual structure and rationale behind each religious cult varied very little. The exception, however, was the cult of Demeter. This goddess presided over the fertility of the earth, over the development of crops and plants. Her particular duty was to guard the annual wheat and barley crops, the lifeblood of ancient Greek society. Thus her role was a vital one, for the goddess of the harvest symbolized in many ways the cycle of life.

Demeter's importance meant that she was a popular goddess and she was worshipped throughout Greece. Some of her most important cult sites were at Delos, Crete, Arcadia and the Argolid, but her greatest centre of worship was in Attica. In this part of Greece the greatest religious festivals of the Greek world took place and they were devoted to the goddess. Athens lay at the centre of the Attic community and was deeply involved in the worship of the earth goddess. In Attica, and in particular at Eleusis, Athens's close neighbour, the cult of Demeter was practised in a unique way that set it apart from the other religions of Greece. A distinct air of mystery and secrecy shrouded the cult. At the same time as it accepted people cut off from the usual religions, it limited worship to those initiated into its secrets. Worshippers were brought into a personal relationship with the goddess and perhaps secured for themselves some preferential role in the afterlife. The Eleusian Mysteries stand out in the study of Greek religion as a paradox.

The foundation of Eleusis was recorded in the Homeric 'Hymn to Demeter', written about 600 BC, and it is likely that the Mysteries were practised even then, though in exactly what form is unclear. The goddess Demeter journeyed to the little town in the guise of an old woman as she scoured the land looking for her daughter, Persephone. Persephone had been kidnapped by Hades, King of the Underworld, with the sanction of her own father, Zeus, king of the gods. As Demeter sat by one of the town's wells, the daughters of the king came across her and invited her into the palace. Engaging in idle conversation, the goddess let slip her identity and so ordered the king of Eleusis to build, below the citadel, a temple to her. When the king had done this, Demeter hid away within it, cutting herself off from the world, and she declared that she would remain within the temple until she again beheld Persephone.

Such was her universal importance that her absence immediately had profound effects on the earth: grain would not grow and all the Greeks were threatened with hunger and starvation. With the future of the human race resting on the matter, Zeus capitulated and allowed Persephone to visit her mother for two-thirds of every year, as long as she returned annually to the Underworld. Demeter then allowed the land to bloom and prosper once more, and before she returned to Olympus with her daughter, the goddess instructed the king of Eleusis in the practice of her secret rites.

Such is the mythical story concerning the origin of the Mysteries, not repeated here out of idle interest in mythography but because the story behind the Mysteries *mattered*. Many other Greek myths were fables – stories designed to explain natural phenomena, the state of contemporary society or the lineage of important families. But the cult of Demeter and the ritual of the Mysteries explained something that occurred every year, that was vital for life, that perhaps explained much more than just why agriculture was dependent on the seasons. Just as Christianity was to do 600 years after the Homeric 'Hymn', the Eleusian Mysteries retold a story about the child of a god and related the emotional and philosophical aspects of the relationship to the worshipper's everyday life. It was more than a legend or a parable; it was a reason for living.

The priest Eumolpus became the initiator of the cult of Demeter and the organizer of her Mysteries. As time passed, Eleusis was drawn into conflict with its powerful neighbour Athens, and Eumolpus led the Eleusians to war against King Erechtheus of Athens. The priest of Demeter died in the fighting, as did his sons. Eleusis was totally defeated and became an Athenian vassal some time around the writing of the 'Hymn to Demeter'. The victor quickly amalgamated its own Demeter cult with that of Eleusis, but Eleusis was able to retain independent control over the Mysteries.

Of course, it goes without saying that we know little of the actual ceremonies and rituals of the Mysteries. By definition, they were a mystery to the uninitiated. But there was more to the cult than secret rituals. The Mysteries had two aspects, one public and processional, the other highly secret and personal. Exactly how secret can be gauged by the fact that the famous Athenian playwright Aeschylus was forced to seek sanctuary at the altar of Dionysus during the performance of one of his plays, because the audience was convinced he had revealed parts of the Mysteries. To do so was punishable by death. Even into Roman times this discipline was upheld. The writer Livy remarks in the *History of Rome* that in about 200 BC two young men from another part of Greece were in Eleusis on the day of the initiations and, unfamiliar with the strict policy against outsiders witnessing the Mysteries, wandered into the Hall of Initiation (called the Telesterion) with the crowds. Their talk soon betrayed them as uninitiated and, after being questioned by the officers of the temple, their mistake was brought to light and they were executed. So harsh was the law, and so jealous were the members of the cult of their beloved Mysteries.

The Telesterion was unlike other classical religious buildings. Normally, a statue of the god or goddess stood within a temple and all ceremonies took place at the front of the building around an altar within the temple's precincts. But at Eleusis all ceremonies took place inside the huge building. The precinct of Demeter was located on the eastern slope of the ancient citadel of Eleusis, but inside the city walls. Two gateways or *propylaea*, built in Roman times, led in succession into the precinct, which was dominated by the square Telesterion. The building had been constructed some time in the sixth century BC and its roof was supported by over twenty columns. Tiers of steps were built into the four walls to seat the congregation of some 3,000 initiates and at the centre of the hall was a separate building called the Anaktoron, or storehouse, which held the sacred objects used during ceremonies.

The two festivals at Athens that incorporated the Mysteries of Eleusis were the Lesser and the Greater Mysteries. The Lesser Mysteries were celebrated annually in Athens during February. Candidates for the Eleusian cult had first to be initiated into these Mysteries, and then seven months later initiation into the Greater Mysteries followed. However, the Greater Mysteries took place only every five years, so initiations also took place every five years, rather than at each Lesser Mysteries. The Greater Mysteries were celebrated in September and began in Athens.

Two days before the festival of the Mysteries began, a great procession of *epheboi* (youths) from the city marched to Eleusis and brought back the sacred objects from the Telesterion to Athens with much ceremony and celebration. A temple called the Eleusinion had been constructed at the base of the Acropolis in Athens to house the relics when they arrived in the city. Whatever the sacred relics were, the eyes of the uninitiated could not look upon them, and so they were conveyed to Athens in round boxes tied with purple ribbons. The objects were small enough to have been carried in their boxes by the priestesses of the cult, and both they and the sacred objects were transported by wagon on the journey, paid for by the Athenian government.

Upon arrival at Athens on the first day of the Mysteries proper (called the 'Gathering'), the candidates for initiation (the *mystai*) assembled in the Agora at a place called the Painted Portico. They may have come from as far away as Thessaly, Crete, Asia Minor and even the Greek colonies overseas, such as Alexandria or southern Italy. So important to the Greek world was the festival that heralds were sent out demanding a truce to allow candidates for initiation to travel to Eleusis. There, a holy proclamation was read to the candidates; also present were the Mysteries' two clans of priests, the Hierophantes and the Diaduchos. Entry fees for the cult were probably paid here, and the amount was quite high: at the cult's peak the initiation fee stood at 15 drachmae, which was roughly equivalent to about ten days' wages for a skilled labourer. Each initiate had to declare that he was fit to enter the Mysteries, that he harboured no evil, that he had not committed any crimes of violence and that he had lived a just life. The word 'he' is used here, but women were as welcome as men, and even slaves were admitted into the Mysteries. Both these underclasses were usually repressed and cut off from normal Greek society, but the Mysteries were refreshingly different. However, the Greeks still retained their loathing of non-Greeks – 'barbarians' – and banned them from entry into this cult. Only the Romans in later times were able to flout this rule. Every step of the way, an initiated cult member guided the candidate through each part of the Mysteries. These *mystagogoi*

27

could be friends, relatives or business associates, and for some were total strangers, but they provided an essential human element in the enrolment, something other religions could not do, and indeed had no need of, since traditional Greek religions *had* no human element.

The second day of the festival was called 'Seaward, Initiates!', and during it the initiates of the cult gathered together and drove on carts to the nearby harbour-town of Piraeus. There they waded into the sea with pigs (the sacrificial animal of Demeter) which were to be bathed and purified in saltwater. After returning to Athens, the pigs would be sacrificed to Demeter and a pork feast would be held by all the initiates. One must have cut the throat of his pig while still in the sea, for it is reported that in 339 BC a shark attacked one of the *mystai* and bit off his legs. This was seen as a bad omen for Athens.

The third and fourth days of the Mysteries were taken up with sacrifices and the initiates' personal preparation for the rituals, no doubt helped by their *mystagogoi*. On the fifth day the festival reached a climax, with the sacred objects journeying back to Eleusis, accompanied by the *mystai* and their *mystagogoi*, the *epheboi* and all the priests of the cult. Also travelling with the procession was a large statue of the young god Iacchus, who quickly became assimilated with Dionysus, the god of fertility. Iacchus even had a priest of his own for the journey, called the Iacchagogos. What part the god played in the Mysteries is still unclear.

The sixth and final day of the festival took place within the Telesterion. Sacrifices were made and the initiates fasted, just as Demeter had done while mourning the loss of her daughter. This fast was broken with a ritual drink called *kykeon*, which was composed of water, flour and the herb pennyroyal (wine was prohibited to members of the cult). At some point during this day the *mystai* were initiated fully into the Mysteries of Eleusis and the true nature of the sacred objects was revealed to them. Formulae were probably repeated, dramas and plays were probably performed that re-enacted the life of Demeter, and the 'meaning of life' would have been shared with the *mystai*. It is likely that the Hierophantes entered the Anaktoron at the centre of the Telesterion and, re-emerging with the sacred objects, were bathed in a bright light that contrasted with the darkness of the hall. Such a highly visual display may have rested at the heart of the initiation; indeed the very highest grade of initiation was called the Epoptai (or 'those who have gazed at something').

The Hierophantes were different in many ways from traditional Greek priests. They wore very elaborate, holy robes of a type found only in Greek tragedies, whereas priests elsewhere wore ordinary clothing. The effect was the transformation of the caste into a kind of royalty; later changes forbad the use of personal names, just as the

Japanese emperor eschewed his personal name in favour of a ritual title. Athenian priests were temporary officiants, members of the congregation drawn by lot to lead the ceremonies for the respective god or goddess, but the Hierophantes were a hereditary caste chosen from the Eleusian family of Eumolpidai, which traced its ancestry back to the early kings of the city. Athens did nothing to change this arrangement, but instituted a new level of priesthood called the Diaduchos ('torch-holder'), who were recruited from an Athenian family in Eleusis called the Kerykes. By not replacing but instead supplementing the official priesthood, the Athenians retained the loyalty of the Eleusian worshippers but were also obviously able to gain some controlling interests.

The reasons why the Mysteries played such an exceptional part in *Athenian* as opposed to Eleusian life, and why Alcibiades could scandalize the city with his behaviour, were to do with the powerful status of Eleusis in the Athenian-controlled Delian League. This was actually an enforced hegemony of allied states owing almost feudal obligations to Athens, and the city flourished under financial, religious and honorific contributions. For the Delian League, and for Athens especially, the absorption of Eleusis (complete with its Mysteries) was of great significance. The Mysteries had become almost pan-Hellenic and attracted a vast number of potential initiates and other visitors. Athens took for itself much of the praise heaped upon the cult, since the city had effectively hijacked it as its own. Athens may have considered the cult a valuable tool in uniting the Greek world around Athens and the Delian League, but it was also a showcase for the best that the city had to offer. All Greeks could witness the spectacle and drama of the vast procession, and participate in the mystery and secrecy surrounding the cult. The Mysteries stood as a symbol of the unity and strength of the Delian League.

This fully explains the hostility which Alcibiades provoked when he parodied the inner rituals of the Mysteries. He was committing an act of treason as well as blasphemy, and in fifth-century-BC Greece the distinction between the two was almost completely blurred. No doubt an attempt to transfer the Mysteries to Athens was made soon after Eleusis came under the city's control, but the attachment of Demeter to the region was too great for this to succeed, and so the great city had to be content with the visit of the sacred objects during the Greater Mysteries. This was a symbol of the new relationship, of the vassal acknowledging its suzerain.

King Kleomenes of Sparta had invaded Attica in the early fifth century BC to ravage the city of Eleusis and destroy the cult centres of Demeter and Persephone. When he later killed himself in an insane fit, the Athenians blamed his madness on divine retribution for his blasphemous attack on the Mysteries. Other states saw it differently, which illustrates how much importance Athens placed on, and how it protected, its adopted cult. Xenophon, the general and writer, praised the Mysteries and their unifying role in the local Attic community; it was at once a religious and a political element in Athenian life, a shared 'secret' that bound the disparate elements of Greece and Athens together. The cult failed to spread its membership across the entire Greek peninsula, however, and Athens failed to achieve the goal of creating a Greek superstate around the Delian League. This ambition was effectively dashed for ever when Greece was torn apart by the devastating Peloponnesian War that saw the Delian League shattered and Athens's status in Greece severely reduced.

However, the Mysteries were not extinguished just because Athenian power in the world was a shadow of its former self. The Roman Empire of later times fully recognized the special role that the Mysteries played in the religious life of the Greeks and the festival began to be attended by Roman citizens. Two Roman emperors, Hadrian and Marcus Aurelius, were initiated into the Mysteries and the Christian emperor Valentian allowed them to continue even after he had suppressed all other pagan cults and Mystery religions. The cult finally came to an end during the reign of Theodosius I in the last decades of the fourth century AD.

And Alcibiades? Whether or not he truly wanted to create disharmony in Athens and the Delian League by parodying the Mysteries, and whether or not his drinking club was partaking of a drunken dare, he felt the wrath of an indignant Athens. But on his return to the city in 407 BC, he more than atoned for his sin by reinstituting the procession to Eleusis, which had been abandoned during the Peloponnesian War due to Spartan incursions. He did this by sheer force, sending out scouts and posting hilltop guards, and surrounding the priests and *mystai* with an armed guard of hoplite troops. The Eleusian Mysteries had never been treated in such a serious manner, contrasting utterly with the scandal of eight years previously. So short a memory did the Athenians have of Alcibiades's impiety that it was decided to refer to his generalship as a 'hierophantship' or a 'leadership-of-the-*mystai*'!

The Orgiastic Cult of Dionysus

Dionysus has already been mentioned in connection with the Eleusian Mysteries, but the god had a strange and mysterious cult of his own. Like Demeter, he became a god of vegetation and of fertility in general, and for this reason his worship took on a similar aspect to hers at Eleusis. The cult was not originally Greek but came from Thrace. It always remained strongest there, and also in Greek Asia

Minor across the Aegean Sea, but it eventually won popularity throughout ancient Greece. As the cult grew in size and changed in outlook, the nature of the god also changed. From a god of wine and simple pleasures, Dionysus became a vegetation deity, a god of civilization in general, and was finally regarded as a supreme god by a Dionysiac subcult called Orphism. The Orphic Mystery religion based its worship around Dionysus, just as the Eleusian Mysteries focused on the trials of Demeter. But there were other aspects and other types of worship of the god.

In Greece, Dionysus's worship originally centred on the region called Boeotia, and his female devotees were supposed to sacrifice a boy to him each year. Later, this festival was known as the Agrionia and the sacrificial victim became a foal rather than a human being. From its earliest days the cult had a sordid reputation, presided over as it was by priestesses called Maenads who engaged in boisterous and emotionally charged worship out in the wilderness. Typically, the Maenads, with their fawn-skins and crowns of ivy, led the female devotees into the countryside. Their arms and faces were often ritually painted and many of the Maenads carried a thyrsus, a sacred wooden wand topped with a pine-cone and entwined with ivy. Others carried burning torches with which to light the way, since their frenzied ceremonies took place at night under the influence of wine and (probably) the intoxicating effects of chewing laurel leaves. During the Maenads' rituals they tore apart sacrificial animals with their bare hands and ate the flesh raw to commemorate the dismemberment of their god Dionysus at the hands of the Titans. No wonder the cult was shunned and feared by the ancient Greeks!

The Athenians worshipped Dionysus annually at a festival called the Lenaia, named, one theory has it, after an alternative title for the Maenads. This festival took place in January, during midwinter, and may have been an attempt to magically revive the plant spirits. Maenads existed in Athens as an organized body, and travelled each year to the sacred city of Delphi, where they met up with other Maenads to carry out their wild orgies. Depictions of these Maenad priestesses can be found on various red-figure vases from the fifth century BC, complete with thyrsus, torches, tambourines and flutes. The absence of mythical satyrs or men of any kind (such as heroes or cult members) indicates that these scenes are depictions of real-life worship, as opposed to legendary fancy. The head of Dionysus sometimes appears atop a pillar, and the phallic symbolism is obvious.

This midnight revelry of drunken women outside the city during the Lenaia continued into the fifth century and beyond, but was overshadowed by a more sedate grand procession and a festival of plays dedicated to the god. Plutarch, a writer of ancient times, tells of a group of Maenads (also called the Thyiades) who carried out their orgiastic celebrations on Mount Parnassus, but were caught in a blizzard and had to be rescued by an expedition from Delphi.

Like the Eleusian Mysteries, the orgiastic rites of Dionysus did not wane with the fortunes of Greece, for the cult gained in popularity following the expansion of the Greek world by Alexander the Great and his successors. It later found acceptance in Republican Rome, reaching the city from the Greek communities of southern Italy by the middle of the second century BC. The Roman Dionysus was called Bacchus, his female worshippers Bacchantes, and his orgiastic ceremonies Bacchanalia. Like the rites of the Maenads, the Bacchanalia was originally an annual festival for women alone, but it began to be celebrated for five days every month, and men were soon admitted, turning the Bacchanalia into a drunken sexual orgy. With rumours that crimes and government-toppling conspiracies were being discussed at these night-time rendezvous, the Senate took action. It ultimately feared a threat to the order of Roman society, along with a breakdown of the moral fibre so vaunted by the authorities. But although measures were taken, the cult was able to establish itself as an acceptable Mystery religion by the time of Julius Caesar.

Death and thoughts of the afterlife figured prominently in the cult's rhetoric, and elements of Bacchic thought appear on cult tombs of the period. A classic Mystery religion, the cult appealed to both men and women, even accepting children into its ranks. Like the Eleusian Mysteries, it focused on emotions and the tribulations of life, paying infinitely more attention to the personal lives (and deaths) of its worshippers than to that of Bacchus himself. As the cult became more refined, its appeal to the upper classes, and to the material needs that they treasured, increased. The highly charged emotion of the earlier days had been subsumed within a cult of sexual gratification, drunkenness and debauchery. The afterlife was often seen as nothing more than this in perpetuation, and thus the cult of the Bacchae failed to provide the spiritual nourishment sorely needed in the dark days of the Empire's decline. It lost out to more exciting and more fulfilling Mystery cults, such as those of Mithras and Cybele, and ultimately to Christianity.

But that is not the end of the story. The traditional medieval Devil, with cloven hoofs, horns protruding from the forehead and forked tail, has its origins in the classical representation of Dionysus. And despite the survival of the 'civilized' aspect of Bacchus to the end of the Empire, the primitive goat-man was the original representation of the god. He was nature incarnate and was associated not just with Pan and the Satyrs, fertility and wine, but also with the dark winter months and the Underworld. The witches' Sabbat may owe as much to Dionysus as to Hecate, since it resembled in many ways the orgiastic rites of the Maenads, with a female congregation, frenzied dancing and the presence of a goat-god.

Even more remarkable is the fact that many medieval witches spoke during their confessions of a 'dark man' or 'black man' present at the Sabbat – a description fitting the Prince of Darkness. Little known is the fact that the ancient Greek Dionysus was given the name of Melanaegis or 'he with the black goatskin' at his shrine at the town of Eleutherai. Worship of the animal god was seen as an essential part of ancient religious life, since it allowed cult members to express emotionally what their human minds could not. Wholeness was believed to be the marriage of the wild and emotional with the civilized and rational.

Elite Warrior Cults

Not all of the Greek cults were purely mystical in nature. The strictly limited citizenry of the Greek kingdom of Sparta in some way qualifies it as a 'warrior cult', as does the Theban Sacred Band of élite warriors who fought in the vanguard of Thebes's citizen army during the fourth century BC. Neither has the religious or magical focus that typifies the other cults in this chapter, but there are rewards in taking a closer look at these two groups.

Spartan citizenship was limited to only a handful of families. They formed a noble élite, known as the *homoioi* (the 'equals'), who indulged in physical sport and preparation for war. Their number varied: in 480 BC, at the peak of Spartan power, there were perhaps 8,000 Spartiate citizens; in 371 BC, following humiliating and costly defeats, the number had fallen to 1,500 and the concept of an élite Spartan citizenry was in crisis. While the *homoioi* retained their tenuous hold on power, the agricultural and industrial work was carried out by an oppressed group called the *helots*. This was a population of state slaves, bound to the Spartan government and working on estates to support individual Spartan families.

The *helots* had been physically conquered and enslaved, and were ready to revolt at the first opportunity; in order to prevent this, the whole of Spartan society was geared for war. Education, politics, eating and sleeping habits, the role of women and the state all combined to maintain a tiny section of society ready to act against the very people supporting it. And each year the Spartan government declared war on the entire *helot* population, thus absolving in advance any Spartan citizen who murdered a member of this slave caste. In fact the murder of *helots* became a method of state terrorism, designed to instil fear into the hearts of the slaves and dissuade them from attempting rebellion. Just as a secret cult adopts violence and secrecy to protect itself, the Spartans defended their puny minority with guile in one hand and force in the other.

33

A tradition called the *krypteia* that had evolved may have begun as a form of initiation for youths into the Spartan citizen cult, but it degenerated into a night-time slave-hunt. Adolescents who had completed state-regulated education were afterwards required to prove their fighting skills and their dedication to the survival of Sparta. They would go out into the night on their own and move covertly across the countryside, hoping to encounter a *helot* who had broken the curfew. When they found one, they were fully within their rights to kill him. This nightly curfew was in all probability a measure designed to prevent slaves conspiring against the state. But curfews had other uses: when a Spartan army assembled to march to war, it left the city during nightfall, thus hiding its size from the *helot* population, which might be tempted to revolt if it knew how few Spartans had been left to guard the city.

Fresh youths eager to prove their manliness by going forth into the night were not the only executioners of suspect *helots*; many slaves were also subjected to organized execution by the state. One such incident is related by the Greek historian Thucydides, who, in his *History of the Peloponnesian War*, relates how the Spartan government proclaimed that the *helots* should choose from among their own number individuals who had best served Sparta, with the implication that these slaves would be set free. Around 2,000 *helots* were selected, and the Spartans, realizing that the most adventurous and high-spirited would be the ones to nominate themselves, murdered all of them, though no one ever found out how. Thus the Spartans rid themselves of individual *helots* most likely to foment rebellion.

Deception and intrigue were the basic building blocks of Spartan home affairs. In many ways the state resembled one of the security-obsessed Eastern European governments before the collapse of Communism or the China of today. Foreigners were closely watched and their freedom of movement was often curtailed; occasionally these unwelcome visitors would be forced out of the country in a mass expulsion. The repression and murder of its own labour force took place on a daily basis, and lies and propaganda were the only forms of freely distributed information. Xenophon recorded two cases (there were undoubtedly more) of a Spartan general who, upon hearing of a defeat for the Spartans, declared the lost battle a victory to his troops in an effort to sustain morale. Such was the preoccupation of the Spartan hierarchy with the covert that it developed a method of secret communication: the *scytale*. This was a stick of a pre-determined length and breadth, around which a leather ribbon was wrapped; a message, such as orders for a general out on a campaign, would be written on the length of leather and could be read only if rewound again on a stick of exactly the same length and breadth to that which the general carried with him.

Spartan citizens trained constantly for war and were forbidden to take up any other occupation. All were soldiers, even at mealtimes, when they joined their *syssitia*, or military-style 'mess'. Every Spartan, including the two kings that ruled over the state, were forced to attend a *syssitia*. Each was a small communal dining group from which a Spartan chose both his friends and his lovers, for the Spartans believed strongly in homosexual partnerships, perhaps as an aid to morale on the battlefield. This calculated manipulation of its members' emotions again reminds us of a modern religious cult that conditions its adherents into accepting a set series of beliefs and behaving in a set way. While the Spartans were as much 'brainwashed' as members of, say, any modern fanatical cult, they accepted the conditioning through a basic need to see the survival of the Spartan *homoioi*, not because of any promised religious or mystical inner teachings. In this they differed from the Triad society, the Knights Templar, the Druids and all the other cults of this book; the Spartan government had more in common with Stalinist Russia than the deadly Assassins.

Eclipsing Sparta's hegemony over much of Greece in the fourth century BC was the city state of Thebes, and crucial to this city's military dominance was the nature of its élite fighting unit. Called the Sacred Band, its troops were all homosexual lovers. As in Sparta, it was thought that warriors who fought beside past and present lovers possessed an almost infinite loyalty to their brethren and would willingly die for them. This bizarre group of men received both the respect and the admiration of other Greek armies, and the nature of the cult earned it a fearsome reputation. Little can be related concerning the rituals of initiation or the customs of the Sacred Band, but it is thought the appellation 'sacred' was derived from the Greek word used in connection with citadels, and that the Sacred Band originally began life as a castle guard. In fact, the unit was garrisoned at the Kadmeia, the heavily fortified citadel of Thebes.

Whatever its origins, the organization had become fully established by the time of the battle of Leuctra, and boasted 300 well-trained hoplite troops led by an elected commander. The inspiration that was supposed to derive from fighting beside one's lover was something remarked on by the philosopher Plato, while Xenophon, who, unlike most Greeks, disliked the concept of homosexuality, could only pour scorn on the idea. But the Sacred Band had a legendary ancestry, for Homer's *Iliad*, the bible of the Greeks, featured the exploits of the warrior-hero Achilles and his lover, Patroclus. Indeed, in the *Iliad* Patroclus dies for the honour of Achilles, spurring the great fighter to battle. It was this 'mythic' quality that elevated the Sacred Band beyond the level of a veteran but still mundane fighting force.

When the Sacred Band suffered severely at the hands of King Philip of Macedon during the battle of Chaironeia in 338 BC, it ceased to be a functioning unit and its troops took their mythic status with them to the grave. Each of the homosexual warriors had refused to give any ground and they fought the Macedonians until they dropped. The victorious king, touched by their valour, is said to have wept openly for them.

CHAPTER 2
Cults of the Roman Empire

Religious life in the Roman Empire was awash with cults, state gods, hero-worship, exotic mysteries and philosophical colleges. Some of the greatest religions of Roman times were in fact imported from the lands that its armies conquered. The most successful were carried to the very top of the social ladder and would be represented by the emperor himself. As the reigning emperors began proclaiming their own divinity, their role in a favoured cult became more that of an avatar, the living embodiment of a god, than a religious leader. Not all foreign cults were warmly welcomed. Those of Bacchus, Isis and Cybele were at first strongly resisted by the Senate and popular sentiment. Eventually, though, they became part of the diverse tapestry of Roman religious life, successfully overcoming prejudice or suppressing the sanguinary rites that they practised. One cult that never made it as far as Rome, and would never have been accepted, despite its contemporary associations with philosophy, was Druidism.

The Druids
In the year AD 64 a great fire swept through the city of Rome, causing untold death and damage. The emperor Nero, suspected by some of starting the fire himself, was under considerable pressure to prove to the people of Rome that other forces were at work. Nero's 'sinister' forces were the Christians of the city; they were to be his scapegoats. Quickly and efficiently, free-speaking and self-proclaimed Christians were arrested, tortured and forced to name others. These too were rounded up. The Christian prisoners, without trial, or any evidence with which to conduct one, were executed for the pleasure of the citizens of Rome. Some were publicly crucified, others were dressed up in the skins of wild animals and torn apart by dogs, while the truly unfortunate were burned alive after dark, lighting up Rome as human torches. Such inhuman barbarity was almost unrivalled in Rome, but would be equalled and even surpassed in the centuries to come.

Far off on the fringes of the Empire, the newly conquered province of Britannia was proving something of a headache for Nero and his advisers. The local tribes, warlike and hot-headed, were led by a caste of fugitive priests called Druids – fugitive because Rome had sought to abolish their cruel and inhuman practices. One of their most spectacular ceremonies involved incarcerating prisoners of war, along with a variety of sacrificial animals, in huge wicker cages constructed in the form of giant men. The wicker men were set alight, burning to death the captives within. These prisoners had become sacrifices to the gods of the Druids, and such a major sacrifice would be made at a time of great need, to appease the gods or call for rainfall, healthy crops or an end to disease. Why had Nero and his predecessors decreed the total suppression of a religion that carried out acts equal to Rome's own? The people of Rome lived to a curious double-standard. They relished flagrant displays of violence in the amphitheatre, as well as the summary deaths of enemies of the state. Death for justice or entertainment, and preferably both, was seen as morally defensible. But to kill a person in the name of a god was considered an abhorrent act, a sinful thing.

In Nero's time, the Druidic elements of Celtic religion had already been forced out of Gaul. At first, the emperor Augustus had forbidden Roman citizens to join the cult, but his successor, Tiberius, went further and expelled the Druids and their rites from the whole of Gaul. Many, it would seem, fled to Britain – at that time unconquered and free. A later Roman emperor, Claudius, totally suppressed the cult in Gaul and it was at his instigation that the Roman army invaded Britain in AD 43. Some modern writers have speculated that the invasion sought to stamp out Druidism once and for all. In fact, the earlier Roman general and adventurer Julius Caesar believed that Britain was the cradle of Druidism, and had spread the practice to Gaul. From there, Druids wishing to be taught the great secrets of the cult travelled back to the British Isles for tuition.

But there was more to Rome's hatred of the Druids than the practice of human sacrifice. The caste of priests constituted a threat to the stability of the Empire in the western provinces. Caesar claimed that the Druids in Gaul met every year at a shrine among the Carnutes tribe and that a single Druid (an 'Archdruid') presided over the meeting; it is likely that equivalent bodies of Druids gathered in Britain and in Ireland. Although the Celtic tribes were distinct and autonomous, the Druidic cult that operated within them was almost pan-Celtic, as though the cult had made itself independent of any individual king or tribal chief. The Druids took care of themselves and accepted only portable gifts, rather than lands that would tie them down to a specific tribal area. The frequent journeys and meetings fostered a spirit of Celtic kinship and resistance, and may have acted as a system of intertribal communication and perhaps, Caesar feared, co-operation, especially in matters of war. Caesar was constantly assessing the threat posed by the Druids, since they were a force he had to contend with in his conquest of Gaul and his later expedition to Britain.

Druids, although exempt from taxes and military service, were often involved in warfare to some extent. They had previously been the arbiters of Celtic feuds and battles, and were able to stop opposing armies from engaging even while they lined up to fight with weapons poised. This obedience in war (and in other matters) is spoken of by the Roman author Diodorus Siculus. Caesar, in his writings, explicitly targets the Druids as political activists, fomenting revolt and organizing anti-Roman resistance. Some writers treat the Roman leader's remarks sceptically, as mere propaganda with which to scare the Roman Senate and exaggerate the Druid threat. Caesar would indeed have stood to gain from such slanderous statements. By giving the impression of Druidism as a high-level resistance movement operating from unconquered Britain and with active members in Gaul, he could get the Senate's approval for a raid across the Channel. He needed the prestige of such a raid and the spoils of war that would come with it. But if Julius Caesar *was* engaged in a mere propaganda battle, the later invasion of Britain by Emperor Claudius in AD 43 and the persecution of British Druids that followed are harder to explain.

Caesar does reveal another side to the Druids, and gives some indication of the power that they wielded within their tribes. They were the political advisers to the Celtic kings and had considerable judicial power in criminal cases. The writer Dio Chrysostom credits the priests with great authority, and not just as advisers. At a tribal assembly, every king had his Druid with him but, it is related, the king could not have his say until his Druid had spoken first. Such was the authority of the Druid! The cult may even have been able to influence the appointment of the Celtic rulers, since Caesar relates how the Druids of the Aedui elected the ruler Convictolitavis and goes on to say that such an election had happened before. The source of their power may have sprung in part from the education and great learning that they received, and was also in part due to their hereditary origins. Apprentice Druids were taken from the sons of the warrior aristocracy, and this would have legitimized the sharing of wealth and power with the tribal nobility.

Caesar may again have been exaggerating the influence of the cult in the tribal hierarchy, but this is unlikely since he was on personal terms with a Druid collaborator called Diviciacus. Also a ruler of the Aedui, Diviciacus had travelled to Rome and had met and talked with the famous Roman politician and writer Cicero; from there he returned to Gaul to aid Caesar in his struggle to pacify the Gallic tribes. The Roman general used Diviciacus as a go-between to mediate with kings and the Druid certainly helped speed Caesar's conquest of the country. Caesar does not explicitly refer to Diviciacus as being a member of the Druid sect, but Cicero certainly does, and also speaks of his powers of divination. That the Roman commander used a turncoat Celt as a mediator between rival tribes is perhaps evidence enough that Diviciacus was no ordinary warrior-chief, but a man skilled in diplomacy and someone who could act as an arbitrator.

The writer Posidonius gives an altogether different account of the priests, not as politicians but as scholars and teachers. Classical philosophers saw in Druidism a system of thought that mirrored aspects of their own, and the Druids were given the status of wise men and 'Magi of the West'. The word 'Druid' as we know it derives from a Latin form of the Celtic original, which in Old Irish is *Drui*. The meaning equates to 'Wise Men' or perhaps 'Knowledge of the Oak', a tree constantly mentioned in connection with the cult. Comparison of the word 'Druid' with the Greek word for oak tree was made by the writer Pliny and he also associates the Druids with the oak tree during their mistletoe-cutting ceremonies.

Strabo, another of Rome's pre-eminent writers, categorizes the Celtic priests as the Vates (or Ovates), who conduct sacrifices, study natural philosophy and foretell the future; the Bards, who are the poets and keepers of tribal lore; and the Druids, who study moral philosophy – that is, the laws and customs of the tribe. It is unclear whether these professions make up a single 'Druidic caste', but it seems likely that both Bards and Ovates were of lesser rank than Druids, and to reach that rank a candidate had first to officiate as an Ovate and a Bard. This would explain both the extraordinarily long apprenticeship and the overlap in role between Druids, Ovates and Bards. Druids (specifically) are recorded as both composers of verses and satires (which could kill a man) and conductors of augury. The classical writers found it difficult to discuss the role of the Druids without superimposing their own ideas on to the priests. Scholars were more interested in classifying and comparing the philosophies of the Druids with those of other priesthoods in Persia, Egypt and elsewhere. Little attention was paid to their important role within Gallic and British life.

One of the reasons that philosophers showed such an affinity with the Druids was the latter's belief in life after death. The Druids taught that the soul was immortal and upon death would go on to another body in the afterlife. Diodorus compared this belief with the teachings of Pythagoras and the 'transmigration of the soul' from body to body on *this* earth. Although Posidonius states that the Druids had assimilated Pythagoras's teachings, there is little evidence for this. But the similarities existed nevertheless, both

Pythagoreanism and Druidism cherishing calendrical and mathematical skills, according women a status unheard of in contemporary cultures, and believing strongly in the existence of another world in which life was regulated by the performance, in this life, of good deeds. On the battlefield the Celtic warrior's courage and blatant disregard for death was attributed by Julius Caesar to this belief that the soul is reborn in the afterlife.

Much of Druidic learning has been lost to us. Secrecy within the cult was paramount and the Druids believed it was taboo to commit to writing any of the order's rituals or teachings. Instead, an oral tradition had evolved and was used by the Druids to teach what they knew to others, especially the sons of nobles. Novitiate Druids, according to Caesar, could undergo training for nineteen years (the Celtic Great Year, which was the time it took for the lunar and solar calendars to coincide). This teaching included tribal history and law, the stories of creation and the gods, astrology, divination (or the reading of omens) and healing. This latter skill encompassed the use of herbs as well as of magic, for in his writings Pliny the Elder makes a reference to 'the Druids and that race of prophets and doctors', which indicates that these priests were always close to the supernatural. A late Irish source specifically refers to the Druids as magicians, as does Pliny, who also depicts them as tribal medicine men who conduct strange magical rituals.

The true nature of Druidism may never be fully known. Were its practitioners resistance leaders, diplomats, philosophers, academics or magicians? Each writer of the time put his own emphasis on the Druids. What is clear is that the Druid cult played an important role in both the mundane and the spiritual world of the Gauls and Britons. The Druids' activities as priests were paramount, giving them both secular and theological power, as well as knowledge of the supernatural.

Central to Druidic practice were the rituals of worship that the Celtic gods demanded. In pre-Roman days, such worship took place in the open air at numerous natural spots that had become sacred to the Celts, and especially sacred were the magical groves deep within the forests. Altars, effigies and ceremonial symbols could be found there, and although animals were routinely sacrificed, occasionally only a human being would do, and prisoners of war or criminals were the usual victims of these rites. The god Esus demanded that human sacrifices be hanged (presumably on a tree within the grove), while Taranis demanded death by fire and Teutates, death by suffocation. Tacitus, whose father-in-law was governor of Britain for a time, relates how the soldiers of Suetonius Paulinus discovered Druidic groves on the island of Anglesey. The altars there were soaked in human blood. Such groves, called by the Celts *nemeton*, were used by Druids across Britain and Gaul. In Lucan's *Pharsalia*, Caesar stumbled upon an ancient sacred grove deep within the forests around Massilia. His army was laying siege to the city and had entered the forests in search of timber with which to build a huge encircling wall. The branches above the grove were interwoven, creating an eerie darkness, and trees all around were splashed with human blood. The legionaries were frightened by the presence of hostile gods, images of which were primitively carved on logs. Their terror increased as strange magic enveloped the clearing. The earth shook, snakes slid across the ground and the trees seemed to burn with a magical fire. Only Caesar, in typical fashion, stood firm as his troops quaked. He took an axe and hacked at a tree, shouting out his defiance of the spirits. His loyal soldiers carried on their work, but with understandable trepidation.

Just as the ban on writing hid the thoughts and ideas behind Druidism, the *nemeton* hid its ceremonies. Of all fears, fear of the unknown is perhaps the greatest, and Romans must surely have felt uneasy about such a clandestine religion. The knowledge that human sacrifice also occurred only strengthened this unease. Besides the burning of the wicker man, there are many other accounts of human sacrifice among the cult. Female prisoners of war suffered cruelly in the holy groves, and Dio Cassius reports that their breasts would be sliced off and put over their mouths to honour the Celtic goddess Adastra. Their bodies were then impaled on stakes and hung in the *nemeton*. Some of the first-born of Celtic families are also reported as victims of the priests, especially in Ireland, where the attendant associations with fertility would bring blessings to the people. The *Dindsenchas* records that the god Crom Cruaich received a sacrifice of 'the firstlings of every issue and the chief scions of every clan'.

Buildings, too, were the objects of sacrifice, a human victim being interred within the foundations to watch over it in future years, or perhaps to placate the local earth spirits. Just as Roman governors had suppressed these practices in Gaul and Britain, St Patrick and other Christian missionaries attempted to put a stop to them in Ireland.

The Roman writers Strabo and Tacitus wrote of a ritual murder carried out by Druids that was not technically a sacrifice. The man's death, as his body reeled from a fatal sword blow, enabled the priests to predict the future, using as a guide the way he fell and convulsed and how the blood seeped from his body. As would happen with a sheep or a goat, his entrails were then scrutinized by the Druids for further omens.

If most Roman rites and political machinations were held in secret, the rituals of Celtic warriors were not. Roman legionaries will have witnessed with their own eyes the Celtic custom of head-hunting that took place after (or sometimes during) a battle. The head of one's enemy was a powerful magical talisman that not only acted as a trophy but also bound the dead man's spirit to his killer. In addition, magical symbolism credits the head with great potency. Specially shaped niches in the walls of some Celtic sanctuaries have been found that were used as 'skull niches' to display the heads of vanquished enemies, and the human head featured prominently in Druidic art as an object of great reverence and arcane power. Presumably this is why some warriors in Roman accounts also drank the blood of an enemy from his skull. Irish warriors had a similar custom, drinking an enemy's blood after washing in it. African magicians used to eat the heart of a lion to gain that animal's strength and ferocity, and it would seem that Celtic blood-drinking reflected a similar belief. But it purportedly went further. The enemy dead were actually eaten by one tribe, according to a report by Diodorus, presumably for the same magical reasons as drinking blood. None of these practices survived in Gaul under the Romans, although head-hunting by Gallic cavalrymen (after they had joined the Roman legions as auxiliaries) was not entirely stamped out. The practice must have been frowned upon.

It is not known exactly what role Druids played during battle. Irish evidence seems to indicate that they bore arms, but there is no record of them joining the fighting ranks. If it took as many as twenty years to fully educate a Druid, then it seems unlikely that he would be wasted in warfare. But the influence of the cult on the battlefield was very strong. The last bastion of Druidism in Britain, following the victories of Suetonius Paulinus, was the island of Anglesey (or Mona). Here there must have been a sanctuary for refugee Druids from British tribal centres across the country, and this cult centre organized a resistance campaign against the Roman invaders. Suetonius Paulinus moved against them, but his troops balked at the prospect of entering combat with warriors who had the support of such a magically adept priesthood. He forced his troops to cross the Menai Strait and begin destroying the *nemeton* on Mona. A large hoard of offerings was thrown into the waters of the lake Llyn Cerrig Bach by the Druids to propitiate their gods. Modern examination of the treasure shows the full extent of the influence of the Druid cult on Anglesey. Items had come from all over Britain. If Britain had its Druidic centre and regular meeting place, then Anglesey must surely have been it. The island had become a religious refuge as well as an important supply base, and it was crucial to Rome that it should be neutralized.

The account in Tacitus of the island's invasion gives us a clear indication of the Druids' ability to organize revolt, as well as instil fear in the enemy by the mere reputation of their magical powers. The Druidic practice of augury has already been mentioned, but they were formidable magicians as well as prophets. Pliny stressed the practice of the magical arts in Britain and rivalled it to the arcane traditions of Persia. As we have already seen, woods and groves played a part in their ceremonies, and oaks and mistletoe were particularly special. Both were highly revered, and the growth of the mistletoe on any tree, but especially an oak, was seen as a gift from Heaven. The plant was considered essential in fertility and medicinal magic. Although Strabo dresses the Druids in embroidered gold and scarlet robes, Pliny says that they donned white robes when cutting mistletoe. This ceremony was conducted on the sixth day of the Moon and a golden sickle was used; as the mistletoe was cut from the tree, it was caught in a white cloth. Two white bulls were then sacrificed. Such a ceremony is likely to have occurred, judging by the Celts' veneration for mistletoe, but it is unthinkable that white robes would have been worn. Surely this is Pliny's way of indicating the magicians' status, with toga-like robes. Similarly, the golden sickle must be a fabrication, since it is doubtful a golden blade would be sharp enough to cut through *anything*; bronze or even iron are far likelier materials.

Magical powers ascribed to the Druids include all kinds of elemental spells, from raising storms to causing magical fires, floods and blizzards. Day could be transformed into night and sunshine and rain could be commanded at will. The Druids of Cormac created a drought across the land but were foiled when a rival fired an arrow into the ground, fresh water flowing from the spot. Even trees and rocks could be transformed into armed warriors. There were other powers available to the priests: one often mentioned is that of shape-shifting into an animal; another was invisibility. And the magical sleep said to be induced by Druids may have been a form of hypnosis, if it existed at all. As the priests cast their spells, they often adopted the ritual stance required of the Celtic magic user: balancing on one leg with one arm outstretched and one eye closed.

When the Christian missionaries attempted to 'do battle' with the pagan gods of the Celts, they needed magic as powerful as that of the Druids, and constantly pitted their magic against that of the cult. St Columba in Scotland and St Patrick in Ireland were endowed by their chroniclers with extraordinary powers; one could even say from such descriptions that they employed Druidic magic at least as skilfully as the Druids they fought. The early Christian writers did not depict this battle as holy faith against pagan sorcery, but as Druidic magic against Christian miracle magic.

As the Romans suppressed the Druids by force, they also cut off the social links that the cult had always depended upon. Roman schools were set up to teach the children of nobles, when they would previously have gone to the Druids for education. The judicial and political systems the Romans installed also isolated the Celtic priests, until they were an out-of-touch and redundant organization. But where Rome had not penetrated, there Druidism still flourished. The religion was not crushed. Sacrifices were still offered, but now they were symbolic, involving the drawing of blood from a human victim rather than murder. Rome made no real attempt to prevent the worship of Celtic gods, just as the British did not outlaw the worship of the goddess Kali in nineteenth-century India. The *ritual practice* can be banned, but a god is only an idea, a thought, and can never be fully suppressed.

Perhaps this was the case with the Druid cult as well. Lewis Spence in *The Mysteries of Britain* puts forward the theory that Druidism survived as a radical Christian sect in the wilds of Britain. The priests of this new cult were antagonistic to any Roman authority and were totally independent. They were the Culdees, who were active in parts of Scotland, England and Ireland from the late sixth century. Culdee clerics occupied hereditary positions and were free to marry, just as the Druids had been. In addition they practised music as well as theology, and celebrated Easter a month before their cousins in Rome. Condemned as heretics in AD 813, the Culdee colleges were continually harangued by Christian scholars. Rather than merely differing on points of doctrine, they had adopted an entirely different doctrine. They condemned the Mass, refused to recognize holy relics or saints, and would not pray for departed souls. The Culdee church was not quickly suppressed but continued to worship in York until AD 936. In Fife, the Culdee sect shared the Priory at St Andrews with the established clergy up until 1124! The cult's Scottish headquarters were on the island of Iona, the Celtic name of which was Inis Druineach ('the Island of the Druids').

It was strange that the polytheistic Roman Empire, which was so willing to absorb and adopt the religions that it came into contact with, clashed so violently with Druidism. One could have expected the wholesale sanctioning of their worship. However, Rome was never tolerant when it encountered cults that dealt as much with political as with theological and philosophical issues. The practice (or merely even rumour) of human sacrifice simply added weight to the argument for a policy of suppression. But if the Roman Senate disliked the political interference of the Druids, the Druids in turn despised Rome's self-imposed imperial cult. As a religion, this state-controlled emperor-worship aimed to unify scattered kings, tribes, towns and cities across a cosmopolitan empire.

The Imperial Cults

The popular worship of a living sovereign was a peculiarly oriental practice that Republic Rome found quite disturbing. The Egyptian

Pharaoh had been worshipped as the son of the god Ra for thousands of years, and Alexander the Great, always fascinated with the East, shocked the Greeks by declaring his own divinity. The Roman state would not stomach living god-emperors for centuries, but the cult began innocently enough with Julius Caesar, who was first deified after his death. This gave his successors a precedent and Augustus, Rome's first emperor, was also made a god upon his death. Such an honour seemed to be the next logical step from the extensive honours bestowed upon the emperors in life.

It was during the reign of Augustus that appeals were made by one of the provinces to raise a shrine to the emperor as he still occupied the seat of power. Whether or not this appeal was actually inspired by Augustus himself is still unclear, but he at least made a pretence of refusing the request before capitulating and agreeing that a dual cult should be created for the worship of Rome *and* Augustus. The cult became established in the provinces, including Gaul, very quickly; at Lugdunum in 12 BC the Roman general Drusus consecrated an altar for the new religion. This imperial cult eventually extended to Rome's empresses, and participation in it became a test of loyalty and obedience for every province. The cult was essentially a fabricated religion, designed for obvious political reasons.

In Britain, the last bastion of Druidism, the imperial cult was not the popular expression towards Roman benevolence it was in the eastern provinces. Following the death (and deification) of Emperor Claudius, the construction of a great temple was begun. According to Tacitus, the temple became a symbol to the British of the Roman conquest and pacification of the country, and was seen as a 'citadel of eternal domination'. In fact, it became more than just a symbol, since wealthy Britons were required to donate large amounts for the temple's upkeep. This imposition on a province only recently conquered and despoiled was seen by another commentator on politics, Dio, as a major factor in the great Boudiccan revolt of AD 60. The Britons were obviously not happy participating in a cult that required worship of one's oppressors.

Even more strongly opposed to the imperial cult were the Jews in Roman Judaea, who were not only oppressed but also openly monotheistic. The constant tension in that land erupted into violent revolt in AD 66, when the priests of the Temple in Jerusalem refused to carry out the daily sacrifices for the emperor and Rome. The sacrifices were an act of loyalty that conflicted with the priests' devotion to God. Fighting broke out between Jews and Romans in a war that lasted until the destruction of Jerusalem in AD 70. Thirty years before, the Roman emperor Caligula had also attempted to violate the temple in Jerusalem but was assassinated before his orders could be carried out. Probably insane, Caligula had declared his own divinity and loyal gentiles in the town of Jamnia had erected an altar to him. When the altar was summarily destroyed by Jews, Caligula became enraged and ordered a giant gilded statue of himself as Zeus to be constructed and placed within the Temple. The desecration, had it gone ahead, would have certainly resulted in rebellion against the imperial cult, the Empire and the emperor. It was only in provinces where the memory of conquest had faded and prosperity under Rome had flourished that the imperial cult found loyal supporters.

During the late Roman Empire religion in Italy and throughout the imperial provinces was undergoing change. Mystery cults had never been more popular, monotheism had taken root and the imperial throne had been split in two. In AD 286 the reigning emperor, Diocletian, appointed Maximian as his colleague and co-regent, and both assumed the title of 'Augustus', indicating possession of almost sacred power derived from the first emperor of that name. These co-emperors chose 'Caesars' who would act as lieutenants and ease the governing of the Empire, but the shift in power had influences on the imperial cult, which became eclipsed by whatever god an emperor seemed to favour. Aurelian had previously proclaimed himself the living embodiment of the Unconquered Sun, and Diocletian followed his lead by adopting Jupiter as his patron god. Diocletian's co-emperor, Maximian, became Hercules; both rulers considered themselves avatars of their patron gods.

The choice of Jupiter as one's *alter ego* was obvious – Jupiter was king of the gods and the ultimate power in the universe. One appellation declared him 'Optimus Maximus' (Best and Greatest). A previous emperor, Alexander Severus, who ruled from AD 225 to 235, had also associated himself with Jupiter, but under the guise of the Romano-Syrian deity Jupiter Dolichenus. Such a fusion of religions was common everywhere in the Empire. Local gods would be equated with a similar Roman deity, and their respective cults would merge. This happened in Syria, where Rome encouraged natives to see Jupiter as a version of their own Baal, or ruling god. So successful was Jupiter Dolichenus with Rome's soldiers that they carried his cult to every corner of the Empire.

Syria was a source of labour (slaves and soldiers) for a thriving Empire and these two classes were probably responsible for the spread of the cult to the West, where it soon became the most popular of the Syrian cults. Jupiter Dolichenus first originated in the small town of Doliche in Commagene, and Roman depictions of the god show him standing on the back of a bull in full military regalia, carrying a double-axe and bolt of lightning. His consort, Juno Dolichena, stands on a hind whenever she is depicted with him.

Sometimes the deity is shown driving a chariot that is being pulled by those two beasts. The cult's sacred animals were the Roman eagle and the Syrian bull, and the twin heroes of Greece and Rome, Castor and Pollux, were holy figures that accompanied the god.

Dolichenus's greatest attribute by far was his martial prowess, and his appeal to legionaries as a god of war was great. But Jupiter Dolichenus also found adherents much higher up the social scale, among the Roman nobility. Senators and equestrians joined the cult, and, as we have already seen, the emperor Alexander Severus identified himself with the god. Not only did the cult have a large sanctuary at Baalbek (Heliopolis) but its biggest temple in Rome was actually on the Aventine Hill. Inscriptions there indicate that the religion was organized into separate dining clubs, which may be derived from worship originally in legionary messes. Alternatively it could point to a Mystery-style organization, with small groups of worshippers sharing the secret rituals of the cult. However, entire units often dedicated themselves to Jupiter Dolichenus, which contrasts with a rival Mystery cult of Mithras, whose members offered up sacrifices on an individual basis. This suggests that Jupiter Dolichenus was not interested in the personal and mystic but favoured an extrovert and open religion.

The worship of Hercules by the co-emperor Maximian was just one step in the sudden rise of a cult that boasted very humble beginnings. The hero-god embodied all the classical military virtues and found favour with emperors and soldiers alike. To the legionary, Hercules was a mortal man who excelled in war; he was a hero engaging in ceaseless tasks and courageous struggles. And for his labours Hercules was welcomed on to Olympus as a god. Of course, Maximum wanted to be associated with this hero. Hercules was a man of action, half-man and half-god – exactly the traits that another emperor, Commodus, saw in himself. This emperor encouraged the growth of the cult as an alternative to the many Eastern Mystery cults current in Rome, and considered himself a reincarnation of the god. A statue of Commodus in the Capitoline Museum depicts him dressed as Hercules, complete with lion-skin and giant club. His obsession with the divine strongman went further. Commodus was killed just as he was about to enter the gladiatorial arena in a test of his Herculean fighting prowess! When paganism surfaced briefly under Emperor Julian, who tried in vain to suppress Christianity as the imperial religion, he was actually hoping that Hercules would take Christ's place. There were definite similarities: Hercules was born semi-divine and performed many miraculous deeds during his lifetime; following an agonizing death, his soul went to the Underworld, but the gods raised him up to Heaven, from where he guided and watched over his worshippers. But the cult had no interest in mysteries or revelations, and its emphasis was on surviving the here-and-now.

Originally Hercules was an Argive folk-hero, with a tradition that encompassed almost every town and village in Greece. As each locality claimed an association with Hercules, the list of his adventures continued to grow. Among his most famous are the Twelve Labours given to him by the mythical King Eurystheus. The worship of heroes like Hercules differed from worship of the gods, and instead they were paid elaborate funerary rites in the hope of gaining their protection. When colonists settled in southern Italy. they took their heroes with them and it was at the beginning of the third century BC that the cult of Hercules reached Rome. At first it caught the imagination of philosophers and scholars, as well as more humble folk. Pythagoreanism and Stoicism focused on Hercules as an example of moral fortitude and strength of character, a figure worthy of admiration and imitation rather than worship. This aspect of personal sacrifice would be echoed in the Persian cult of Mithras, the sun god who also found favour among the legions.

Syncretization with the Unconquered Sun god was a future that several popular Roman cults, including that of Hercules, looked forward to. Roman philosophers regarded Hercules as a devotee of Apollo, the Greek god of light. Some even believed he was an actual incarnation of that god.

It was the emperor Aurelian who first established a cult of the Unconquered Sun in AD 274 and elevated him almost to the rank of Rome's foremost deity. Aurelian had been inspired by Rome's emperor of some fifty years before, the Syrian boy-priest Elagabalus, who reigned briefly from AD 218 to 222. The youth had so attracted the Syrian legions that they made him an emperor and took him to Rome, where he immediately established the cult of his native sun god, Elagabal. This was the sun god from Emesa who originally began as a Syrian Baal but followed the trend for the growth of sun cults. The sun had commonly come to be appreciated as the most powerful of the heavenly bodies, and the supreme symbol of divinity.

While he reigned, Elagabalus had little grasp of imperial politics, throwing open the Senate to all races and describing the members of that august body as mere slaves. The fourteen-year-old priest even imported to Rome from Emesa the god's sacred black stone, which was associated with Elagabal's worship. With theology uppermost in his mind, he began the process of usurping all other religions and placing at the Empire's head a single god and a single unifying faith. Two temples were built for Elagabal in the imperial capital, but young Elagabalus was assassinated before the cult could really take root. However, the idea of a single, all-powerful deity that encompassed every other and was represented on earth by a god-emperor would not go away.

Mithras, Lord of Light

It would be Christianity in the end that became the official religion of the Roman Empire, but the pagan sun gods did not give up without a fight. Constantine, the first Christian emperor, had previously been a devotee of the Unconquered Sun, Helios. He had replaced the head of the huge statue of the god Helios in the Forum with his own, and his associations with the sun god were numerous. Constantine repeatedly equated Christ with the pagan Helios; he saw a great similarity between the two religions.

There was one sun god in the later centuries of the Roman Empire who seriously challenged Christ for state recognition. The Persian sun cult of Mithras competed with Christianity, and lost . . . just. Contemporary writers sometimes thought of Mithras as a mere shadow, a pagan copy of Christianity. There *were* definite similarities, if not links, between the two religions, and this relationship is remarkable, since Mithras was primarily a cult of warriors not pacifists. On many levels, in fact, the worship of Mithras stands out from that of both the traditional Latin gods and the many imported Mystery cults. It was a Mystery religion with massive appeal, a religion made for the traveller and soldier, a religion that seemed to capture the very essence of the *imperium*. Mithraism was the state religion that should have been.

The cult, like many in the late Empire, was an import from the East. Mithras is commonly depicted wearing a forward-swept 'Phrygian' cap, which identifies him as coming from Asia Minor, Rome's major contact point with the East. It was a land long familiar with Mithras. In the first century BC his name was popularly taken up by local kings, such as Mithridates of Pontus, as well as those in Commagene and Cappodocia. The god also appears on a relief on the mausoleum of Antiochus I (king of Commagene) at Nemroud Dagh. It was during the military campaign against the pirates of Cilicia in the mid-first century BC that Romans first encountered this god. Plutarch records in his *Life of Pompey* that the pirates made sacrifices to several of their oriental gods on Mount Olympus, one of which was Mithras. In the first century AD, in his poem *Thebais*, the poet Statius mentions Mithras and his famous struggle with the mythological bull from which it would seem that the name of Mithras was common knowledge at about this time.

When worshippers of Mithras began establishing temples in the city of Rome, there was little public outcry and no senatorial condemnation or fuss. Unlike several other Mystery cults, such as those of Isis, Bacchus or Cybele, Mithraism became accepted almost overnight. It had been carried to Rome by the vast population movements occurring on a daily basis throughout the Empire. Most of this population was enslaved, and much of the traffic was from east to west. As the slaves travelled, their faith came with them, for as slaves they had nothing else. When large concentrations of slaves were put to work together in Italy on the large state-owned farms or in workshops, it is hardly surprising that old religions from homelands far away were re-established and worship began once more. So it was, too, with those provincial legionaries forced to leave their native soil and spend a lifetime marching from one end of the Empire to the other.

The old Roman frontiers have been the source of many inscriptions and dedications from soldiers to Mithras, and the movements of these troop units can often be tracked back to a station in the East. Mithras travelled with these people, and temples were eventually to be found around the entire Mediterranean. Many were clustered in the ports and cities on important trade routes; it was there that slaves, soldiers and other converts would meet and establish a local temple for worship. In Rome, forty-five temples of Mithras (Mithraea) were in use; similarly, at the great cosmopolitan centres of Alexandria, Carthage and London Mithraea were in abundance. The ports of Piraeus, Puteoli and Ostia also had temples of Mithras. Although the god's name originally meant 'light', it later came to be associated with the word 'contract' and Mithras became popular with traders and merchants as a deity of oaths and obligations. Undoubtedly the greatest spread of Mithraea was throughout the legionary forts and camps of the Roman army. Only a small proportion of these have survived to be identified, but the soldiers of the Empire were the most numerous worshippers of the god. And his appeal was strong.

Imperial acceptance of the god was never very significant. The first to acknowledge Mithraism was Nero, who invited Tiridates, the king of Armenia, to Rome. According to Pliny the Elder, the king (who was also a high priest of the cult) was accompanied by members of a Persian priesthood called Magi. They initiated the emperor into magic banquets, which must have been the sacramental meal that was eaten by worshippers of Mithras.

In some ways, Mithraism and the plethora of other Mystery cults were attempts to rekindle something that had been lost in Roman religion. The traditional gods of Rome when it was no more than a single city state had at first been local, the worshippers members of the same tribe or district, and the rituals personal. The rise of the vast Republic had turned these religions into state organizations that appealed to Roman citizens and subjects far and wide. They became impersonal, extrovert and very public. Perhaps it was the sheer size of these official religions that allowed the Mysteries to gain a foothold. In addition, they provided worshippers with answers – about the universe and life itself. Some, such as the cult of Bacchus, offered immortality to the faithful and divine punishment for the uninitiated. The establishment feared them, not least because they promoted licentiousness and an emotional emphasis to worship. Mithraism was certainly one of these Mystery cults, but it was at the same time remarkably different. The initiates were bound to follow the god's moral guidelines of truth and chastity. Mithras himself was not just a spiritual force but had a detailed life history, beginning with his birth from the rock and culminating in his heroic struggle with the sacred bull. This is the most common depiction of Mithras, standing astride a bull with a dagger plunged deep into its neck. It is the Tauroctone, the god's sacrifice of the cosmic bull for the benefit of humankind. From the animal all life and fertility flowed. With sadness, the hero carried out the duty given to him by Ahura-Mazda, supreme god of light. Mithras's trials and labours were all well known, but none of his life had been ritualized, as was usual with the Mysteries. Unusually, there was no annual drama celebrating the birth, death or life of Mithras. Perhaps an important factor in the lack of a rebirth drama lay in the fact that Mithras didn't die each year, like Adonis or Bacchus or Persephone in the Eleusian Mysteries. He had died once and been reborn as a god; he had become immortal and, with perseverance and sacrifice, so would his initiates.

The Mithraic aspect of sacrifice and asceticism did appeal to Rome's soldiers, and much of Mithraism mirrored army life. With its emphasis on austerity, toil and struggle, the cult spoke directly to the tough legionary. He could identify with its ideals, as opposed to the self-consuming and contemplative cults of the intellectuals. Mithras was not a god of violence and killing, but of soldiering in general. For the soldier, Mithras was the unconquerable god; one of his later titles was 'Sol Invictus', the Unconquered Sun. The god had struggled through many adversities, but his courage and determination guaranteed him success. For initiates of Mithraism, life itself was seen as a battle between good and evil, angels and demons, and his worshippers could easily have seen in the great wars of their time some cosmic significance. The cult was able to elevate the warrior from apologist for his crimes to fighter on the frontline for the destiny of the universe. And for initiates this conflict continued even in death.

The cult's military-style organization revolved around seven ranks that a worshipper could pass through; the membership was all-male and the emphasis was on ordeals and initiation trials. Initiates had to match Mithras's toughness and austerity, especially during the ritual tests for entrance and promotion. It is difficult to say whether Mithras 'the Warrior' was worshipped in Asia Minor, from where he originated, or whether this aspect of the god was an invention by the Romans, but the martial nature of Mithras certainly flourished and developed with the legions. One of the ranks, attainable by passing a test, was actually called 'Soldier'. The worshipper had to push a crown from his head so that it fell to his shoulder. As he did this he would state, 'Mithras is my crown.' Other ordeals tested the initiate's courage and determination and allowed him to prove himself to his god. One test involved the aspirant's hands being tied behind his back with chicken guts, then he would be thrown across or have to jump a water-filled pit while blindfolded. At the Mithraeum excavated at Carrawburgh a pit used for this purpose has been found. Other horrible rites took place in the temples, including ritual brandings and tortures. Bloody swords are reported and depicted, to be used in a ritualized mock murder. But rumours were circulated of actual human sacrifices during ceremonies. Whether true or false, the emperor Commodus insisted that an actual execution be carried out during his initiation. The emperor's extravagance was a blasphemy; the ordeals and staged murder were an invention to create fear for fear's sake, not to enact a Mithraic fable. The ordeals would have helped the new member to feel a sense of personal achievement and a bonding that was far stronger than that created by mere attendance. Again, this was a military reinforcement, somewhat similar to the harshness of basic army training, seemingly so cruel, pointless and brutal, but for a purpose.

The titles of the initiation levels were all masculine, which reflects the restriction of membership to men, and their meanings were astrological, each rank representing one of the planets. These levels, in ascending order, were:

Raven The Raven was Ahura-Mazda's messenger and represented Mercury. On frescos and mosaics the initiate holds a cup and the *caduceus* (the winged staff with two serpents entwined around it).

Bride Since the congregation was all-male, this title had a masculine ending. The Bride carried a lamp, and wore a diadem and yellow veil, representing Venus.

Soldier Unsurprisingly, the rank of Soldier was equated with Mars, and initiates at this level are depicted in brown clothes and carry a spear and legionary's pack.

Lion The Lion represented Jupiter and he clutched a lightning bolt in one hand and a rattle in the other. He was associated with fire. Since water was hostile to fire, honey was used to wash with during Lion initiations. It was commonly regarded as a magical substance that preserved and sweetened, cleansed and purified.

Persian Initiates who had attained this rank are depicted in grey clothing and wield the implements of agriculture: a scythe, a sickle and ears of corn. Astrologically, the Persian was the moon.

Messenger of the Sun As the title would imply, this rank was associated with the sun. In mosaics the emblems of a crown radiating light, a burning torch and a whip are featured. The whip was used to drive the sun's chariot across the sky each day.

Father This was the highest rank in Mithraism. The Father was usually chosen by the worshippers of that temple and he presided over worship, initiations and the astrological destiny of the cultists. He is represented as a red-robed figure wearing a Phrygian cap and holding a sickle and a staff. He is Saturn.

It is tempting to think that during ceremonies worshippers would have donned the clothing and paraphernalia appropriate to their rank, but for that there is no evidence. Together the congregation would gather in the small Mithraeum and conduct its sacred rituals. Few excavated temples could hold more than 100 worshippers; most were much smaller. The oblong temples were symbolic caves, imitating the mythical cave in which Mithras slew the sacred bull. To this end a Mithraeum was usually of a sunken design or a converted cellar. Long benches lined the sides of the tiny room, and at the far end stood a statue of Mithras wrestling with the sacred bull, flanked on either side by his retainers, the *dadiphori*. These torch-bearers accompanied Mithras in much of the cult's artwork. Reliefs and altars also decorated the end of the Mithraeum and the room would have been filled with the sweet smell of pine-cone incense. Mithraism actually practised baptism and the members ate a sacramental meal. Other ritual acts included the imitation of animals sacred to the god – initiates flapped their arms like the raven and growled like lions. Reliefs in Mithraea that have been excavated show worshippers wearing animal and bird masks to support these reports. It is likely that some of the ceremonies ended with the sacrifice of a bull to the god. Much as Mithras enriched the world with the life-giving fertility of the dying bull, so too his worshippers would kill a bull, not for the benefit of the god but for the benefit of mankind.

The Tauroctone was the central event of Mithras's life and provides the theme for much of his worship. He was given the task to capture the first living creature – the sacred bull – by the Persian supreme deity, Ahura-Mazda, who sent the order via his Raven messenger. Both Mithras and Ahura-Mazda fought on the side of good against evil, represented by Ahriman, Lord of Darkness, and his army of demons. The entire basis for Mithraism is the dualism of light and darkness: the eternal fight between good and evil. When Mithras had captured the bull, he dragged it into a cave and, against his wishes, he slew it. Many statues and paintings preserve this moment, often with the sun and moon flanking the struggle, sometimes along with the two torch-bearers, Cautes and Cautopates. Mithras's faithful hound accompanies the god, while Ahriman's demons, Snake, Ant and Scorpion, attempt to poison the dying bull and prevent this miracle of life taking place. Mithras is dressed in typical 'Persian' costume, with long trousers, tunic and pointed Phrygian cap. There is a look of sorrow on his face. To the cult, this event has as much importance as the Crucifixion – from death life is born. Although there were several concurrent interpretations as to the meaning of the Tauroctone, the central idea is that all life flowed from the bull. To release it, the bull must be killed. Some representations of the bull depict corn-stalks flowing from the knife wound, or give the bull three stalks of corn where his tail should be. This symbolizes the fertile nature of the bull and illustrates its importance in agrarian societies. Mythologically, bull's blood is magically potent, even poisonous. An inscription in the Sancta Prisca Mithraeum in Rome reads: 'And you saved us by having shed the eternal blood.'

The death of the sacred bull allowed all life to flourish, including the first human couple. Mithras protected them from the ravages of Ahriman and then made ready to depart the mortal world. He brought together his disciples, Cautes and Cautopates, and ate a celebratory Last Supper. This event was remembered in Mithraism by a ritual meal of bread and wine. Then Mithras ascended to Heaven in the sun god's chariot, and from Heaven he continued to watch over his followers. Some accounts tell of his eventual return to destroy the world in fire and lead the faithful to Heaven.

The cult had an interest in astrology, no doubt brought from its origins in Persia. The advancement of initiates from planet to planet and further into the Mysteries was seen as the ascent of a ladder up which the soul travelled. The ultimate goal was Heaven. Ladder-shaped amulets of bronze have been discovered in tombs, along with incriptions bearing the names of the planets.

There are two opposing accounts of Mithras's birth into the world. Usually he springs from the Generative Rock, fully armed with knife and torch and ready for action. His alternate birth is from the Cosmic Egg (often surrounded by the zodiac circle, in Mithraic iconography). This account clearly indicates some Greek influence in later Mithraism. Greek influence in the religion began almost as soon as the West learned of its existence. Mithras as bull-slayer is also not a Persian artistic idea, but may have been directly copied from a Greek Victory sculpture at Pergamum in Asia Minor. The cult never did have a unified mythology, since there was no unified cult. Each Mithraeum carried out its worship independent from the rest. The different monuments and inscriptions show little consensus of symbolism, although the character and nature of the cult seem to have remained geographically uniform. It would appear that some Fathers of Mithras did not understand what their artisans were painting or carving. For example, in some instances Mithras is put in opposition to the sun, in others he is the sun. As to his birth, is he born of rock or egg?

At the time of the emperor Commodus, who ruled from AD 180 to 192, Mithras was becoming increasingly associated with the sun.

The god's solar aspect went back over two centuries, and his increasing popularity had led to his assimilation of Ahura-Mazda. To the Romans now he was Mithras the Warrior, and also Mithras the Lord of Light and Supreme God. As we have already seen, other sun gods would also find popularity in the Empire, merging to become the single 'Sol Invictus' that was championed by Elagabalus, Aurelian and Licinus. The sanguinary interest of Commodus with the cult did not dissuade potential initiates; rather, the religion expanded further, becoming ever more popular. One definite advantage for Mithraism was the religion's relaxed approach to the worship of other gods. Mithras was not a jealous god. In fact, sculpture and reliefs devoted to other gods, such as Aion, Cybele and Serapis, have been discovered in Mithraea.

Some scholars have likened Mithraism's non-alignment, coupled with its secrecy, to that of Freemasonry. It crossed social, political and religious borders, yet bound together the initiates with both fear and camaraderie. Like the Masons, devotees of Mithras pledged to help each other no matter what, forming a close-knit brotherhood. Whether a worshipper was a senator or the lowest legionary, he had a chance of reaching the rank of Father and leading the rituals. Even educated slaves and freedmen were among the initiated. Women, however, could never join the cult, but it is doubtful that a Roman female would find the god appealing. The Mystery cult of Cybele, which had close links with Mithraism, will have instead catered for Roman women. As an alternative, Christianity also welcomed women into its congregation.

Christianity offered the same cross-class equality as Mithras. It, too, required its worshippers to live morally upstanding lives. But, unlike Mithras, it welcomed women, who were attracted by the religion's tenderness. This was a trait that was denied by Mithraic worship. By the third century AD both cults found themselves in competition with one another for the status as the major religion of the Roman Empire.

The similarities between Christianity and Mithraism may not seem significant, until certain aspects of the warrior god's mythic past are examined. Mithras was born on 25 December and, one account has it, shepherds were present at his birth. Throughout his life he strove to help humankind, and constantly fought on the side of light against the evil forces of darkness. His greatest deed was a cosmic sacrifice – a murder carried out so that all life could prosper – and before he ascended to Heaven with the aid of his master, he ate a sacramental meal with his followers. When the end of the world is close, Mithras will return to engulf it in fire and he will lead his worshippers to immortality. Only those loyal to him in life will join him on this journey. The similarity is quite striking. Did Mithras borrow from Christianity or was Mithras the inspiration for the worship of Jesus Christ? Ancient writers also asked this question, and came up with few answers. In Celsus's *True Discourses* (dating from *c.* AD 178–180) the writer directly compares the two religions. Justin Martyr believed that the pagans had copied the Christians and incorporated myth and ritual into their own worship. More modern thought favours the reverse, particularly in connection with the Last Supper and the practice of baptism. In addition, early Nativity scenes depict the Magi in 'Persian' costume, with Phrygian cap and long trousers, rather than as kings. It is unlikely, however, that wholesale plagiarism occurred. As Christianity grew, it obviously took its converts from other religions, and these were most probably (since they had much in common) other Mystery cults, of which Mithras was one. It was not difficult to imagine ex-Mithraists taking with them ideas about the universe, and how this could be translated into ceremony, across to Christianity. In the eyes of the ancient world, Christianity must have seemed to be just another Mystery cult, offering some of the same comforting rituals and beliefs as the others.

To support this idea, it is an interesting fact that the Christian apologists, so virulently anti-pagan, bitterly attacked the Mysteries and thoroughly condemned them. This may at first not seem to be proof that many early Christians had connections with the Mystery cults, but it was the resemblance of Mystery rituals with Christianity that frightened and disturbed these writers.

In the end the religion of Mithraism could not compete with Christianity. As paganism battled with its rival, Mithras was syncretized with the other sun deities, namely Apollo, Helios and the Syrian Baals. Aurelian's newly fashioned Unconquered Sun, or 'Sol Invictus', and its cult became virtually monotheistic, absorbing the characteristics and attributes of the other pagan gods. When the Roman emperor Constantine, a staunch devotee of the Unconquered Sun, became a Christian, the demise of the traditional gods and of Mithraism as the prospective state religion was final.

This is not to say that some elements of the cult's beliefs and teachings did not survive. Christianity absorbed much from the pagan West, including the cosmic struggle that was Mithras's *raison d'être*. The concept of the opposed forces of light and darkness provides Christianity with its basic moral theme, the defeat of the Devil. One of the early Christian scholars, Augustine, reflected this dualism in his *City of God* and *City of the World*. In addition, it was taken up not as a theme but as a definitive religion in its own right by the heretic Christian cult of the Gnostics. The Gnostic teachings penetrated deep into the heart of Christianity and were important in the thoughts and beliefs of later medieval groups such as the

Cathars, Bogomils, Waldensians and the Knights Templar. This latter group were, much like the warrior initiates of Mithras, dedicated to soldiering as well as to God. And it is strange to think that, although separated in time by over 700 years, they may have shared some common beliefs and traditions.

CHAPTER 3

The Order of the Knights Templar

The greatest military adventure of the Middle Ages, the Crusades, had by 1099 culminated in the defeat of hostile Arab forces and the capture of Christendom's most holy city, Jerusalem. From there other realms were carved out by the knights and lords until a loose chain of Crusader territories existed in Syria and Palestine. The Holy Land was an important prize for the Christian nobles who were settling there and beginning to raise families. But the Crusader states were never to be permanent kingdoms and were constantly menaced by the Muslim states surrounding them. Crucial to their defence was a group of pious knights, small in number but highly disciplined and skilled in combat. They were the Knights Templar.

This knightly order constitutes a medieval conundrum. Its origins, its activities and beliefs, and finally its ignominious demise are all shrouded in mystery. Much has been written about these warrior-monks who fought in the Crusades to defend Jerusalem from the marauding Arabs. Few of the questions asked have been satisfactorily answered. In fact, views of the order have varied throughout history. Nineteenth-century writers often depicted the Order of the Knights Templar as a satanic brotherhood dedicated to Devil-worship and the practice of heretical and blasphemous ceremonies. More recent scholars have tended to look upon the order with some sympathy, seeing in its persecution and fall the machinations of European power politics. A more radical theory contends that the Knights Templar were involved in an age-old conspiracy to discover and guard the Holy Grail, not an actual cup or chalice but some secret concerning the real events surrounding Jesus's death and the survival of his bloodline into medieval times.

Whether occult practitioners or holy warriors, the Knights Templar were indisputably extremely powerful. No other body or individual equalled or exceeded them in authority apart from the Pope. Blessed by this pre-eminent Bishop of Rome, the order was also destroyed by the Pope's own Inquisition. Rumours and stories circulated of a vast Templar treasure, of a planned Templar state, of high-level diplomacy between European kings, as well as attempts at reconciliation between Jews, Muslims and Christians. These stories have a firm basis in truth; yet the order began most humbly.

The Knights Templar were inspired by an already existing knightly order, the Knights Hospitallers. These were performing generous and charitable services for the thousands of pilgrims who were flocking from Europe to the new Christian Jerusalem. Many, however, did not make it to the city, but were attacked and robbed or even killed on the roads. Arab bandits were proving a constant threat to travellers, and in response the French nobleman Hughes de Payens formed a group of knights to ensure the safety of Christian pilgrims. At first only nine men strong, the tiny order called itself the Soldiers of Christ. It may have been active from as early as 1111, but by 1118 the group was granted part of the king of Jerusalem's palace for use as its headquarters. The part given over had previously been a mosque of great significance and was thought to be the site of the Temple of Solomon. Because of this latter association, the order became known as the Order of the Knights of the Temple of Solomon in Jerusalem, or the Knights Templar. Why King Baldwin II should have given over a portion of his palace to nine bedraggled knights on a mission to make safe the roads of the Holy Land is still a mystery.

The great strength of this new order was its permanence. Local soldiers were part-time warriors fighting to defend the land that had become their home. Other knights and their vassals from Europe fought for a short period and then returned to their estates. But Jerusalem needed a standing army of devoted soldiers if it was to survive, and it seemed that the Knights Templar were to be that force. But only nine men? The Holy Land covered a vast area, much of it inhospitable wilderness, criss-crossed by ancient travel routes. How could nine men defend such an area or watch over the thousands of pilgrims making their way to Jerusalem?

However they performed their avowed task, the Templars were eminently successful, mixing martial ardour with vows of poverty, chastity and obedience. Such morality was unequalled among knights of the period, who seemed to favour ostentatiousness and competition. A measure of the order's poverty and brotherhood is signalled by a seal of the Temple which depicts two knights mounted on a single horse. Clothing worn by the order during the first few years was second-hand, and nothing that could encourage pride was allowed; humility and obedience were the central tenets of the cult. Frequent references to 'the poor fellow soldiers of Christ' are made in official Templar documentation, as if to emphasize the order's humble philosophy. Other self-imposed restrictions existed, all revolving around the unique loyalty that the order owed to the Church. Hughes de Payens visualized his knights as a body of warrior-monks, devoted to God and the Church, as well as to the art of warfare.

Funding for the fledgeling order was quickly forthcoming. King Baldwin II had already granted part of his palace to the Templars, and various sections of the Church in the Holy Land followed his generous lead. When Hughes journeyed to Europe, he was warmly met by members of the clergy there. The founder of the Cistercian Order, St Bernard, the Abbot of Clairvaux, was an immediate supporter of the Templars and continued to be so until his death. In fact, Bernard's uncle, André de Montbard, was one of the group's founder members. Bernard ranked as perhaps the most influential ecclesiastic in Christendom, being able to advise (and even make nominations for) the Pope. It is this man's considerable influence with the papal authorities that gained the Knights Templar such close links with Rome. Western nobility, too, paid generously to support the activities of the order. All thought the cause a worthy one, since by funding the Templars, they were helping further the cause of the Crusaders in the Holy Land and could be ranked among the friends of the monastic order without actually going as far as to join it. The practice of religious orders depending on the charitable donations of influential patrons was a common one in medieval times, and gifts of territory and money were readily forthcoming. It seemed that every influential lord wanted to display his piety, wealth and commitment to the fight against the infidel by making a donation.

By far the greatest gift that was bestowed upon the Order of the Knights Templar was papal blessing, first from Pope Honorius II and then from Pope Innocent II. In the twelfth century, all nations, all kings, looked to the papacy as the ultimate authority in Christendom, and to have the Pope's blessing meant a great deal. The ties with established religion would grow as the order itself grew. At first, the knights had followed the Rule of the Order of St Benedict, but the rapid development of the order required that a separate and specific rule be created to cater for the order's unique mission. King Baldwin II encouraged Hughes de Payens, as the leader of the knights, to approach the papacy and seek a new rule. The mediator was to be Bernard of Clairvaux. His influence with Pope Honorius II was strong, but the Pope was already well disposed to the knights and saw in them great potential for the Church, both in the newly conquered Holy Land and in Europe. If the papacy were to take the Templars under its wing, it would at last have a fighting force independent of the feuding kings and princes. The Templars had already shown themselves an effective and popular force in Jerusalem, and one that could support the development of papal authority in Syria. Honorius may even have seen in the warrior-monks the flowering of a papal army capable of marching against any secular opposition.

In 1128 the Knights Templar received their rule. The Council of Troyes, which decided the matter, was attended by the most influential men in France, with the exception of St Bernard, who was ill. The Abbot was involved in the drafting of the new constitution, however, and the rule incorporated much of what was already in the Benedictine Rule. Hughes de Payens was pronounced the first Grand Master of the order, and a say in the order's affairs was granted to the Patriarch (or Bishop) of Jerusalem, as well as to the Pope. The rule was long and its seventy-two articles covered every aspect of daily life. Of paramount importance was the emphasis on monastic matters. The order would be entirely communal, sharing food and material goods; even personal letters, if received, were to be read aloud before the Master of the order. Prayers were to be said several times each day, as in any other monastic order, and meals were to be eaten in strict silence. New articles were later added. In fact, modifications were made several times and hundreds of new articles were eventually added to the rule. The Master of the order was fully authorized to modify the Rule of the Temple.

With the recognition by the Pope of the Knights Templar as a monastic order, the power and wealth of the group grew rapidly. The Council of Troyes had given a seal of approval to the order and the number of recruits and donations of both money and land increased. Hughes de Payens donated all his lands to the cause, and new recruits, the young nobility of Europe, were expected to do likewise. Almost immediately the Templars changed from a tiny group of less than a dozen knights and hardly any land to an international organization with estates, lands, officials and a capital in Jerusalem. Hughes de Payens and other influential knights of the order travelled to all the major European kingdoms to drum up support. They were very successful.

By the middle of the twelfth century, the Knights Templar were one of the most wealthy and influential bodies in Europe. They owned large tracts of land in England, Scotland, France, Spain, Portugal, Germany and Austria. These estates were sources of revenue vital for the order's survival, for they were not simply donations of land but of farms, animals, bondsmen, mills and other elements of the rural economy. While the Temple of Solomon site in Jerusalem became the order's headquarters, these European territories were its money-making colonies, providing not just financial help but food, political support and personnel. Only the papacy itself could boast more extensive international connections. Preceptories were established as local bases from which to administer the Temple's lands and admit new recruits. The order's first preceptory was founded at Troyes on land donated by one of the councillors.

Some of the distinctive hallmarks of the Temple were not adopted immediately but came to the order some time later. The white robes worn by the Cistercians were copied as a symbol of the purity of life that was expected of the knights, and the famous emblem of the red cross came during the start of the Second Crusade. This may have served a dual purpose, as much to differentiate themselves from the Cistercian monks as to advertise the knights' special relationship with the Church. In 1162 this relationship became even more special with the issuing of a papal bull by Pope Alexander III that granted the Knights Templar freedom from all tithes and taxes and awarded them the unique judicial position of being unable to be tried in a court of law. Knights of the order were legally responsible only to the representatives of the Pope. This edict set up the Temple as virtually a church within a church. It even possessed its own burial grounds and chaplains, and was able to receive tithes from its estates, just as the Church did.

The Growth of Templar Possessions

Jerusalem became the headquarters of the Knights Templar from the moment they moved into the king of Jerusalem's palace. It became the first of many Templar possessions and a base from which others could be founded. The portion of the royal residence granted to them had, prior to the conquest of Jerusalem in 1099, been the Al-Aqsa mosque. This in turn was built on the presumed site of the great Temple of Solomon, centre of ancient Israel. The king's palace was dominated by the distinctive Dome of the Rock, and this latter building featured on the seals of the order's Master. The Dome of the Rock influenced the Templars both architecturally and symbolically, since it was built by Islamic architects with eight interior walls designed to hold up the famous golden dome. The octagon within the circle became an important geometric symbol to the order, and octagonal chapels were constructed in imitation throughout Europe on Temple grounds.

Preceptories, the local headquarters of the order, sprang up in every region where there were estates to be managed. These land-holdings were organized into large Templar provinces, each commanded by a Master who was appointed by the order's Grand Master. This latter position at the very head of the cult was automatically given to the Master of Jerusalem, the region which was, after all, the most powerful and influential of the Temple's provinces. By far the most productive province was France, but good relations were not always maintained with the French throne. In the end it was the French King Philippe who pounced on the Templars in 1307 and utterly destroyed them. The reaction of other nations to the sudden growth of this wealthy military and monastic order was varied. Spanish Templars were well liked by their government, principally because of the need in that land for a well-armed fighting force to challenge the Muslim armies of the south. Attacking originally from North Africa, the Arab invaders had been a thorn in the Spanish side and the defence of Christian lands had constituted a ready-made crusade. The Templars there were rarely shipped out to the Holy Land or elsewhere; after all, there were infidels in abundance to be killed right there in Spain. That each Spanish Templar swore an oath of fealty to his king gives some measure of the degree of co-operation between the two.

During Hughes de Payens's visit to England in 1128 to advertise the existence of the order, he was warmly welcomed by King Henry I. Two preceptories were conferred upon the Grand Master at this time, one at Dover and another at Shipley, in Essex. An English Master was also established to oversee the new (and rapidly widening) territories being donated. Hugh d'Argentein was the first Master. He was followed by Osto de St Omer and he in his turn by Richard de Hastings. In Britain, as in other European countries, power was secured at the very highest levels, ensuring that the order was well connected and in a position to get what it wanted. The English Master of the Temple was given the right to sit in on the government's Parliament, mainly due to his position as one of the major landholders of the realm, and he was also head of all the nation's orders, not just his own.

Henry I's successor, Stephen, was even better disposed towards the Knights Templar, since his father had been one of the leaders of the First Crusade. King Stephen allowed the organization to spread across the entire country and preceptories were established on lands donated by such august personages as the Earl of Derby, the Earl of Warwick and even Stephen's wife, Mathilda. London became the centre of Templar operations in England, with the first headquarters, the 'Old Temple' at Holborn, forming a self-sufficient community. It was quickly replaced by the 'New Temple'. Today this is known as Temple Bar, and the original round church used by the order still stands. The Master of England assembled the country's chief officers here for an annual meeting, and the Templar precinct was important not just for the Templars but for London as a whole. It was the presence of the Temple and its wealth that helped the city become an international centre of finance.

The next king, Henry II, remained on good terms with the knights, and they in turn tried their best to defuse the ecclesiastical row with his archbishop, Thomas à Becket. But the close association between the Temple and the English monarchy reached a peak during the reign of Richard I, known as the Lionheart. He took the throne in 1189 and spent much of his life in the Holy Land, as a prominent participant in the Third Crusade to recapture Jerusalem from the Muslim leader Saladin. It would have been unusual, then, if Richard had not been familiar with, and strongly allied to, the Knights Templar. In fact, he seems to have been something of an associate member, able to make use of the order's facilities and ships, but not required to take the obligatory monastic vows. When the king fled from the Holy Land, accused of plotting the murder of a Christian ally, he wore the uniform of a Templar and travelled incognito with members of the order. The assassination had been connected to Richard via a mercenary sect of Muslims called the Assassins, who were thought to have been commissioned by the king, and the Templars had relations with this group too. Chapter 4 tells the story of this strange cult and the way in which it could have been linked to Richard. The king had numerous dealings with the Knights Templar, and after he had captured the island of Cyprus, he sold it to the knights for use as a base. For a time, the island did become a Temple stronghold and the centre of its eastern operations.

Extensive properties across England were the source of the order's power in the country rather than special political affiliations with the government and the crown. Such relationships existed and were closely bound, but they were based on real power in the towns and villages of the land. The holdings of the Temple are impossible to calculate today, encompassing as they did hundreds of farms, churches, villages and small estates. Modern estimates suggest that there were seventy-four major Templar possessions, and there were thirty well-established preceptories in England. But the knights did not depend on land-ownership alone for their income. Their need to transport knights, horses, supplies and arms to the frontline in the Holy Land had meant the development of an entire Templar naval fleet. With the tremendous business acumen that characterized their existence, the Templars employed the large vessels as cargo ships for exporting wool sheared on their lands. Pilgrims wanting safe passage to Jerusalem put their faith in the military might of the Templars and sailed with them, but were required to pay handsomely for it. La Rochelle was the centre of Templar naval activities on the Atlantic coast, and it saw much traffic both to and from the Holy Land. The last leg of the journey to England ended at either the Thames wharf of the London preceptory or at Bristol. At this latter port, the Temple dominated much of the local economy, since it based the greater part of its naval strength there while it sat in English waters.

While Bristol depended on the Knights Templar for a great deal of its prosperity, there were other, smaller, towns that owed their very existence to the order. Baldock, a village in Hertfordshire, was founded by the order and derives its name from the Old French for

'Baghdad', reflecting the single-minded obsession of the organization. The common occurrence of the word 'temple' as a place-name even today testifies to the prevalence of their possessions in England. There were tracts of Templar land and Templar buildings in Scotland and Ireland also. The major Scottish preceptory was near Edinburgh, at the modern village of Temple, and another preceptory is known to have existed at Maryculter, near Aberdeen. In Ireland there was a preceptory at Dublin and at least five others existed elsewhere. The details of many other holdings in both Scotland and Ireland are now lost to modern historians.

In England the Templars were able to gain unprecedented powers, the most fundamental being the ability to receive tithes while being immune from the tax-collector. Metal Templar crosses adorned all their buildings, warning away the collectors. Unfortunately for the crown, some enterprising city-dwellers also mounted the Templar crosses outside their own houses in an attempt to avoid paying taxes. However, the subterfuge did not go unnoticed and Henry III tried to put a stop to it. Exemption from taxes was not the only privilege enjoyed by the knights. They were not liable to pay tolls on roads and rivers, they created their own local law courts and ran Templar fairs. Such power had never been seen before, and the Knights Templar obviously wielded considerable high-level influence to be able to ignore such basic laws of the land.

Power and Prestige

The Church during the Middle Ages had developed considerable prestige and extraordinary authority, but it did not possess a physical presence with which to back up its power, lacking troops, commanders in the field and a fleet. It was primarily due to the Church that the Knights Templar were able to receive all of these things. That a small body of worldly knights would devote their lives to the way of God was seen as a spiritually uplifting phenomenon. But the hard political facts behind the theological trumpeting were stubbornly secular. The Pope had seen in the first glimmerings of Hughes de Payens's order a thoroughly loyal fighting force, divorced from petty national squabblings and dynastic conflict. Like the established Church, the Temple took on some of the former's money-making powers and, coupled with its own formidable military might, it became an international banking organization, creating wealth for the sole purpose of keeping its troops in the field. It had no subjects to feed in times of famine, no cities to maintain or duties other than to itself. The order existed to fight for the freedom of Palestine, and the profits from every farmstead, orchard, tithe, court fine or sale of wool were poured into this endeavour. Money became such an important aspect of supporting a permanent Crusader army that it seems to have blurred the order's focus later on. Greed and the tendency to avoid open conflict became a characteristic of the knights who vowed to remain poor and suffer hardship.

One of the greatest paradoxes of the Knights Templar was the initiates' vows of poverty and their abandonment of all material comforts while at the same time joining the richest organization in the world. Their wealth was legendary, as was their haughtiness and pride. The phrase 'to drink like a Templar' was current in medieval times, and it is unlikely that they stopped at drink, despite initiates' vows of celibacy. Such wealth was not a fleeting thing, gained in a flurry of donations and spent on failed Crusades. The Templars may have been responsible for the financial institutions that we know today, since they took the creation of wealth deadly seriously, even establishing a type of international medieval bank with the ability to lend money and grant credit. In fact, the sophistication of the system was such that a depositor could take away with him a letter of credit from one Templar preceptory and present it at another. There, if the secret codes used to identify the depositor were validated, he would be able to withdraw the sum on the note. Only a well-established and highly competent international group could have run such a system.

Many other financial dealings were undertaken; loans were made not just to merchants and minor property-owners but to lords and kings. In theory this practice was forbidden to the Knights Templar, since usury was not allowed by Church law. But the compulsive desire to make money, coupled with clever wording in the definition of money-lending, overrode this obligation and the Temple began to dominate this traditionally medieval Jewish occupation. English kings often made use of the order's copious funds. King Edward I borrowed and repaid Templar money, as did King John and King Henry III. The latter got so heavily in debt as a result of the constant warfare during his reign that he actually pawned the crown jewels to the Knights Templar for a period of six years. This indicates great trust in the order's security – so much trust, in fact, that part of the French royal treasury was based at the order's Paris preceptory; the knights there guarded their own treasures as well as those of the French crown. A similar arrangement was established in England, with the London preceptory serving for a time as one of the country's treasuries. The order's immunity from taxes has already been mentioned, but as if that were not enough, the Temple also collected the taxes and donations due to the Pope, as well as a portion of those due to the crown. In fact, along with more mundane debt-collection, the Temple seems to have been involved in virtually every type of financial transaction. Trust funds, pensions, dowries and inheritances all concerned the cult, and anyone with money entrusted it to the Temple.

Investors could deposit sums of money and be sure that it would remain untouched for years to come, even after their death. Such monies were inviolable. Even kings, who tried on occasion to lay their hands on the funds of disgraced lords, were rebuffed. As well as being secure, the Temple preceptories were discreet, allowing nervous nobles to hide there. King John spent quite some time in one or other of the order's preceptories, and so did Richard the Lionheart. Other dignitaries, from diplomats and minor lords to archbishops and representatives of the Pope, were welcome guests of the Knights of the Temple of Solomon. One Templar who sought the protection of the preceptory in Sidon did not enjoy its security for long, for he was kidnapped by soldiers acting for the king of Jerusalem. The knight, one Walter of Mesnil, had broken a treaty with the sect of Muslim fanatics called the Assassins and the secure preceptory was not secure enough to save him.

As the Temple grew in power and strength, and as kings entrusted both their kingdoms' wealth and their own lives to the order, the knights became arrogant about their place in the world. They realized that few individuals or organizations could challenge their financial might. Unlike other knights or rich landowners, the Templars lived the frugal lifestyle of monks. According to the rule, members of the order possessed few items of value besides their arms and armour, their horses and riding tack; and those who undertook agricultural work, usually the sergeants, also had the use of farm implements. But nothing was above the sturdy and practical, and even food was basic and bland, with a little wine and some salted meat. The Knights Templar sought not to squander the vast revenues that they were accumulating. The ever-spiralling costs that resulted from the maintenance of a permanent army in Palestine had to be met. By hard toil in the rural areas of Europe, by trade and commerce, by a multitude of tithes and taxes, and by the generous donations of lords, kings and archbishops, the Temple was able to meet this cost.

Soldiers of Christ

What service had the Knights Templar promised to perform that prompted such largesse? The cult's original directive was to protect all pilgrims in the Holy Land. This in itself was a worthy cause, but with an initial membership of only nine knights for the first nine years, it would seem to have needed a force of new members more than an abundance of gifts. There are two mysteries surrounding the foundation of the Templars: the first concerns the exact date that this occurred. The Crusader historian Guillaume de Tyre, writing decades after the event, declared that the order was founded by Hughes de Payens in 1118, and goes on to say that the Templars accepted no new members for nine years. However, other sources state that a handful of knights had joined the cult in the years before 1126, the earliest being the Count of Anjou in 1120. If Guillaume de Tyre is correct in his assertion that nine years passed before new recruits joined the fledgeling order, then the Knights Templar may have moved into the king of Jerusalem's palace in 1111 or before. The second mystery is the fact that Guillaume wrote of the Templars' activities in around 1180, but King Baldwin II's own chronicler, Fulk de Chartres, who wrote about all minor and major events in the Holy Land at the very time of the order's inception, fails to mention it at all. Hughes de Payens, his holy knights and their much-lauded mission to protect the pilgrims against Muslim raiders go unrecorded. Why?

The Order of the Knights Templar began as a secret organization, but upon emerging into the limelight of the Second and Third Crusades became a small cadre of élite warriors engaging in both military conflict and negotiation with the Muslims. What set the cult apart from other Christian forces was not their martial skill (they did lose battles as well as win them) but their discipline, *esprit de corps* and independence from greater powers. Charges of collusion with the infidel were brought against the Temple in the last years of its existence and these charges helped precipitate the order's downfall. Unlike some of the other charges wielded like swords by the Inquisition, these had a definite foundation in truth. The Knights Templar may have set themselves up as champions of Christendom and the protectors of Palestine, but did in fact have little compunction about dealing with the enemy, co-operating and allying with the Muslims, and even fighting other Holy Orders.

By the time that the Temple had become well established in Palestine and Europe, rumours began to circulate of pacts made with Saracens and of unholy practices. Even the Pope began to doubt the order's commitment to the Church. The rumours became fact when the Templars allied themselves with the Emir of Damascus in 1259 against their arch-rivals, the Knights Hospitaller. Other pacts were formed. The order became familiar with the communities of Muslim fanatics called Assassins that occupied fortresses close to Templar territory and it eventually forced them to pay regular tribute. Unfounded rumours were current that even accused the Templars of hiring the sinister cult to commit political murders. The death of Conrad Montferrat at the hands of the Assassins, and the way in which King Richard I, an associate member of the Templars, was implicated in the murder turned rumour into plausible speculation. If Richard *had* paid the Assassins to kill his rival, would he not have negotiated such a deal through the Knights Templar, who were not just neighbours of the sect but regular extorters of money from them?

Deals, alliances and diplomacy in general became the order's trade far more often than their skill in battlefield carnage. The Templars in Palestine were often well disposed towards the neighbouring states, whether Christian, Muslim or Jewish. Part of the answer to the order's tolerance of its sworn enemies must have been the regular contact that it had with Arabs and Jews. The latter's domination of scholarly and financial institutions brought them into regular contact with the order, and in Jerusalem Masters of the Temple often took Arab secretaries into their employ. Many knights actually learned Arabic, sometimes as a result of being held as prisoners of war, and all Templars wore beards in the fashion of the Muslims – the only Christians in the Holy Land to do so. One story of a visiting Arab to the Temple indicates this close relationship between the order and the Muslims. The Arab wished to pray at a small shrine that had survived the Templar takeover of the Al-Aqsa mosque and was freely allowed to do so by the knights; however, a new Templar recruit saw the man and tried to stop him praying to Mecca, insisting he pray as Christians do. Several times other knights tried to hold back the recruit, until he was eventually removed from the area and the Muslim continued to worship.

It is not impossible to envisage this tolerance as one of the initial ideas behind the Knights Templar, for it is unlikely that the avowed purpose of the Templars, to defend the Christian pilgrims as they travelled, was seriously pursued. But as guides and scouts, the Templars may well have played a crucial role. The cult was a permanent force and was well placed to learn much about the nature of the terrain, the enemy and the politics of the region. The close proximity of the Muslims and the long-standing relationship that the order had with them, while other Christian forces came and went, testify to a new kind of strategy. In its secrecy, low membership and sometimes questionable alignment, a picture is painted of an armed diplomatic mission rather than an élite fighting force. There are modern-day examples of well-trained soldiers becoming so deeply involved with the natives of the land they have invaded that they prefer *their* ways to those of their fellows. The war in Vietnam provides us with an analogy. Elite Special Forces personnel from the American army were sent to live and work alongside the primitive mountain tribes on Vietnam's border in an effort to train them to resist the invading North Vietnamese. These Special Forces often saw in the tribesmen's tough fighting spirit and plain, uncluttered way of life something that had already been instilled into them during training. In comparison, the conventional US Army soldiers were thought of by many Special Forces as crude and ignorant of local ways. And the élite forces of any war, not just those in Vietnam, are taught to fight like their enemy to be victorious – to become accustomed to the terrain, the language, the clothing and lifestyle of the enemy to such an extent that when fighting occurs, the élite troops are forearmed with local knowledge and an understanding of the enemy's methods.

As a fighting force, the Knights Templar were far superior to any other Frankish (i.e. Christian) army in the Holy Land. Such strength came not from numbers, for the Temple never had a large standing army, but primarily in determination and discipline. Each knight was forbidden to retreat from a foe unless he was outnumbered by at least three to one. The knights' tenacity in battle was legendary, their courage unswerving. It was as though they had adopted the Spartan system of preparation for war almost wholesale. Like the Spartan men, the Templars lived in enforced poverty, away from women, constantly training for the battlefield and loyal to their brothers unto death. Templar castles and strongholds were the most impregnable known at the time, for war was their trade and the order never lacked for opportunities to practise it.

Newly arrived in the Holy Land, the Templars joined King Baldwin II in his attack on the Muslim city of Damascus in 1129, but victory for the Frankish forces was not forthcoming. The Order of the Templars was not seriously damaged by the defeat, however, and the disastrous Second Crusade some years later gave the knights the opportunity to really show their mettle.

Both King Conrad of Germany and King Louis VII of France set out from Europe to restore the Crusader kingdoms after the Christian state of Edessa had fallen to the Arabs. After an abortive march to the Holy Land, the two kings launched an attack on Damascus in 1148. It did not go well. At first the Franks seemed in an ideal position for a siege and wore down the defenders inside Damascus until victory seemed likely. Suddenly a command was given to shift a large portion of the siege army to the south-west, under the guidance of (so some rumours purported) the Knights Templar. No food, water or shade was to be had in the new position and the Franks began to complain bitterly, eventually striking camp and marching unvictorious from Damascus. Charges were later levelled at the Templars, accusing them of taking bribes from the besieged in Damascus and advising the change in position while knowing full well that, as a permanent and knowledgeable force in Palestine, their suggestions would be heeded.

Despite such sinister accusations of complicity and bribery, the Knights Templar had pledged to obey every command of their own Master and vowed never to retreat in battle. For this, and for their steadfast courage, King Louis commended them. He wrote that he could never have 'existed even for the smallest space of time in these parts' without the aid of the Temple. It seems that the Frankish cause in Palestine would have come to a dismal end there and then had it not been for the heroic efforts of the Templars. But the rumours that circulated concerning the order were kept alive despite King Louis's praise, and they were to follow the Temple to its destruction. In 1153 the Egyptian port of Ascalon was blockaded by the Frankish army of Jerusalem and an impressive force of Knights Templar that had been mustered especially for the siege. The city was successfully captured but not without incident. Part of the city's walls had collapsed due to mining operations undertaken by the Franks, and the Christians rushed forward to enter Ascalon. However, according to one account, the Templars passed through the wall first and prevented their allies from joining them. Bernard de Trémélai, the Master of the Knights Templar, led thirty-nine other knights into Ascalon, intent on securing the richest booty for themselves. Greed turned into disaster as the Egyptians rallied their forces and turned on the tiny force of Templars, killing them all. Other eyewitness chroniclers only praise the work of the Temple in securing Ascalon, which suggests that the story just told may have been yet another rumour – an alternate version of events believed by few and remembered by many.

Not every military incident was followed by accusations and bad-feeling towards the Temple. Jerusalem had always been the very heart of the Crusader kingdoms and in 1152 was in serious danger of being captured by a surprise force of Saracens, who had advanced in a series of forced marches to camp in secret on the Mount of Olives. The daring plan was well timed, for King Baldwin III of Jerusalem and the Master of the Knights Templar, Bernard de Trémélai, who had not yet led his troops to their death at Ascalon, were away fighting other Muslim armies. Baldwin III was at Tripoli and Bernard was at Nablus with a contingent of knights. Fortunately, the Muslim army was spotted and the remaining Templars at Jerusalem joined with knights of the Hospitallers and a hastily raised citizen force to ambush the Saracens at night while they slept. The Christians were able, by dint of a surprise attack of their own, to rout the Muslim forces and crush them as the fleeing soldiers tried to cross the River Jordan. Again the valiant Templars had saved the Crusaders from a catastrophic defeat.

The Templar Ritual and Religion

Every aspect of life within the Order of the Knights Templar was carefully regulated and controlled. The rule by which its members lived followed closely that of the Cistercian Order, led by St Bernard of Clairvaux, who was so prominent in championing the virtues of the Templars in the first place. Both Cistercian and Templar orders grew in wealth and importance at a prodigious rate, and it is quite possible that their fortunes were linked by such powerful personages as André de Montbard (who was also St Bernard's nephew) and the Count of Champagne. When a Templar desired to leave the order he had but one option open to him, to enter an even stricter monastic order, and the Cistercian monasteries accepted many Knights of the Temple of Solomon, including an ex-Master, Everard de Barrés. He had secured many benefits for the Templars but did not wish to live out his entire life in Palestine. Unfortunately, the position of Master of the Temple required that the leader do just that and no exceptions to the rule could be made.

The rule touched on every aspect of life, from daily work to prayers and punishments for misdeeds, and also to details of organization and the obligations of rank. The members of the Order of the Knights Templar were roughly divided into three 'castes': knights, sergeants and chaplains. The knights were all of noble birth, warriors and men of deep commitment to the cause who brought with them to the Temple their lands and property. Sergeants were members of the middle classes and formed a fully fledged infantry force that accompanied the mounted knights into battle. Some estimates put the number of sergeants to knights as high as nine to one, and unlike the knights, who wore white mantles, the sergeants wore tunics of black. The sergeants also acted as a kind of rear-echelon group, preparing the knights for war and carrying out a wide range of tasks within the order, being also farmers, grooms and stewards. Sergeants formed bodyguards for important Templars and were able to reach positions of importance; they were not a despised underclass. The governor of the port of Acre was always a sergeant, and a member of this rank carried the order's famous standard into battle. Fear was struck into the hearts of the Saracens when they saw the half-black and half-white standard called Beauséant unfurled. Across the standard were written the words: 'Not unto us, O Lord, not unto us, but unto Thy Name give the Glory.' Beauséant also became the war-cry of the charging Templars.

Knights were allowed up to three horses, while the sergeants, ranking below the knights, had only one mount each. Charged with the non-military aspects of the organization were the Templar chaplains, who were the official priesthood, ministering to knights and sergeants alike. The chaplain's role also included the non-military tasks of administration.

At the very head of the Knights Templar was the Master of the Order of the Temple of Solomon of Jerusalem, to give him his full title. Later historians often, and erroneously, refer to him as the order's Grand Master. In his tasks and powers the Master of the order played much the same role as an abbot would in a traditional Christian order. As the pre-eminent member of the most powerful international empire in existence, he was extremely influential, but his decisions were not always fully his own, for in some matters the Master consulted a small chapter of knights. Knights also formed part of his personal entourage: there were two champion knights on his staff, a cook and a blacksmith, a secretary, a chaplain and an interpreter. In addition, a sergeant and two servants attended to the Master's safety and other needs. An officer titled the Seneschal was the Master's executive officer, deputizing for him in times of need. Below the Seneschal was the Marshal, responsible for military matters first and foremost. The burden of this position was great, encompassing as it did the distribution and maintenance of horses, weapons and armour, the supplying of the order's knights, and the formulation of battle plans and overall strategy. When the Templars rode into the fray, the Marshal was expected to be at the very front of the charge. These three offices in essence formed the hub of the order, the heart of a web of command and control that spread commercial and feudal links out from Jerusalem to other Holy Land cities, to Eastern Europe, Germany, France and beyond.

A second tier of ranks administered this sprawling empire, beginning with the Commander of the City of Jerusalem. The Commander had very little to do with politics but was primarily concerned with the day-to-day needs of the Templars in the Holy City. As the Templars expanded, the Commander's duties widened too, and he became responsible for the protection of pilgrims along the highways of the Holy Land. It is strange that the single *raison d'être* of the Templars was now a side-mission delegated to a local commander.

What was now the basis for the Master's grand strategy? What single objective drove the order onwards and justified the lavish donations? Rumours of the Templars as guardians of the Holy Grail were rife during the Middle Ages. Whether they did in fact possess this object is a matter of pure speculation, but the order did own a fragment of the True Cross upon which Christ was Crucified. It fell to the Commander of the City of Jerusalem to safeguard this holy relic, perhaps the most valuable object in Christendom at the time.

Other regional commanders lacked the prestige of the Commander of Jerusalem but in their own territories were highly influential people. The Holy Land boasted two very powerful local Knights Templar, the Commander of Antioch and the Commander of Tripoli. These were virtual Masters in their own regions, and in Europe their equivalents were actually called Masters, so there was a Master of England, a Master of France, etc. The Templar structure was also duplicated in each province, so there was a provincial Seneschal and a provincial Marshal, and every Master had an officer called a

Draper who undertook to organize the clothing and bedding of the knights in his care. With the vast revenues that originated in Europe, the Masters of these provinces were responsible for immense sums of money and the fortunes of entire kingdoms. Only if the Master of Jerusalem entered the country did the provincial Master relinquish his control.

Parts of the province, divided up into castles, estates, farms and other holdings, were properly called 'houses'. There were several offices concerned with administering these houses – the Commanders of the Houses who were responsible in all matters to the Master, and the Commanders of the Knights who were in their turn subordinate to the Marshal of the province as lieutenants of the warrior-knights. The knights themselves formed the cutting edge of the Templars on the battlefield, but were little more than simple monks when out of their armour. They were drawn from the sons of European nobles, a class that continually trained for war, using tournaments and jousts as a substitute for battle. A noble wishing to dedicate himself to the Knights Templar brought to the order not just his warrior skills but also all of his lands and estates. In this way the order forced the recruit to 'burn his boats', by making it almost impossible for him to return to the life he had known before.

Glory and pride were the central ideals that every recruit had to abandon if he were to adhere to the rule and become a Knight of the Temple. By relinquishing his lands and his wealth, the noble would enter the cloistered world of poverty, humility and obedience. Without money, he had to rely on his fellows and on the order itself. Becoming a Templar set the knight above all others, but the price he had to pay was that of personal glory, for there was little that the outside world had to envy in the lifestyle of the warriors. Like all monks, the Templars rose early and put on a simple robe over their underclothes. The knights neither ate nor washed, but went directly to prayer. Because expeditions, training or other tasks would take them away from the preceptory's chapel, it was common for the knights to say all of the morning's prayers in one session (unlike traditional monks, who prayed frequently during the entire day). Daily chores were exceptionally *un*-monastic, with military training, lessons in tactics and the regular maintenance of weapons and body armour, horses and riding gear. Typical Templar gear included a full coat of chainmail, with a surcoat carrying the red Templar cross, a shield, a spear and a long sword. Other weapons found their way into the knights' employ, ranging from hideous forms of poleaxes to maces and flails.

It was not until late morning or even midday that the knights had their first meal of the day, and it was always plain but filling, and eaten at long wooden tables. Every man provided his own cup, knife, spoon and bowl and no conversation was permitted during the meal, just as in other monastic orders. Instead, passages from the Holy Book were read out to the diners and any conversations that took place at the dinner table were via sign language. Meat, when available, was rarely served more than three times in a week. As the heart of the order, the knights ate first, followed by their comrades-in-arms, the sergeants, and then the lay servants, who carried out the menial tasks within the preceptories and houses but were not actually members of the order. The last to eat were the native mercenary warriors who joined in the escapades of the Templars without enduring the severity of full membership. A second meal would follow the afternoon's activities and the second period of prayer, which was then followed by even more prayers as the knights prepared for bed.

When the knights gathered together in an assembly to discuss matters, it usually occurred on a Sunday in the chapel during a weekly chapter. Here members were encouraged to confess any misdemeanours that they may have committed that week. Those not owning up to a crime who were then challenged by the preceptor or commander suffered severer punishments than those who owned up when given the chance. On a greater scale, and with far more important matters to discuss, general chapters would be convened. These were rarely scheduled and involved high-level officers of the Temple in discussion about policy, strategy and the organization and running of the order.

Templar chapters allowed the concerns of the order to be addressed and must have had mixed agendas, for at one and the same time the Temple was a church, a business and an army, with none of these elements dominating. Between daily worship and military practice, the knights gave alms to the poor and sold wine, wool and grain from their farms.

The Templars were notorious for their seeming disregard for traditional Christian beliefs. Charges levelled against them by the Inquisition continually referred to satanic rites, and the rituals of initiation were said to involve repudiating Christ and spitting or urinating on the Crucifix. What brand of theology the order followed has perplexed historians from the time of the Crusades to today. Did their shadowy rites and ceremonies hide nothing more sinister than the Freemasonry of modern times, or were they specifically designed to hide secret and abhorrent rituals? There is reason to suspect that the order had links with a powerful schism that had developed in the Church and had its centre in southern France. This heresy of Catharism predated the Order of the Knights Templar and may have 'infected' the latter during the twelfth and thirteenth centuries. As the Cathars were being systematically wiped out by a

Papal Crusade, numerous survivors found refuge in the Order of the Temple, and Cathars played a prominent part in the running of the Temple in the Languedoc region.

The Templar Stephen de Staplebrugge, who confessed the crimes of the order in 1311, said that the Knights Templar had picked up their heretical beliefs from the Agen region of southern France. Agen had been one of the Cathar strongholds during the Albigensian Crusade and was part of the Templar province of Provence. In fact, one of the Temple's Masters of Provence, Roncelin de Fos, had for a time been the Master of England, and may have spread Cathar theology to that country. During the Inquisition, the Preceptor Geoffrey de Gonneville alleged that the heresies that so afflicted the Knights Templar were introduced by just one man, referred to in the testimony as Brother Roncelin. Was this Roncelin de Fos? If indeed it was, then it may date the influx of heretical practices to 1248 (when Roncelin became Master of Provence). Some of the order's other senior officers were actually from well-established Cathar families, including one Master of the order, Bertrand de Blanquefort, and both Cathars and Templars were rumoured at different times to be the guardians of the Holy Grail. Finally, both incurred the wrath of orthodox Christendom and were harried and persecuted by the forces of the Pope.

Nestled in the fertile lands of the Languedoc region in southern France is the small town of Albi, and it was here in 1165 that a council of eminent clergy condemned the Cathars for their heretical beliefs. The established Church had reason to fear the Cathar sect, which had virtually displaced Catholicism from southern France. It had to be stopped, and with this in mind Pope Innocent III declared a Crusade against the Cathar strongholds – subsequently known as the Albigensian Crusade after the town of Albi. The military expedition marched into Languedoc in 1209 and began a campaign of destruction that would last for forty years. The 30,000 troops waged a war as fanatical as any against the infidel Muslims, because, according to the Pope, the Cathars were 'infidels'. All came under the sword, men, women and children, Cathar and Christian alike. When one Crusader asked how he should distinguish Cathars from Christians, he was told by papal officers: 'Kill them all. God will recognize His own.' Cities were put under siege, captured, sacked and despoiled, among them Béziers, Narbonne, Carcassonne and Toulouse.

What was it about the Cathar faith that persuaded knights from across northern Europe to march into Languedoc and exterminate it utterly? Besides the intrinsic power that the Cathar 'Church' had gained at the expense of Catholicism, the heresy was slowly spreading northwards into Champagne and Germany. It harboured plans to revise orthodox Christianity and remodel it according to the Cathar system.

Both the Cathars and the Knights Templar were influenced by the Persian doctrines of Manichaeanism as well as by early Christianity. It seems likely that Catharism grew from the traditions of Manichaean schools that had long been established in Spain and southern France. The Manichees were a Christian sect that had been established by a Persian mystic called Mani in the late Roman Empire. Mani had absorbed the Gnostic teachings of his father and created a fusion of Christian and Persian ideas. The new cult incorporated elements of Persian Zoroastrianism and the far-reaching warrior religion of Mithras. He taught that faith should be replaced by personal illumination, and that light and darkness were in eternal conflict for the human soul. Mani was executed in 276, skinned and beheaded, but his cult survived and spread across Europe, to the south of France in the west and to China in the east.

Among the Cathar priests (or 'Perfecti') was a belief that flesh was intrinsically corrupt and that the purpose of life was the elevation of the human spirit. Cathar theology claimed there were two equal and opposite gods representing good and evil, light and darkness. The good god held sway over the immaterial, the spiritual and the emotive, while his opposite ruled over the material world and the universe as a whole. The battle between these two deities involved the struggle for human souls, and the renouncing of the material world for the principles of love. The great stumbling block with Christian orthodoxy was the fact that Jesus claimed his own divinity while manifesting in a physical body. Cathars rejected the material as evil and so too rejected that Jesus was the son of God. By the same token, the Perfecti renounced the materialistic Catholic Church, with its wealth, influence, property and elaborate ritual. It aimed to replace the established Church (and society in general) with one modelled on the Cathar cult, with its emphasis on personal worship and knowledge of God rather than pure faith. This radical and revolutionary concept threatened the secular world just as much as the theological, and provided the Pope with the arguments he needed to galvanize European nobility against the Cathars. As with the Crusades to liberate Jerusalem, it was not high-minded piety that convinced the knights and their lords to spend years away from home, risking life and limb; it was the material gain to be had. As well as ridding Languedoc of the Cathar heresy, the rich territories of the region would be available for plunder and annexation.

Rituals that were supposedly carried out by the Cathars and that were confessed during torture often matched closely the testimony of Templars sixty years later. This may indicate a similarity of beliefs between the two organizations, but any evidence originating from the barbaric and horrific torture chambers of the Pope's Inquisition must be suspect. Even so, alleged rituals, such as spitting on the Cross, denying the divinity of Christ and wearing the 'little cord' (*cordula*), and the practice of the obscene kisses of initiation, bear witness to a degree of identity between the two. Crucial evidence to any connection was the testimony of Brother John of the Order of St Benedict, which stated that the Templar, at his initiation, was presented with the 'little cord' which he then wore at all times over his mantle. Brother John may not have recognized the meaning of this evidence and its heretical nature, for the *cordula* was the Cathar badge of faith.

It was aspects of the initiation ritual which so disturbed the investigating medieval Inquisitors, but how much was actually fabricated by them to provide material with which they could prosecute the order is not known. Knights confessed to holding initiations in candlelit chapels at the dead of night, behind locked doors and under guard. The recruit was forced to deny his faith, to spit, trample or urinate on the Crucifix and hear the leader of the ceremony denounce Christ as a false prophet. If true, the act of defiling the Cross may have directly reflected the Gnostic and Cathar belief that, as the symbol of Christ, it was inherently evil, representing the death of a mortal Jesus and the evil machinations of the materialist God, called by the Cathars 'Rex Mundi'.

More mundane elements of the initiation included the taking of a vow of obedience by the candidate following a serious discourse in the stringent requirements of the order; the hardship, the chastity, the poverty and the obedience that were expected of all Templars were bluntly described. In return the candidate was asked if he had already taken vows to other orders or a vow of marriage, or had an outstanding debt that required paying. Even the existence of any diseases had to be disclosed to the examiners. It seems that most Templars were illiterate and depended upon their examiners for full administering of the rule. Even some chaplains lacked a full knowledge of Latin and required that the rule be translated into French – this occurred in 1139 under the Master Robert de Craon. Interestingly, a strange amendment was made to the rule during translation. The Council of Troyes's original rule stated that a knight who had been excommunicated from the Church could not join the order; in the new rendering the rule stated explicitly that the Temple was to actively seek out excommunicated knights! This hardly seems to be a translator's or copyist's error, but a distinct policy change (the Master did have the authority to rewrite the rule at any time he so wished). By accepting men who the Church had rejected, the Temple was asserting its almost total independence and setting itself up as a rival.

According to the testimonies of many Templars under interrogation, the induction climaxed with a series of obscene kisses. The candidate kissed his initiator on the mouth, navel, penis and anus (or alternatively in the case of the latter, with deference to magical symbolism, the 'base of the spine'). For many modern historians, the accounts of the kisses are purely the product of a desperate Inquisition constantly forced to fabricate more and more un-Christian acts with which to pillory its enemies. Others see in the kisses an occult tradition stretching back to Zoroastrian and Sufi lore. According to various Eastern schools of mysticism, the navel, genitals and perineum (the area at the base of the spine between the anus and the genitals) are the chakras or psychic centres of the human body. Could the Templars have absorbed aspects of Eastern philosophy during their stay in the Holy Land? A further practice was alleged to take place during initiation, namely an act of sodomy with the officiating chaplain, but it is impossible to ascertain the truth of this and other aspects of the rituals. Between the élitist affectation of secrecy and mystery (compare the strict anonymity of the British Army's Special Air Service élite troops, even when appearing in the courtroom) and the virtual psychopathic fantasies of the Inquisition, the real truth behind the theology and beliefs of the Knights Templar may never be known.

The most bizarre accusation made by the Inquisition, based on the accounts of many Templars, was that members of the order worshipped a false idol named Baphomet. Too vague and abstract to be the invention of the Church, Baphomet was real, a Templar belief that defies explanation, although many have tried. The Inquisition could make no sense of the matter either, but established that some sort of 'cult of the head' had existed and that Baphomet was part of it. Although tortures produced confessions that referred to Baphomet, similar information was extracted without such radical measures and the name was also encountered by agents of the king of France, who had secretly infiltrated the order to obtain incriminating evidence. References to holy idols in the form of heads repeatedly occur in the testimonies of knights, and it is thought that Baphomet was a skull or the image of some symbolic head worshipped by the order. Apparently it was believed that the head was able to make the land fertile, enrich the people and secure prosperity in general. This echoes almost exactly the properties prescribed to the head of the Celtic war hero Bran the Blessed, as well as the famous Holy Grail, legends of which were contemporary with the Knights Templar. What exactly was this supposed to represent? The head of Jesus Christ? The head of the cult's founder, Hughes de Payens? An interesting theory put forward by Ian Wilson speculates that the head could have been the

Turin Shroud, the funerary cloth that covered Christ after he was taken from the Cross and which bears an image of him. Folded and displayed as the face of Jesus, it may well have been an object of worship for the Templars, who would not conceive of their veneration as heresy. It is known that the Templars took pride in collecting holy relics, and the Shroud could have come into the order's possession following the sack of Constantinople. By a strange coincidence the Turin Shroud appeared in France long after the dissolution of the Temple in the possession of the family of Geoffrey de Charnay, the Preceptor of the Temple in Normandy, who was burned at the stake, along with the last Master of the order, Jacques de Molay.

The origin of the word 'Baphomet' is shrouded in mystery and speculation. One of the more commonly suggested theories is that it is a rendering of the phrase 'Prophet Muhammad', and is an allusion to the Templars' dealings and suspected sympathies with the Muslims. Far more likely is a derivation from the Arabic word *abufihamat* (which in Moorish Spanish becomes *bufihamat*), which can be translated as 'Father of Wisdom'. Such is the title of a Sufi master, an Arab religious mystic. In fact, the venerated fount of all wisdom for the Arab cult of Assassins with whom the Temple had so many dealings was the Imam, the living embodiment of God's wisdom on earth. Not all Templars came from Europe. The Master of Jerusalem, Philippe de Milly of Nablus, was born a Syrian who was elected to lead the Temple in January 1169; he and other local knights may have brought into the order facets of the Sufi teachings that remained hidden beneath the order's cloak of secrecy.

It was not just the Temple's beliefs and initiation rituals that were kept secret, but even the rule of the order was only known in its entirety to the higher ranks. Such subterfuge was an unnecessary trapping of the cult, one that would give the Temple's enemies more than ample fuel to destroy it. But something was needed to set the knights apart from the secular warrior nobles, something other than stringent duties and high-quality training. As has already been noted, modern-day élite units, like the British SAS, the American Special Forces and Russian Spetsnaz troops, revel in the mystique granted to them. Such troops wear uniquely coloured berets, often remain anonymous on operations and are allowed simple freedoms denied to the rank and file. Elite units have always required some special ceremonies or practices to set them apart from the traditional soldiery. What worked against the Knights Templar was their constant emphasis on their own legendary status, as sorcerers and alchemists, and on their position as guardians of the mysterious Holy Grail. In *The Perlesvaus*, a medieval Grail romance, the Knights Templar are depicted as the mysterious and occult initiates charged with the protection of the fabulous object. The Knights had little reason to suppress this propaganda.

The Downfall of the Order

As mysterious as the sudden rise of the Temple is the obscure demise that it suffered at the hands of King Philippe IV of France. It is impossible for historians to pinpoint the exact reasons behind the persecution of the Knights Templar. Several theories have been put forward, and it is likely that it was not just one but the sum total of these reasons that persuaded Philippe to act. A major turning point in the life of the order was the retaking of Jerusalem by the Saracens in 1291. This was soon followed by the expulsion of all Crusaders, including the Templars, from the entire Holy Land. A last stand at Acre failed to create the centre of resistance that was hoped for, and the order found itself without a home, without an enemy, without a cause. The security of Palestine and the Crusader states had been the Templars' very reason for existence, and with that gone the massive fund-raising efforts throughout Europe became the pursuit of wealth for the sake of wealth itself. Other orders weathered the storm. The Teutonic Knights, for example, had gained territories in Germany and established themselves there, away from the great powers of the age. The Hospitallers, always rivals of the Knights Templar, were able to fall back on their public service of healing the sick and caring for the old and infirm. Similarly, the Cistercian and Franciscan monastic orders had a place within the communities that they served, unlike the Temple, which had set itself outside the community, and above all laws but the Pope's. With no Crusades on the horizon, the nobles and monarchs who had given so much to the Temple began to ask what it had all been for.

For a time the order retreated to the island of Cyprus, but this proved wholly inadequate as a place from which to attack the Muslims. So the Temple looked back towards its rich hinterland in western Europe with the idea of creating for itself an independent Templar kingdom. This is what the Teutonic Knights had done in the harsh wilds of northern Europe, but the Knights Templar were not willing, as the Teutonic Knights had been, to live on the fringe of Christendom. Their power and wealth lay in England and France, and in particular in the south of France, in Languedoc. Here the Cathars had held out against the forces of the Pope, and it seemed that the Templars found the region both economically and culturally to their liking. The connection of the Knights Templar with the Cathars has already been mentioned.

King Philippe IV of France, known as Philippe le Bel (the 'Fair'), was not predisposed towards the idea of an independent kingdom being carved out of his territories and ruled by arrogant, haughty knights who were still extremely wealthy and also formidable opponents in battle. The Templar arrogance and greed had previously been tolerated, since the order was the most powerful fighting force in Palestine, and perhaps the only thing that stood between the Saracens and the fall of Jerusalem. But now that the order had been humbled by its losses, the continued arrogance and secrecy of the knights provoked angry reactions from the Western kings. Philippe in particular saw the Temple as a part of his great strategy for European domination, and unlike previous kings, who would not challenge the Pope's favoured knights, he had successfully subverted the papacy with his own candidate. If he chose to fight the Knights Templar, no one would stand in his way, for now that the Pope was his, the Order of the Knights Templar had no friends willing to support it.

No other king had ever gone as far as to plot the downfall of not one but two Popes and effectively create his own papacy. Pope Boniface VIII had been in constant conflict with the French crown, with charges being constantly levelled at each other. A kidnap attempt by the king failed, but Boniface died in mysterious circumstances soon after. So too did his short-lived successor, Benedict XI. In 1305 the king was able to force his own papal candidate on Rome, Bertrand de Goth, who became Pope Clement V; Philippe also ensured his survival by transferring the papacy to the French city of Avignon. This unheard-of move created the so-called Avignon Captivity and produced both a string of rival Popes and a papal schism that lasted for sixty-eight years. Philippe had shown himself to be ruthless and ambitious, and his plan to dominate the European kingdoms had moved one step closer. He had secured the papacy; now he needed to secure the downfall of the Knights Templar.

Not only were the Templars themselves plotting to create their own state on French soil, which may have been reason enough to oppose them, but they had personally snubbed Philippe. Several nobles had been honoured by the order by special lay membership, conferring upon them the use of preceptories, Templar bodyguards and suchlike. Perhaps the most important lay member had been Richard I, king of England. Philippe's bold initial plan revolved around becoming a member of the Templars and, as a warrior-king with the order at his side, attempting to unify the European kingdoms into one Christian super-state. But the Templars were not willing to play along and snubbed the king's request for honorary membership. If he needed any other excuse to destroy the order, then the vast wealth guarded by the knights could provide it. The king was approaching a financial crisis. He owed the Templars vast amounts of money and risked bankrupting the country. In addition, he had seen for himself the vast wealth that the Templars had accumulated when, in 1306, he was forced to seek shelter in the Paris preceptory from a rampaging mob. The wealth of the Temple was legendary and proved too much of a temptation for King Philippe.

When two fugitive members of the Knights Templar approached the king in 1307 looking for protection from the order, Philippe granted it on the condition that they provide incriminating evidence with which he could charge their fellows. The king got his damaging testimony and proceeded to plan a mass arrest of all Templars in France. He prepared charges against the knights using the reports of the two fugitives and the information supplied by royal spies within the order. The king struck suddenly and without warning on Friday, 13 October 1307. His officers around the country opened sealed orders simultaneously and marched on preceptories to seize both the knights and the treasures they found there. However, the great treasure of the Templars seems to have slipped through Philippe's fingers and the Paris preceptory, the great prize of the order, yielded little for the greedy king. Rumours circulated of the preceptory's treasurer fleeing France in the company of a bodyguard. Later confessions by knights confirmed the story and reported that the treasure of the Templars had been loaded aboard eighteen Templar galleys bound for an unknown destination. Somehow the Temple had foreknowledge of the king's actions and thwarted his attempt to capture Templar treasures.

Almost immediately, knights of the order were put on trial and interrogated. Torture was a popular tool of the prosecution, and was used openly and without mercy. As the testimonies of the knights were collected, the secrets of the order became apparent: the worship of the strange head called Baphomet, the obscene initiations, homosexual practices, the denunciation of the divinity of Christ . . . the list grew longer, incited by the agents of King Philippe. Somehow, the king had to arrange matters so that none of the knights could re-form the order and strike back at him, and to this end he had to convince his royal cousins abroad also to begin persecuting the Templars. Pope Clement V was quickly brought in on the Templar scandal and forced to back up the accusations made against them. This fuelled persecutions outside France, as the governments of other countries saw that it *was* possible to attack the Knights Templar without papal retribution. Everywhere the temptation of the order's treasures was too great to ignore. For close on 200 years the Order of the Knights Templar had stood firm as one of the immovable pillars of medieval Christendom. It had become a permanent fixture in the economy of every European land and one of the most distinguishing features of the Crusades.

With the papal authorities involved in the scandal, serious pressure was put on the gaoled knights. A papal bull was issued that attempted to force the kings of Europe to follow King Philippe's lead in arresting the Templars and confiscating their estates and properties. Full legal proceedings were begun that lasted for several years. In this time many of the imprisoned knights died, either from the terrible conditions in which they were kept or the wretched agonies of torture. The trials proper began in April 1310, and in the French town of Vienne many of the knights, having confessed to the acts already mentioned, recanted and were burned at the stake for their change of mind. Many other knights who had confessed their sins and stuck by their testimonies were allowed to walk free. In several instances the freed knights were allowed to draw a pension to sustain themselves, since from March 1312 the Order of the Knights Templar had been disbanded by the Pope. Part of the Inquisition's twisted psychology was to burn only those Templars who refused to confess to the charges laid against them and to set free those who openly admitted their guilt. As the trials dragged on, the plundering of the order's lands was pursued vigorously by Philippe and the Knights Hospitaller, who had always been rivals of the Templars. At the trial's end, no verdict was satisfactorily reached, since the trial was, after all, only a weapon of execution. It mattered little by 1312 whether the verdict had been guilty or innocent; the strongest of the Templars had been burned alive, the weakest made dependent on pensions, and the order's material assets seized by greedy nobles. It was as if a suspect had been summarily executed midway through his trial.

An air of utter finality settled over the last of the trials two years later in 1314. The Master of the Order, Jacques de Molay, was now on trial with the Preceptor of Normandy, Geoffrey de Charnay. Both recanted previous confessions, De Molay claiming that he had willingly admitted his and the order's guilt but 'out of fear of horrible tortures'. Both Jacques de Molay and Geoffrey de Charnay were tied to stakes on the tiny Ile de la Cité, in the middle of the River Seine. There they were slowly roasted alive, and as they died it is said that De Molay uttered a prophetic curse on those who had brought the order to its ignominious end. He cursed both Philippe and Pope Clement V, that they should follow him to his death within the year. Adding to the growing mystique of the Temple, Clement was overcome with a fatal illness before the month was out, and Philippe died mysteriously within the year that De Molay had predicted. Whether supernatural or not, these sudden deaths fuelled the image of the Temple as an occult coven and highly secret band of magical initiates. By the time of the French Revolution, almost five centuries later, when Paris was awash with secret societies, the legacy of the Temple again surfaced. As King Louis XVI's blood-spattered head dropped unceremoniously into the basket below the guillotine in 1789, a member of the vast crowd climbed on to the scaffold and dipped his hand into the dead king's still-warm blood. He flicked it out over the crowd and shouted 'Jacques de Molay, thou art avenged!' There is no need to see in this tale any survival of the order down the ages, but just the absorption of the Templar mystique into the French Freemasons, a member of whom the man on the scaffold is likely to have been. However, some historians have sought links between the refugee Knights Templar, fleeing from papal 'justice', and the first Freemasons.

Across Europe the Order of the Knights Templar had been destroyed and its members killed or persecuted to varying degrees. But nowhere were the knights as brutally treated as in France. In odd places, in fact, the authorities actually aided the escape of the knights rather than follow the dictates of the papal bull which called for their immediate arrest. The German Templars marched fully armed into the courts where they were to stand trial and intimidated the judges by a show of force into pronouncing their innocence. In Germany, Spain and Portugal the knights disbanded the order and either joined others, such as the Knights Hospitaller or the Teutonic Knights, or formed new orders with different titles. In Lorraine, then part of Germany, the Preceptor gave orders to his knights to mingle into the local population and keep their identities hidden. For this task they had to shave off their distinctive beards and abandon their white robes for more mundane costumes.

Trials in England were proving so fruitless that the Pope actually sent representatives of the Inquisition to extract confessions. Arrests had been carried out with little energy, prisoners had been kept in degrees of comfort or quickly released, and most with access to any resources had made their escape. On 9 January 1308, the Master of England, William de More, was arrested and held at Canterbury castle in some luxury, but was soon released. Only at the end of the year was he rearrested and subjected to a harsher custody. As in other countries, most knights either joined different chivalrous orders, hid among the population as civilians or fled the country. When the Inquisition arrived in England, it found that the Knights Templar who were being held prisoner by King Edward II in the Tower of London and the castles at Lincoln and York were mainly old men, retired knights of pensionable age. The body of the order still roamed free, and the king himself wrote of knights in secular garb living in the towns and villages. Some were even marrying into the populace, blending perfectly into ordinary medieval life. The Pope made repeated complaints to the king and the Archbishop of Canterbury, but little action was taken against the renegades. Those unfortunate enough to be imprisoned were eventually tortured by the Inquisition, which was becoming frustrated by the lack of progress, but still confessions were not forthcoming. By 1310 the papal legates were pressing (unsuccessfully) for the transportation of the incarcerated Templars to France, where professional torturers could be set to work on them.

In 1311 the papal representatives were able to gather a solid confession from a member of the order. Torture had no part to play, however, since the confessor spoke of his own accord, claiming to be a renegade Templar. The knight was Stephen de Staplebrugge, and he confessed to having been forced to deny Christ during his initiation into the order, but Stephen claimed he had spat only near the Crucifix, not at it, when directed to do so. Although he had admitted to almost all of the charges laid before the Temple, Stephen appealed to the mercy of the Church. A second knight and a previous Master of England, Thomas Tocci de Thoroldsby, came forward soon after to assert that he too had spat near a Crucifix during his initiation. He also told his examiners that the Templars had often favoured the Muslims in the Holy Land rather than the Christians, and that the Master of the order had often spoken of Christ's mortality. A third man, John de Stoke, who had been the Temple's treasurer in London, joined in the attacks on the Knights Templar. John's testimony carried some degree of weight since he would have known personally both King Edward I and King Edward II, as the London preceptory doubled as one of the royal treasuries. Soon, other knights were offering up similar confessions, often as part of arrangements made before the trials, when punishments had already been decided upon. There were no mass executions in England, and those who confessed were mostly forced to join monasteries.

The Temple Survives

In Britain most of the able-bodied knights were able to make their escape, just as they had in Spain and Germany. The French surprise raids precluded the escape of the Templars in that country, but even there, as we have seen, the Paris Preceptory (housing Philippe's treasury) was empty when his bailiffs arrived. The treasure, so coveted by the king, had been smuggled to the coast and not one of the Temple's ships was ever captured, despite the existence of a vast fleet. The fleet had been put to use transporting military supplies and pilgrims to and from the Holy Land, and, as already noted, exporting wool from the houses of England for sale elsewhere. It was a mercantile as much as a naval force and was supported by private wharfs and ports. How could this fleet just disappear? If it was involved in a desperate attempt to ferry the remaining Templars to freedom, where would it have sailed to?

The authors of *The Temple and the Lodge*, Michael Baigent and Richard Leigh, have proposed that the Templar fleet, laden with men, materials and money, sailed around Ireland and to the Argyll region of Scotland. Here Robert the Bruce, already excommunicated by the Pope, had begun a guerrilla war against Edward I's armies in 1306. Such a state of affairs may have been to the order's liking; Bruce's Scotland was a region cut off from established authority, free from papal bulls, and in need of a well-trained cadre of knights. One of the English Knights Templar did indeed state that members of the order had fled to Scotland, and Bruce would surely have welcomed fugitive knights from England, Ireland, France, Germany and Spain. The remaining Templars could have formed a training cadre, passing on their valuable experience in warfare, their discipline and their tactics to the Scottish rebels. When the forces of Edward II and Robert the Bruce met in battle at Bannockburn in 1314, the English were soundly defeated, in part due to a mysterious 'fresh force' that appeared on the battlefield to save the day for the Scots. Baigent and Leigh contend that this 'fresh force' may have been composed of, or at least led by, a number of Knights Templar.

Some other Templar survivors also put their formidable military skills to good use and established their own warrior bands. One such knight, Roger Flor, founded a ragged band of warrior-mercenaries, called the Catalan Company, who waged war in southern Italy on behalf of the kingdom of Aragon. Most members of the company were either Catalan, Aragonese or Navarrese soldiers. The small force later fought against the Turks while in the service of Byzantium, but eventually turned to outright robbery and brigandage in Greece.

The Portuguese Templars also formed a new order, but one eminently more successful than the short-lived Catalan Company. The Order of the Knights of Christ, an organization that lasted well into the sixteenth century, was built on the foundations of the Temple's experience in naval and navigational matters. Its vessels began a series of exploratory voyages that culminated in the expedition around Africa by a Knight of Christ called Vasco da Gama. The order even sailed under the famous red cross formerly attributed to the Knights of the Temple. When Columbus sailed across the Atlantic Ocean and into the history books, he too sailed under this cross. He was married to the daughter of a former Grand Master of the Knights of Christ and it is quite likely he was able to make much use of his father-in-law's documents. There is speculation, and some evidence to support the idea has been put forward, that the Knights Templar were in league with the Venetian sailors of the period to explore the North Atlantic coastlines of Greenland and Nova Scotia. The order was intent on establishing an independent state following their defeat in Palestine, and the writer Andrew Sinclair has suggested that the remains of two failed colonies on the American continent were the tentative first beginnings of such a state.

There is convincing evidence that what became modern Freemasonry derived in part from the survival of Templars in Scotland. Similarly, in Germany, where the Templars had infiltrated the Teutonic Knights in great numbers, the famous secret society called the Illuminati may have had its origins in the remnants of the Order of the Temple. As the memory of the political power squabbles of the day faded, the Templars became an object of emulation: both the Jesuits and the Scots Guard (the personal bodyguard of the French king) were founded on Templar principles of combining military strength with high-powered diplomacy and an élite status.

More recent connections to the long-dead Knights Templar have been made, most ominously at the turn of the twentieth century, when the activities of the Order of the New Templars were bound up in the future of Aryanism and the growth of the German Nazi Party. An outgrowth of the *völkischen* cults, which glorified the history and mythology of the German race, the New Templars were anti-Semitic and dedicated to the eradication of Jews in the German Fatherland. The order's founder was Adolf Lanz, a former Cistercian novice who once met Adolf Hitler and recognized in him the spirit needed for Germany to gain a formidable position in the world. It seemed as though any occult or mystical society could not be taken seriously without at least some allusion to the Knights Templar.

The last Templar incarnation (quite literally) was the Order of the Solar Temple, a Swiss-based religious cult that involved itself in magical rites and financial double-dealing. While other Templar societies claim a ritual heritage from the original medieval order, Joseph Di Mambro, the cult leader, actually claimed to be the reincarnation of a Knight Templar. His followers were respectable professionals, not naive and easily-led youths, and they joined Di Mambro in carrying out the cult's rituals.

During these ceremonies they would don the costume of medieval knights, while Di Mambro wielded a holy sword that he claimed had been given to him during his time in the Crusades. His daughter Emanuelle, he boasted, had been conceived without sex and was the 'cosmic child', a crucial part of his grand design. Also part of his plan was the order's Centre For The Preparation For The New Age, but Di Mambro had doomed the Templar cult to destruction. According to a senior member of the Solar Temple: 'Death can represent an essential stage of life', and in October 1994 some 53 members of the cult committed suicide simultaneously. The enigmatic Di Mambro was rumoured to have faked his own death at one of the two mass suicides, ensuring that his order would, like the original Knights Templar, be forever associated with controversy, impropriety and mystery.

Such is the alluring and powerful legacy of the order that in 1991 one of its commanderies in Britain was re-established in the revivalist spirit that had previously seen the modern foundation of the Order of Bards, Ovates and Druids. The commandery of the Knights Templar in Templecombe has its headquarters in the village's manor house, the very site used by the original knights as a base and training centre. Four years after its official re-inauguration, the Prior of South England, Major General Sir Roy Redgrave, led the official investiture in Sherborne Abbey of the Templars' first-ever Knights and Dames since the order's dissolution at the start of the fourteenth century. This new organization, without the motivation or the aims of the original, is a modern link with the past, and an attempt to recapture something of Britain's lost heritage.

The ideological and eponymous survival of the Order of the Temple in later historical movements and pseudo-religious cults (even today) is testament to the real power of the Templars. As a medieval organization they involved themselves in every aspect of life, from politics to religion and finance. Their story was one of intrigue and mystery, and their demise was made all the more shocking by the Templars' seemingly permanent and indestructible nature. Despite the order's size and power, nothing could harm it, or so it seemed. But, like the Assassins with whom the knights had such close contact, when the knights lost their focus and determination to fight for the objectives set at their foundation, then the order became vulnerable.

The charges of collusion with the Muslims deeply wounded the order, but they were well-founded accusations, for the Temple had discovered that no amount of force could vanquish the armies of the infidel. Divide and rule, and a policy of conciliation, had been the strategies of the order, rather than the rash, bludgeoning approach of the early Crusaders. Since the cult of the Assassins had been feared as much by the Arabs as by the Christians, it may have been the Temple's plan to encourage and develop links with this schism, allowing the fanatical murderers to create chaos and terror among the enemy. The Inquisitors who brought the Temple to its knees never forgot the order's numerous connections with the Arab world, and would always remember that their first headquarters had been one of the most pre-eminent mosques in Palestine. It was the Temple's unique approach to the fight for the Holy Land that provided the weapon with which the order's enemies at home were finally able to destroy it.

CHAPTER 4

The Assassins –
Political Killers of the Medieval Middle East

The Crusades had given many Frankish nobles the chance to establish themselves in a land far from the squabbles of Europe. But the newly conquered lands were only a tenuous acquisition, gained by force of arms and held by constant preparedness for war. Exactly how fleeting such gains were was brought home to the Crusaders when the Muslims made a series of significant military gains that culminated in the fall of Jerusalem in 1187 to the army of Saladin, the Sultan of Egypt.

This Arab general was the third in a line of powerful Muslim leaders dedicated to driving the Christian 'infidel' out of Syria and Palestine. He was born in Baalbek and ruled over Egypt, where he consolidated his power and from where he began to harry and threaten the Christians. Saladin was a pious Sunni, a follower of the established Islamic faith, but he commanded an army and a country that had followed a heretical offshoot to orthodox Islam. The Fatimid Shiites in Egypt had often been at odds with the rest of the Islamic world and had always resisted the religious decrees coming from the city of Baghdad – the heart of Sunni Islam. However, by Saladin's time the Fatimid Caliphate had lost most of its power and ability to stand against the forces of orthodox Islam. The new Sultan of Egypt had plans for the country and began an attempt to unite the Muslim world under his leadership; from 1184 he started to proclaim himself 'Sultan of Islam and the Muslims'. Only two things stood in the way of his becoming the undisputed leader of an Islamic Middle Eastern empire. First, there were the European Crusader states along the coast of the Mediterranean, and then there was a heretical Shiite sect that had originated in Egypt but taken root in the mountains across the Muslim world. This vehemently anti-Sunni sect was called the Nizari Ismaili, more popularly known as the Assassins.

Saladin had personal experience of this cult and of its fanaticism. Its members opposed the established Islamic faith with a will and for them Saladin embodied this establishment. In 1175, when Saladin was putting the city of Aleppo under siege, the city's ruler, Sa'ad ad-Din Gumushtakin, hired the Assassins to murder Saladin and so bring an end to the siege. Members of the cult entered the

Sultan's camp in disguise and prepared to kill him, but an Arab emir who had himself dealt with the Assassins recognized them. As he foolishly approached the cult members to question them about their presence in Saladin's camp, the Assassins killed him, giving away their presence. The ensuing struggle to capture the Assassins ended bloodily, with a multitude of dead, including every one of the Assassin cult members. Saladin himself was unharmed.

It was during the siege of Azaz, just over a year later, that the Assassins attempted to kill Saladin a second time. Again they had entered the general's camp in disguise, this time dressed as soldiers in his own army. The disguise seems to have been surprisingly successful, since Saladin was physically attacked by the knife-wielding cultists. By a stroke of luck his armour protected him from any harm and the Assassins were eventually killed by Saladin's companions. As before, several of the Sultan's defenders died in the fight. Saladin now realized how vulnerable he really was to this fanatical and unrelenting cult. His well-founded paranoia resulted in the adoption of several measures against assassination: he would allow only people with whom he was familiar to approach him, and he took to sleeping inside a specially constructed wooden tower. Being a soldier, he also decided to bring about the end of the cult by marching against the most important Assassin citadel, Masyaf. The siege of Masyaf was not decisive, and Saladin quickly withdrew his forces. One story, told to explain this strange reversal, has it that during the siege he woke one morning to find a poisoned dagger on his bed along with some hot cakes of a type only baked by the Assassins and a piece of paper on which a threatening verse was written. It was obvious to Saladin that an Assassin had been into his tent, if not the Assassin Grand Master himself, Rashid al-Din Sinan. Understanding the awesome power that the cult had over his own followers, he wisely chose to leave Masyaf and the other Assassin castles in peace.

Old Man of the Mountains

This episode illustrates perfectly the mystique possessed by the Assassin leader; his reputation as a sorcerer and conjuror had spread to every kingdom, both Christian and Muslim. Sinan was considered able to charm any man or woman and was said to possess the powers of telepathy and clairvoyance. To contemporaries, Rashid al-Din Sinan was a magical evil genius leading a cult of fanatical killers: a 'medieval Moriarty'. He was thought of as presiding over a sinister web of informants and agents, bound together by dark conspiracies and evil schemes.

Sinan, as Grand Master of the Syrian Assassins, was known as the 'Old Man of the Mountains', a term used to describe many Syrian

Grand Masters, as well as some of the Persian Assassin leaders. But the title properly belongs to Sinan, who took control of the Syrian cult in 1162 and held it until his death in 1193. When the chroniclers of the time (both Muslim and Christian) mention the 'Old Man of the Mountains', it is to Sinan that they refer. The origin of this fascinating appellation is ambiguous, but it may be connected with the name 'Mountain Chief' (or Sheikh'l-Jabal), which became translated as 'Old Man of the Mountains' by Western writers like Marco Polo. Alternatively, it may have been a title used to signify the great knowledge and wisdom of the Grand Master, the 'old' referring to a long and well-established tradition.

With his skill and cunning, Sinan took the Assassins to the peak of their success and notoriety, and in part this meant they were constantly defending their castles from Muslim armies as well as Crusaders. Under his leadership, the Syrian Assassins created a small but unified 'state' and fortified the castles that they held. Although their territory was always fairly limited and their numbers few, the cult was well placed to negotiate with all the major powers in the Holy Land.

The power of the Assassin cult did not lie in troop numbers or wealth, but in the unique form of warfare that they waged. They were masters of infiltration and surprise, and their members were cold, calculating killers incapable of being bought or warned off by their targets. The strength of purpose that drove the Assassin 'devoted-ones' (*fidais*) was so overwhelming that the deadly retribution which always followed a successful murder was actually welcomed. The families of the *fidais* thought it an honour that their son be killed on a mission; consequently it was considered a great dishonour when a son returned home from a suicidal mission on which his colleagues had perished. This single-mindedness served to fire the imaginations of European writers and Crusaders when they arrived in the Holy Land. Initially there was very sparse contact between the Crusader states and Sinan's Assassins, but dealings became gradually more commonplace. This hesitancy can be put down to the Assassins' obsessional hatred of the Sunni faith and their belief that the Europeans seemed to offer little threat to their brand of Islam. Such mutual ignorance came to a sudden and bloody end in 1152, when Assassin devoted-ones murdered the Christian Count Raymond I of Tripoli.

Medieval Europe would never forget the word 'assassin', mainly because of Count Raymond's death, and the Crusaders fought with the Assassins interminably from that point on. The cult began to lose prestige and fighting effectiveness due to pressure from the Christians, so much so that they were obliged to pay tribute to the most powerful of the knightly orders, the Knights Templar. Although it seemed not to help the Assassin cause in any way, the attempts to assassinate Crusaders continued. In 1192, Conrad of Montferrat, the Prince of Tyre, was walking through that city on his way home after a visit to the Bishop Beauvais. As he turned a corner he was met by two youths known to him, who pulled out concealed knives. In the attack that followed Conrad was mortally wounded, while his bodyguard was able to kill one of the Assassins in retaliation. One source says that Conrad was carried to a nearby church as he clung to life, but that the very same church had been the second Assassin's refuge! This devoted-one emerged from hiding to administer the final blow to Conrad. Unlike the murder of Count Raymond, which had no real benefit for Sinan and his gang of Assassins, Conrad of Montferrat was influential and ambitious and was seen as the ideal man to oppose Saladin. It was thought at the time that he might have been able to lead the Christians back into the city of Jerusalem, which had been in Muslim hands since Saladin's conquest of 1187.

Christian and Muslim sources differ on the supposed financier of Conrad's demise. According to some, the Sultan Saladin approached Sinan with an offer of 10,000 gold pieces and a request to assassinate both the immensely successful Richard the Lionheart and also Conrad of Montferrat. The story goes that Sinan accepted, but only in the case of the latter nobleman. Unfortunately for King Richard, he was suspected by public opinion in the Crusader states of hiring the Assassins himself to kill Conrad. Charges against Richard were laid after he had left the Holy Land in secrecy, and he did that dressed in the white robes and armour of a Knight Templar. That such conspiratorial rumours were current indicates the degree of complicity that had developed between the Syrian Assassins and all the powers and territories around them. Much of the gossip and rumour may have been put about by Richard's arch-rival, King Philippe Augustus of France. Whether true or not, the connection of the king of England with the Syrian Assassins became one of many legends that were woven around the cult and still survive to this day. One French poet immortalized this connection in a poem that has Richard teaching English boys the murderous techniques used by the Assassin cult.

The regular contact between the Assassins and the Knights Templar has already been mentioned in Chapter 3. The growth in power of this knightly body into the foremost military force in the Holy Land meant that the threats of the Assassins held few terrors for them. In fact, as we have seen, following Raymond's murder the Knights Templar were able to force the Assassins to pay a regular tribute of 2,000 gold byzants to them. This arrangement rankled with the cult until Sinan decided to negotiate with the kingdom of Jerusalem to try and stop the tribute. His envoy, Abdullah, was dispatched to the court of King Amalric I with an offer of an alliance. As a sign of good faith, Abdullah promised that the Assassins would convert to Christianity in return for the lifting of the Templars' tribute. King Amalric was perhaps not thoroughly convinced by such an offer, but he was delighted at the prospect of having such a band of killers standing at his side rather than behind his back. Abdullah was sent back to Sinan in 1173 with full acceptance of an alliance, but he never made it to the cult's castles. On the dusty road back, his party came face to face with armed and armoured horsemen, complete with footmen: Templars! The knights attacked the Assassin group and one of them, wearing an eyepatch, struck down Abdullah, killing him. This knight was Walter of Mesnil, acting for the Templars to ensure that the tribute they received from the cult continued.

King Amalric was greatly displeased and, in contravention of the judicial privileges that Templars enjoyed, called for Walter's arrest. The Templar Chapter in Sidon, where Walter was hiding, refused to give him up, claiming (rightly) that only the Pope could pass judgement on him. But the king's soldiers attacked the building and kidnapped the knight, whom they then imprisoned in the city of Tyre.

Although both orders were at odds in this episode of Crusader history, there were times when Assassins and Templars had similar goals. The two groups seem alike in many ways, and this fact was not lost on the papal Inquisition that put the Knights Templar on trial over a century later. Both the groups followed a similar system of organization, with three lower ranks: lay brothers (the Assassin *lasiq*), sergeants (*fidais*) and the knights (*rafiq* – a word, like 'knight', which means 'companion'). Again both sects had three upper ranks: the Templars had priors, grand priors and the Master; the Assassins had the *dai*, *dai'l-kabir* and *dai'd-duat* (who was the Grand Master). Like the Christian Templars, the *rafiq* cult members, too, wore robes of white with red trim.

The Templar castles of Chastel Blanc and Tortosa were among the closest to the Assassin territories, and they used them in a classic Assassin strategy. The castles were not the basis for a feudal kingdom, but only armed forts used as jumping-off points for raids and campaigns. For example, little effort was wasted on denying enemy movement between Templar castles. Assassin citadels were employed in exactly the same fashion. The proximity of Assassin and Templar 'states' only adds to the numerous points of similarity between the two organizations. Inevitably, questions of interaction and influence have been asked, but none have yet been satisfactorily answered. As permanent residents of the Holy Land, with an armed presence that continued as long as the Crusaders remained there, the

Knights Templar must surely have absorbed aspects of the culture around them. It was natural that the pious warrior sect saw in the Assassins something of themselves.

The Templars were also involved in perhaps the most remarkable encounter of Assassins with the West, when the king of France had several meetings with prominent Assassin members. The meetings were spread over several years and began when the Syrian 'Old Man of the Mountains' sent two trusted *fidais* to assassinate King Louis IX in Paris. News had reached him that the king was planning a new Crusade, with the usual help from the French Knights Templar. The Templars and Louis were on good terms with each other, which may explain why the 'Old Man' then changed his mind and sent two more senior Assassins to stop the murder. Had the Temple convinced the Assassin Grand Master to call off the killing? When Louis prepared for a Crusade in 1244, seven years later, the Templars did indeed organize a great deal of the financial aspects. In the event, the two high-ranking Assassins caught up with their brethren at the French port of Marseilles; legend has it that a grateful King Louis sent the Assassins back to the Holy Land with extravagant gifts and peace offerings.

Not all of King Louis's dealings with the cult were resolved so easily, for he was met in Acre by three Assassins in 1250, just after he had been released from captivity by a later Sultan of Egypt. These Assassins exploited the king's vulnerable position to the best of their abilities, hinting at the dreadful fate awaiting him if he should not decide to pay a tribute to the cult. They emphasized that some of the other European nobles were already paying tribute and were now immune from the deadly knives of the Assassins. Among those paying protection money, they claimed, were the emperor of Germany and the king of Hungary. King Louis wisely promised to reflect on their threats. At the following meeting the king made sure that he was well supported by Masters of the Knights Hospitaller. It was not their physical presence which may have intimidated the Assassin envoys but rather their acquaintance with the ways and methods of the cult.

The knights were great rivals of the Knights Templar and, like them, established a castle close to Assassin territory in 1142. The immense fortress of Krak des Chevaliers lay just a single day's ride from the Assassin stronghold of Masyaf, and this intimidation paid off, since they too were able to demand (and receive) a tribute from the Arab sect. The Assassins, now the ultimate mercenaries of the Holy Land, were once caught between the rival knightly orders in 1213. The Knights Hospitaller had hired the Assassins to murder the son of Prince Bohemond of Antioch. In return the prince marched against the offending Assassin castle with a force of Knights

Templar. As usual when under siege, the wily Assassins negotiated an end to the conflict.

King Louis's final meeting with the persistent Assassins ended peaceably for both sides, although it began badly when the envoys were threatened with being thrown bodily into the sea! The indignation of the king's advisers seems to have had unexpected results: gifts were exchanged and King Louis sent a cleric, Brother Yves, to visit the 'Old Man of the Mountains' and learn the philosophies and beliefs of the sect. The idea that the Assassins actually had a theological doctrine of their own will have seemed unbelievable to the Crusaders, who considered them despicable mercenaries and rogues intent on doing evil and spreading terror. In that belief, the Crusaders were probably correct, but they knew little of the cult's origins, its inner beliefs or *raison d'être*.

A Policy of Murder

The Assassins, more properly known as the Nizari Ismaili, were a dissident religious sect that formed a heresy within the Islamic faith. The first and greatest schism in Islamic religion was between the established Sunnis and the opposing Shias. The Sunnis believe absolute power and authority rest with the Koran as presented by the Prophet Muhammad. The Shias, on the other hand, believe that each age has its own great leader and that this leader, or Imam, is the voice of God on earth. His wisdom is God-given and he possesses almost superhuman powers. Beginning as a small but growing heresy, Shiism resorted to secrecy to survive and as the Shiite movement started to fragment, an array of subcults and related religious sects were created. One of these was Ismailism. The Ismaili secret sect was named after Ismail, the son of an Imam, and his father's supposed successor as the seventh Imam – the rightful heir to the wisdom and authority passed down since Adam. Both Sunnis and Shias regarded Ismail as a criminal, unfit for the Imamate and rightfully passed over by the succession. For following Ismail the sect was persecuted by the established Arab world, although for some time the Ismaili heresy did become the official religion of Egypt during the Fatimid Caliphate (AD 909–1171).

At that time, Cairo was the centre of Ismailism and the heart of opposition to the Sunni faith. It was to this capital that students flocked, receiving instruction in the whole range of academic subjects, as well as Ismaili doctrine. Under the banner of Ismailism, the Fatimid Caliphate made enormous political gains, conquering Syria, North Africa and areas in Arabia. By the end of the tenth century, Ismailism seemed set to conquer the Muslim world. Its greatest obstacle was the Seljuk Turks, who had quickly come to dominate the Muslim states of the Middle East. They ruled Persia and gave support to the heart of the Sunni religion: the Caliphate of Baghdad. Egypt's role as the great champion against the Sunni Muslims soon declined, and the country was effectively run by the army. The activities of the military in the affairs of state would eventually be responsible for yet another, final, schism. Before the Caliph Al-Mustansir died in 1094, he had nominated his son Nizar to succeed him. The Caliph's general had other ideas and placed on the throne Nizar's brother, whom he had married to his own daughter. This tore apart the loyalties of faithful Ismailis. Those in the sect who had settled in Persia refused to acknowledge the new Caliph, and established their own breakaway sect called the Nizari Ismailis. They declared their allegiance to the ousted Prince Nizar and, under the leadership of a dynamic and wily revolutionary named Hasan-i-Sabbah, this Persian cult flourished as the Assassins!

Hasan-i-Sabbah was a religious leader who had studied Ismailism in Cairo. There, a 'Hall of Wisdom' was attended by Hasan and others who wished to acquire academic knowledge and learn the intricacies of the faith. Hasan had been raised as a Shia, in the Persian city of Rayy, but in his early years he had met an Ismaili missionary (or *dai*) called Amira Zarrab. This man was also known as 'the Coiner' from his disguise as a tradesman – all secret missionaries adopted disguises. Little by little he undermined Hasan's faith and introduced him to the tenets of Ismailism. It was a subtle conversion, a process whereby the missionary encouraged the convert to question his own faith, while simultaneously providing answers. Only when he had come to agree with and understand the new way of thinking did the missionary reveal his Ismaili origins. Hasan later studied under the *dai* Abu Najim Sarraj ('the Saddler') and began to learn the deeper secrets of the sect. The young Hasan was soon compelled to leave Rayy, perhaps on a spiritual journey to Egypt, perhaps because the heretical beliefs he preached were frowned upon.

Hasan travelled extensively, always learning, teaching and forging contacts, and he spent three years in Cairo studying at the Caliph's court. There he gave his support for the Caliph's eldest son, Prince Nizar. After his return to Persia at the start of the 1080s, the skilled Hasan-i-Sabbah began to put down roots that would support his secret sect in the years to come. As an Ismaili *dai* he found support among the local Persian Ismailis and immediately made an impact. Hasan had a keen mind, the *dai*'s grasp of oratory and theology, knowledge of philosophy and a rigid moral code that impressed those he spoke with.

His missionary work in the remote mountains of Persia proved fruitful and Hasan began to look for a permanent headquarters from which to operate. The land he and his converts travelled was the inhospitable mountain district of Daylam, in the north-west of Persia, a region difficult for the government to control yet perfect for the type of guerrilla war that Hasan had in mind. For ten years he organized the Persian Ismailis and promised the overthrow of the Seljuk Turks who ruled the land. The long-term goal was the destruction of the centre of Islamic religious authority, the Sunni Caliphate in Baghdad. Hasan chose as a base the isolated but impregnable castle of Alamut, north-east of the Persian city of Qazvin in the Elburz Mountains. But first he had to seize it.

Alamut (from *aluh-amut*, the 'Eagle's Nest') was more than just a castle; it was a fortified village and the centre of the Alamut valley and its villages. The Alamut River drains into the Shahrud River and thence into the Caspian Sea. In fact the Elburz range, and therefore the citadel of Alamut, occupied a strategic position between the Persian plateau and the route down to the Caspian. Alamut had virtually impregnable natural rock defences that made it an ideal location for the secret cult Hasan was establishing. The fort was originally built as a hide-out, some time around AD 860–61, by religious refugees from the Abbasid Caliphs. It had not only formidable defences but an array of outlying forts and look-out posts across the valley.

The castle of Alamut was occupied by Hasan-i-Sabbah in 1090, using the guile and cunning that were to characterize both his later thinking and that of his cult. Rather than lay siege by traditional force of arms, Hasan sent out his own *dais* one-by-one to convert the inhabitants of the villages in the Alamut valley. Soon his missionaries were able to preach Ismaili doctrine inside the castle itself, making numerous converts to the faith. At one point Hasan was smuggled into Alamut and lived there in disguise under the name Dihkhuda. When the castle's ruler discovered the subterfuge, there was little he could do about it since by then the residents were almost all loyal Ismailis. Hasan allowed the Alamut's former ruler to leave and stepped into his place as lord of the valley and its people.

This first success would be repeated many times as Hasan sent out his *dais* to infiltrate and take control of towns, villages and castles near and far. Such a strategy would become a standard of guerrilla warfare for centuries to come. Slowly and surely the provincial population is overcome by a combination of propaganda and anti-government sentiment. Mao Tse-tung used these tactics in China in 1949 and Ho Chi Minh used them against the Americans during the Vietnam War. The persuasive *dais* preached politics and religious doctrine in the same breath.

New castles were taken by force and a few were built by the Assassins themselves. Following successes in Daylam, the south-eastern district of Quhistan came under the influence of the Assassins; rebellious elements there were inspired to rise up against the Turks and Quhistan became the second centre of Ismailism in the country. The third area was centred on Girdkuh, south of Damghan. The spread of the cult throughout Persia was inexorably carried along on a wave of revolution and defiance of Seljuk authority. The Seljuks would not turn a blind eye to the dissident sect for long, though, and Hasan prepared for the day when their armies moved against him. He implemented a policy of strengthening the defences of Alamut and other castles that the cult had recently occupied. In 1092 the Seljuk Vizier Nizan al-Mulk sent armies against the two Ismaili strongholds of Alamut and Quhistan, but neither could dislodge the cult. The besieged Ismailis had used their local influence to good effect and called on help from the surrounding population. Those at Alamut were able to rout the Seljuk army by carrying out a successful ambush against it. This small victory spurred Hasan-i-Sabbah to formulate new and more adventurous plans for the overthrow of the Seljuks. Rather than continue a policy of fostering popular support in the outlying districts of Persia, Hasan-i-Sabbah began instead a campaign of terrorism. This entailed the use of systematic assassinations for political purposes and would eventually propel Hasan's up-to-now minor sect into the consciousness of the entire world.

The shift from a guerrilla war to a terrorist campaign was one that was eventually to ensure the cult's failure. Rather than gain territory, the loyalty of whole villages or representatives in the government power structure, terrorists, then as now, inspired terror and crudely eliminated individuals standing in their way. Not only were their attacks haphazard but the randomness and brutality of them served to alienate the population. People felt frightened and powerless, cut off from making any difference themselves. Hasan's Assassins and their methods would have been scorned by the Russian revolutionaries Lenin and Trotsky, who, like all successful guerrilla leaders, realized that to overthrow an oppressive dynasty (be it the Seljuk Turks or the Romanovs) the loyalty of the people actually under subjugation was needed. At the most basic level the local villages and towns could be used as hide-outs for members. Not so with the Assassins; there were few places they could show themselves without being arrested and executed. Terrorism (even international terrorism) can be said to have started with Hasan-i-Sabbah and his first murder victim.

This first target was to be a man with whom Hasan had reputedly been good friends before his conversion to Ismailism. He was Nizam al-Mulk, the Vizier to the Turkish Sultan. Legend says that Nizam and Hasan had originally been old friends and associated with

Islam's most famous poet and astronomer, Omar Khayyám. The story is apocryphal, but it is interesting because of the light in which it casts Hasan. The three men were students together and it was suggested that whosoever achieved fame and fortune first would promise to share them with the other two. This was agreed, and after some time had passed Nizam al-Mulk became the first to achieve the honours of high office in 1073. He had managed to find a position at the Turkish Sultan's court. As agreed, his two schoolfriends soon came to visit – Omar Khayyám was presented with a pension and a quiet place to study, but Hasan asked for power and Nizam foolishly granted him a place in the Sultan's court. It was not long before Hasan incurred the displeasure of the Vizier; perhaps Hasan desired even more power and began to plot against his friend to gain Sultan Malik Shah's favour. The man who would later be the leader of the Assassins was forced to flee from the court and was hunted by Nizam al-Mulk for many years.

Whether true or not, the story tries to explain the enmity that existed between the two men in the following years. Nizam hunted high and low for his old friend in an attempt to catch and kill him. This obsession with Hasan-i-Sabbah ended in 1092, with the sudden demise of Nizam al-Mulk at the dagger-point of an Assassin. Hasan had achieved power of his own devising and, with the murder of Nizam, he showed that he was not afraid to use it. This first cult assassination had all the hallmarks of later murders: the Assassin, Bu-Tahir Arrani, dressed in disguise as a Sufi holy man and carried out the killing during the holiday of Ramadan. Immediately after he had committed the deed, Bu-Tahir was cut down by Nizam's bodyguards. This use of disguise and deception, the exploitation of religious festivals or buildings, and the suicidal attack with a knife all echo down the corridors of Middle Eastern history until the very last days of the cult in the thirteenth century.

Two years later the Ismaili Caliph of Egypt died and was replaced by his commander-in-chief's preferred choice. The legal claimant (and spiritual leader of Hasan-i-Sabbah), Prince Nizar, was arrested and later killed, prompting Hasan to break away from the Ismaili religion that centred on Fatimid Egypt. He announced that his Persian Ismailis would recognize the late Nizar as Imam and rightful heir to the Ismaili leadership. From then on Hasan's Ismaili cult became the Nizari Ismaili, a secret sect within a secret sect!

After 1094, Hasan-i-Sabbah consolidated both his territorial gains in the Persian wilderness and the doctrines of his theological teachings. His sect was now isolated, both religiously and politically, and the path he chose to go down was that of a policy of murder to achieve his aims. We cannot say that Hasan invented political assassination, but he institutionalized the act and created from the usual murder for power, greed or revenge a systematic policy of assassinations on a strategic scale that aimed to overthrow not just an oppressive dynasty but an entire religion.

In the years to come, the leader of the Syrian Assassins, Sinan, was known and feared as the commander of a gang of killers. His men carried out their grisly trade for financial gain. Not so Hasan and the original Nizari Ismaili – their assassinations were a battle royal with the Islamic establishment. Hasan was no wheeler-dealer either, but a stoic thinker and philosopher who gained his converts not with money or threats but by the force of his personality and his persuasive arguments. The Syrian Assassins, when they began to operate in the twelfth century, achieved a notoriety and a mercenary reputation that was not truly deserved of their Persian brothers.

The very name 'assassin' was never used of the Persian Nizari Ismaili by contemporary writers. The title was used only of the Syrian branch of the cult when it became established at the opening of the twelfth century. Most historians agree that the modern etymology of the word 'assassin' is derived from the drug hashish, used exclusively by the Syrian Assassins. Because of the popularity of this drug with the Assassins, they were also called the 'hashishin'. Known also as cannabis, marijuana and ganja, the drug was used by the Assassins for the sense of spiritual uplift and enlightenment it can bring. Hasan's austerity and inhibited way of life would have precluded its use by his Persian followers. The leader had both of his sons executed; one of them, Muhammad, was put to death after accusations were made that he had drunk wine. Liberal drug use, therefore, would have been highly unlikely.

The Assassin Strength of Faith

The cult that Hasan-i-Sabbah now presided over was an ascetic one to say the least. But the very austerity of such sects is what at times can prove most appealing, as the modern-day popularity of cults like Hare Krishna attests. All forms of drugs, including alcohol, seem to have been banned from the Assassin castles, and absolute and unquestioning loyalty was expected from all of the sect's members. Such devotion was a requirement of a movement that had been continually harassed and persecuted, as the Nizari Ismaili had. Hasan refined this faith to turn members who would stick by the cult through adversity into members who would murder for it, even if in the process they would be killed themselves. In part this loyalty was fuelled by devotion to Hasan as a charismatic leader and in part also by the nature of the cult as a secret body of initiates that inspired a feeling of comradeship and group loyalty.

The basic doctrines of the Assassins were derived almost wholly from the parent Ismaili sect and comprised a fusion of Greek thought (mainly Neoplatonic and Pythagorean) with various Semitic ideas. The fifty-one epistles, known as the *Rasa'il*, were the authoritative text of the Ismaili, and may have constituted current Ismaili theology at the time. It is known that the Syrian Grand Master Sinan studied the *Rasa'il* in depth, which suggests that it did indeed play an important role in Assassin thinking. Part of this thinking was the concept of 'levels' of knowledge that could be attained by passing through seven grades of initiation. The number seven had an important significance within the cult: there were seven ranks of initiation as well as seven Imams.

The seven grades in the Nizari Ismaili began at the lowest level with the rank of *fidai* (devoted-one), who had taken the oath of loyalty to the Grand Master and Imam, but knew nothing of the cult's inner secrets. Members of this grade were the rank and file of the sect and performed the assassinations that gave the Assassins their notoriety. Above the *fidai* was the *lasiq* (adherent), who may have had more duties and responsibilities than the *fidai*. Neither was properly initiated. The members who were had the title of *rafiq* (comrade) and knew something of the mysteries and doctrines of the organization, but still lacked the full understanding and authority of the next three grades: the *dais*. Above the first of these, the *dai* (missionary), there was the *dai'l-kabir* (superior missionary) and *dai'd-duat* (chief missionary). This last rank was that of a Grand Master, an ultimate leader who controlled the entire Nizari Ismaili cult from the fortress of Alamut. Hasan-i-Sabbah was the first Assassin *dai'd-duat*. He commanded his superior *dais* and they, in turn, commanded their own village or fortress. The *dais* were the fully initiated members of the Assassins, capable of preaching the doctrines of the cult and spreading the Ismaili faith. In them was vested the spiritual health of the Assassin communities.

At the pinnacle of this organization stood the Imam, the Shia's legitimate heir to the teachings of Ali and Prince Nizar. These official teachings of the cult were referred to as the *da'wa* and they replaced the previous *da'wa* of the Ismailis. Hasan-i-Sabbah was the arbiter of the knowledge and acted as the Assassins' link with God; such a one-man priesthood exaggerated the Assassins' loyalty to him. Faith and belief went unchallenged and kept alive the cult's spirit of absolute dedication and self-sacrifice. Western writers went to great lengths to try and explain this mesmeric grip that the 'Old Man of the Mountains' was supposed to have on his followers. The most popular explanation was the use of hashish to instil the calm killing mind and cold-blooded obedience, but the drug actually has the opposite effect. Hashish created intoxication and a feeling of quiescence. It is unlikely to have been used by Assassins just about to murder someone. Faith was likely to be a stronger drug.

Chroniclers of the Crusades also attributed Assassin fanaticism to the magical powers of their Grand Masters. It was thought that both Hasan-i-Sabbah and Sinan dabbled in the occult. Sinan, in particular, was given power over men's minds and skills in alchemy and magical practice. It is highly likely that both branches of the Nizari Ismaili performed alchemy, astrology and magical ritual. In the world of medieval Islam, such practices were entering the scientific sphere and Hasan the thinker and philosopher was also reputed to be an expert alchemist. Few today would accept the view that the Grand Master of the Assassins held sway over his cult through occult means. As history and the other cults in this book attest, fanaticism is most powerful when an inner belief overrides the cult member's own social or moral conscience.

Two stories often repeated by European writers in connection with the Assassins illustrate why people were fascinated by this sinister and unfathomable group. The first maintains that when the Grand Master had selected a group of *fidais* to perform an assassination, he had them drugged with hashish and then carried into a secret garden. The young men would awaken to find themselves in a beautiful paradise, with splashing fountains, pavilions and well-watered trees and flowers. Every need was catered for by attractive maidens – music, wine, delicious foods and love. This Garden of Paradise was supposed to be a foretaste of the Paradise in the afterlife that awaited the *fidais* upon their death. Once drugged again and transferred from the garden back into the harsh realities of the Assassin castle, they were told that to die in the service of the Grand Master would mean they would be borne back to Paradise by angels. Such a subtle form of mind control may well have taken place, and its brainwashing effects are illustrated by the story of the Death Leap. Count Henry of Champagne had visited the Assassin citadel of Kahf to accept the apology of the Grand Master there for the cult's murder of Conrad of Montferrat. While he was there, Henry was walking with the Grand Master and was told by the Assassin leader that no Christians were as loyal to their masters as his devoted-ones were to him. To prove the point he made a signal to a group of *fidais* high on a battlement. Without hesitation, two of them threw themselves off the edge and plunged to their deaths. Obedience was everything to the Assassins.

The Grand Masters
Hasan-i-Sabbah had been the first *dai'd-duat*, or chief *dai*, of the Nizari Ismaili from the point when the legitimate Ismaili Imam Prince Nizar was deposed and murdered. That year, 1094, was the official beginning of the Assassins as an independent organization. For the next thirty years Hasan worked to extend his state by

infiltrating and occupying castles, by sending *dais* to new areas of unease and by the strategic application of assassination. The Alamut valley became the centre of this state, and Hasan's home right up to the time of his death. It was said that until that day he left the confines of his house only twice, and that was to go on to the roof! His work involved fasting, praying, reading and analysing the reports of his spies. The regime was tough. One Assassin was exiled from Alamut for playing the flute, and, as already noted, both his sons were executed. One was accused of the murder of a *dai* and was summarily killed; it is not known what Hasan's reaction was when he discovered that his son had in fact been innocent. Only the spread of Nizari influence concerned him; the control of towns and castles would eventually provide a solid base for future rebellion.

The identity of many of the smaller Assassin citadels has been lost to us, but the greatest have been located and explored. Crucial to Hasan's tiny mountain empire were the castles of Samiran, Lammassar, Maymun Diaz, Shah Diz and the lesser strongholds of Damghan, Turshiz and Girdkuh. The valley of the Assassins held the cult's three most important castles: Alamut itself, Lammassar and Maymun Diaz.

Samiran, which occupied an important military position in a valley further north, and the impressive Shah Diz were the two other notable Assassin sites. This latter castle was located far from the Alamut valley, eight kilometres from the city of Esfahan. Shah Diz was not long in Assassin hands, though; following a siege in 1107, it was lost to the Sultan Muhammad. The Sultan had fought with the Nizari Ismaili all across Persia and destroyed Shah Diz when he eventually took it, probably to deny the place to the Assassins in the future. Of course, the Assassin commander of the castle, the *dai* ibn-Attash, used every bit of his sect's skill and cunning to end the siege. One story says that he negotiated with the Sultan of Persia and secured the withdrawal of the army, but carried out an ambush against the soldiers as they marched away. Another records that he volunteered to surrender the castle after his plan to assassinate Sultan Muhammad ended in failure.

Hasan-i-Sabbah died on 12 June 1124. His place as Grand Master of the Assassins was taken by his own nominee, Buzurgumid, the loyal and experienced commander of the Lammassar fortress. Hasan had the foresight to choose a successor before he died, thereby preventing the Nizari Ismaili fragmenting, just as the original Ismaili religion had done. Buzurgumid proved to be an able and skilled Grand Master, fending off Seljuk armies sent against his Assassins. The great Seljuk Empire of the Turks now encompassed a large portion of the Middle East and the Sultan was dedicated to eradicating the Assassin 'state-within-a-state' that existed in Persia. A new Sultan had by now succeeded Malik Shah. Sanjar, who ruled the Seljuks from 1117 to 1157, proved to be a bitter opponent of the cult after an initial truce. But the Assassin *dais* were still being dispatched on their missions and ominous threats against Sanjar were made. Eventually the Sultan sent his armies against Buzurgumid's strongholds. The commander of the force assaulting Quhistan was the Vizier Muin al-Mulk. He quickly fell to the knives of two *fidais* who had disguised themselves as stablehands. Other murders were to follow; the Assassins no longer needed Hasan to provide them with the motivation to kill.

When Sanjar's brother asked for an Assassin envoy to negotiate a peaceful settlement to the fighting, the envoy was killed. In a frenzy of revenge, the cult murdered 400 people in the town of Qazvin, close to Alamut. Other murders, rather more politically motivated, were also carried out. The most important murder of Buzurgumid's reign took place in 1138, the year he was to die himself. The arch-enemy of the Assassins, the Caliph of Baghdad, had been captured in battle by one of Sanjar's commanders. The Caliph had joined a coalition opposing Seljuk power in the region and for his crime he was placed under arrest in the Seljuk camp. Such a sitting target was hard for the Assassins to resist and the camp was easily infiltrated by *fidais*, who then murdered the Caliph.

Like Hasan, Buzurgumid was also able to nominate his successor as lord of Alamut, and he chose his son, Muhammad ibn Buzurgumid. This Grand Master ruled until 1162, facing a conspiracy against him at Alamut. The religious direction begun by Hasan and continued by Buzurgumid seemed to have waned during the third Grand Master's rule. The teachings of the cult took second place to a defensive campaign of military raids aimed at consolidating Alamut's hold on the local area. Territories away from the Alamut valley were left to fend for themselves and the aggressive preaching and murdering that characterized the Assassin campaigns lapsed. Murders were still carried out – most importantly, the son of the Caliph who Buzurgumid had ordered murdered in 1138 was killed – but reconciliation not revolution characterized the cult's relationship with the Seljuks.

A growing body of Assassins became disenchanted with Muhammad ibn Buzurgumid's approach and looked to the Grand Master's son, Hasan II, for a return to the old ways. Unlike his father, this Hasan was young, personable and persuasive. He studied the work of earlier Ismaili writers (including Hasan-i-Sabbah) and at some point became convinced that *he* was the next Imam who Hasan I had prophesied in his writings. As the young Hasan's popularity increased, that of Muhammad ibn Buzurgumid declined.

Drastic measures were taken. His son's supporters were tortured and killed. In one murderous rage he had 250 of Hasan II's supporters executed and 250 more exiled from Alamut, forcing them to march down the mountain carrying their dead comrades on their backs.

When Hasan II did take the throne at Alamut, it would be only for a brief four years, but he would totally transform the theology of the Nizari Ismaili during that time. He declared himself an Imam and radically changed the cult doctrines, declaring that a Resurrection would take place that involved the returning to life of all the dead. Only those who truly believed would rise again to immortality. He instituted his own deeply heretical rituals, which flouted many fundamental tenets of Islam. Contemporary Muslim writers began to refer to them as the Malahida (the Heretics). In fact, the new Assassin religion introduced by Hasan can barely be called Islamic at all. Much like the witches' Sabbat, the cult 'reversed' many aspects of orthodox worship to create an anti-Islam. For example, in the middle of Ramadan, the Islamic month of fasting, Hasan established a Festival of the Resurrection that included a feast with music and wine. As if that were not enough, the worshippers prayed to God with their backs to Mecca.

Hasan II's enthusiasm seemed boundless, and although Muhammad ibn Buzurgumid had allowed Alamut to become isolated and cut off from the other Assassin regions, Hasan sent out *dais* to preach the Resurrection and teach the new ceremonies. It is surprising that Hasan II was able to get so far with his audacious reforms in such a short period, but they seem to have been accepted by the majority of the Nizari Ismaili. Some cult members loyal to the memory of Hasan-i-Sabbah left Alamut, never to return, forced out by the newly established death penalty for continuing the old teachings. Perhaps the Assassins had resigned themselves to the utter futility of converting the vast Sunni population of the Islamic world and were happy to hear that a reward for their struggles was not far away. The doctrines of Resurrection that characterized Hasan II's reign at Alamut would outlive him. Hasan died in 1166, at the hands of his brother-in-law, but his son, Muhammad II, quickly assumed power, thus ensuring the survival of the new religion. He was a more loyal son than Hasan II himself had been, and he carried on and consolidated the teachings of the Resurrection for another forty years. He proclaimed the existence of the divine spirit in himself and his successors, transforming the leader of the cult from the *dai'd-duat* (chief missionary, or Grand Master) to Imam. In other matters Muhammad II seems to have played almost no role in Persian politics. Assassinations were rare and Alamut was again cut off from the other Assassin citadels. The limelight was now shifting to the Assassin colony in the Syrian Jabal Bahra mountains. As we have already seen, these Nizari Ismaili were achieving great fame for their skulduggery against the Christians and Muslims.

From the reign of Muhammad II, the Persian Assassins became an insular and introverted sect continually on the defensive, lacking clear objectives and with many deadly enemies. In some ways they resembled the heretical sects of the Christian West, such as the Cathars or the Bogomils, but without their popular support. Life was becoming difficult for the heretics, which may have explained why Muhammad's son Hasan III made another dramatic series of changes to the Assassin doctrine. From his succession in 1210, Hasan III transformed Nizari thought and perplexed the Muslim world by converting to Sunni Islam. The very object of Assassin hatred was embraced wholeheartedly by them. The defeat of the Sunni faith was, after all, their *raison d'être*, but Hasan III was perhaps more politically astute than either of his two predecessors. The Assassins were coming under pressure from the Caliph of Baghdad in the west and Muhammad Khwarazmshah in the east. Perhaps Hasan III was tempted to move to orthodoxy for the security that it provided. Whatever his reasons, the Nizari Ismaili now became just another Sunni faction, complete with newly built mosques and traditional ritual practices. The Resurrection was never totally abandoned, though, and when the reforming Hasan III died, his son Muhammad III continued to support it, alongside the practice of the cult's Sunni teachings.

Muhammad III became lord of Alamut as a young boy in 1221 and as he grew to maturity he began to move the Assassins back to the Ismaili faith. The Resurrection still figured in this doctrine but began to play a lesser role. In fact, the Assassins seem to have lost their missionary zeal altogether under Muhammad III, and their powerful position within Persian society had evaporated. The cult still had its divine authority and clung to its independence, but the end of the Assassins was in sight. The Mongol hordes were massing on the steppelands to the east and attacks on the Middle Eastern realms were becoming more common. Muhammad seems to have been an unstable ruler, determined to stand up to the military might of the Mongols, although many Assassins, including his son Khwurshah, disagreed with him.

Like Hasan II before him, Khwurshah found support among the Assassins at Alamut, who suggested that he reign as regent while his father was placed under arrest. The cult needed a strong, clear-headed leader in this moment of crisis and Muhammad III was not to be it. He was an ill-tempered drunkard who flew into violent rages on receiving bad news. Such a ruler was effectively cut off from events in the real world and the decisions he made were almost useless. In the end, the Grand Master of the feared Assassins was killed by his homosexual lover. Khwurshah succeeded his father in 1255, and in doing so became the last Grand Master of the cult. His chief inheritance was to be the impending destruction of the Assassin strongholds by the Mongol Hulegu, brother of the Khan Mongke. His vast armies had invaded Persia and, like the other Mongol armies on the march to the north, would stop at nothing less than total world domination.

The Great Khan had received news that the Assassins would be a terrible thorn in the Mongols' side, a ready-made guerrilla army, fierce and fanatical. His troops, through warfare and the open threat of a display of military might, were able to force the surrender of most states, and the majority of Persia was conquered in this way by Hulegu's armies. Within a year Khwurshah and his Assassins faced the Mongols on their doorstep. Like his predecessors, the Grand Master at first attempted negotiation, since the cult lacked any sort of military power. However, the tactic of stalling for time only frustrated the Mongol leader, and the siege of the Assassin citadels began. Until now no army had succeeded in taking an Assassin castle in the Alamut valley, but the Mongols had such immense resources that they were able to rain constant fire down on the first of the doomed castles: Maymun Diaz. Catapults, crossbows and siege engines were used in the assault, and as the defences of the great castle wavered, a band of fanatical Assassins refused to surrender and continued the fight to the end. Finally Maymun Diaz fell. The vast army then moved to encircle Alamut and the terrified Assassins surrendered almost immediately. By the end of 1256, the Persian Assassins were broken. Alamut was sacked and its library of Ismaili texts (including Hasan-i-Sabbah's autobiography) was pilfered and then summarily burnt by the Mongol historian Juvayani.

The young Khwurshah had an ignominious end, although his life in captivity at first seemed to indicate some kind of favoured status. This last lord of Alamut was married to a Mongol wife and received presents from Hulegu. He then began to accompany the Mongols on their conquests. It is almost certain that the Mongol leader first bribed and then used Khwurshah to help him negotiate the surrender of the remaining Assassin citadels. As the last bastions of the Nizari gave out, there were stories of Khwurshah's heir being spirited away to live a life in exile, thus preserving the Imamate. Perhaps in order to save himself as well, or to preserve something of the Ismailis, the Assassin leader travelled to the Mongol capital at Karakorum, where he was to meet with the Great Khan. When the Mongol chief learned of Khwurshah's presence in the city he ordered his removal, probably because stories of the ease with which Assassins murdered heads of state still carried great force.

And even though the cult was now smashed, there had been rumours that Assassins had entered the city on a mission to kill the Great Khan only two years before.

Rebuffed, Khwurshah made his way back to Persia, but without the status and authority he had up to now enjoyed, he was grimly beaten and murdered by his own travelling companions. But the Assassins were not dead yet. The Syrian Nizari Ismaili were held up in the mountains of the Holy Land, struggling with a foe even greater than Hulegu. But within twenty years of the fall of the Assassins in Persia, the last of the Syrian castles fell to the all-conquering Sultan Baibars.

The Cult in Syria

The Syrian Assassins had made quite an impact on both the Western and the Muslim world, and they reached their height under the leadership of Rashid al-Din Sinan during the Crusades. Sinan had been one of those eager devotees of the divinely inspired Hasan II, who introduced the radical doctrine of the Resurrection. It was this young Grand Master who sent Sinan to Syria to spread the new teachings there. In 1162 Sinan became the independent Grand Master of the Syrian Assassins and the legendary 'Old Man of the Mountains', initially establishing himself at the castle of Kahf. A different account tells how Sinan was one of the supporters of young Hasan II during the reign of his jealous father, Muhammad ibn Buzurgumid. In one of the purges of his son's friends, Muhammad forced Sinan out of Alamut and from there he fled to Syria. When Hasan eventually usurped his father, he made use of Sinan by giving him control of all the Nizari Ismaili in the Holy Land.

It is known that the doctrine of the Resurrection was received at the Syrian branch of the cult, and that the Assassins altered their theological teachings accordingly. But Sinan seems to have finely judged his loyalty to Alamut – at least once Assassins were dispatched to kill the Syrian Grand Master. Sinan ignored much of what Hasan II's son and heir, Muhammad II, decreed, causing an almost unbridgeable rift between the two Assassin communities. In fact, he may have thought of *himself* as Hasan II's legitimate successor, perhaps even as an Imam, especially once relations with the next Alamut lord broke down.

Sinan was not, of course, the first Assassin lord in Syria: there were Assassins established in the region soon after Hasan-i-Sabbah took control of Alamut. Other Ismailis had been hiding away there for centuries and this relative isolation among the mountains provided the Nizari Ismaili with some measure of security. Ismaili influence in Syria had waxed and waned with the fortunes in Egypt of the Fatimid dynasty, who for a while had held Jerusalem.

At about the time that Hasan-i-Sabbah was consolidating his hold over the Alamut region, Seljuk power in Syria was divided. The fragmented politics of the region meant instability and a degree of lawlessness that would last for almost 200 years. It was this internecine fighting that allowed the Assassins to prosper later in the history of the Holy Land, and also to gain their initial foothold. One Seljuk lord actually invited the Assassins into his realm, ostensibly to fight other Seljuks (commanded by his brother, Duqaq). The lord was Ridwan, ruler of Aleppo, and a supposed Ismaili convert. He may have feared the killers almost as much as he valued their presence, especially when they began to flaunt their power in the streets, arguing, robbing and murdering with impunity. The first Assassins from Alamut to settle in the city of Aleppo in about 1103 were led by the *dai* Al-Hakim al-Munajjim.

Murders carried out by the sect for payment began early in Syria, almost as a necessary method of survival in such a war-torn land. The local rulers who called on their grisly services could also provide shelter and patronage. Of course, the real mission, to acquire castles and communities of their own and use them in a guerrilla war against the Seljuk Turks, would always drive the Assassins onwards. But first the cult had to gain a permanent base and hang on to it. More immediately, the mercenary Assassins earned their keep quickly enough by murdering an enemy of Ridwan. The rival who required killing was the ruler of Homs, and he was set about during prayers by Assassins dressed as Sufis. As often happened, the killers had absolutely no chance of escape and were themselves killed.

Aleppo was used as a base from which to expand. Under a new leader, Abu-Tahir as-Saigh, the cult managed to occupy castles in the local area. These gains were not to last, however, and the Assassins were forced from them by a combination of Crusader and Seljuk attacks. Simultaneous with these depredations were the Sultan Muhammad's assaults on the Assassin territories in far-off Persia. The weakening of the cult and the loss of prestige that this had caused resulted in a mass killing of Assassins on the streets of Aleppo. Abu-Tahir, Assassin leader of the Syrian branch, was also arrested and executed during the massacre. But even after Ridwan's death the cult was not totally expunged. His successor, Alp Arslan, allowed the Assassins free rein in Aleppo until the pressure from Sultan Muhammad to force the cult members out of the city became overwhelming. The round of arrests and murders, however, meant that from then on Aleppo was to see little of the Nizari Ismaili.

A new centre of operations sprang up under a new Persian leader called Bahram, in the mountain range of Jabal as-Summaq, to the south-west of Aleppo. Missionaries went out from this area to search for other potential sites, and eventually the ruler of Damascus, Tughtugin, invited them into his city and allowed them to build a 'House of Propaganda', much like the one they had established at Aleppo. Like Ridwan, this Arab leader wanted to use the Assassins as a fighting force in battle rather than as an assassination unit. Tughtugin, as their new patron, called on the cult and its *fidais* to join his army against the Crusaders in 1126. This marks the first use of hired Assassins in wartime, but it was not to be a common occurrence. Soon, the events of Aleppo repeated themselves in Damascus, with the Assassins being forced from the city in 1128, following Tughtugin's death. The cult also had to give up Banyas, a single castle that they had acquired and held for only a short time, but that Crusader forces demanded as the price for allowing the Assassins to leave the region unharmed.

After thirty years of mercenary work, the Syrian Assassins still had neither an established base nor a haven from persecution. But that would all change in 1132, when the cult actually bought the castle of Qadmus from the emir of Kahf. Territory here, to the north of the Crusader county of Tripoli, was often untenable and opportunities for conquest were ripe. The Assassins needed only a handful of castles to establish themselves, where other states required land, a rural population and so forth. The emir, for his part, was glad of a buffer between Muslim and Christian lands – castles owned by anti-Sunni Muslim fanatics were better than castles standing empty and waiting for Christians to occupy them. Other castles were taken one by one, and by a variety of methods. Within three years the Nizari Ismaili had also purchased the citadel of Kahf and could begin to make claims of an Assassin 'state', tenuously strung out among the Jabal Bahra mountains. The years from 1140 to 1160 were a period of consolidation and strengthening of the newly acquired castles. From now until the end of their existence in Syria, the cult occupied, on average, ten castles, and manned them with a total population amounting to something like 60,000 people. It was from these bases that the Assassins began the mission first put into motion long ago by Hasan-i-Sabbah in 1090, and in doing so they used their infamous tactics against the Muslim and Christian forces surrounding them.

These Syrian Assassins were forced to make frequent pacts and alliances with Crusaders and Arabs alike. They were caught in dangerous crossfire, and on occasion even acted as the weapon! In part they were protected by their reputation as well as the defences of their castles. The greatest of the Syrian castles was Masyaf; others included Banyas (for a short period), Kahf, Khawabi, Mainakah, Rusafah and Ullaikah. No one castle served as the cult's Syrian headquarters in the way that Alamut did for the Persians. The Grand

Master moved around, from locale to locale. This would enable him to receive intelligence directly, as well as dramatically reduce the risk of his being assassinated by an outside state.

It was at this period, following the recent settling of the Assassins into Syria on a permanent basis, that Rashid al-Din Sinan arrived from Alamut. Without a doubt his immense skill shot the Nizari Ismaili to unprecedented heights and worldwide fame. It is thanks to Sinan and his exploits that we know anything at all of the history of the Assassins. The Muslim writers considered the cult a heretical and therefore undocumented religion, but the Crusaders found the Assassins in the Holy Land a fascinating and mysterious subject. It is through Sinan and his adventures that the word 'assassin' entered both the imagination and the vocabulary of European nations. His successors, however, did not lead the Syrians as effectively. There are few documented Grand Masters and few notable events in which they are involved. Each leader was sent directly from Alamut, and his rule reflected the current thinking of the Persian Grand Master. For example, when Hasan III declared the reversal of Assassin doctrine and acceptance of the Sunni faith, the same religious policy was implemented among the Syrian Assassins.

The decline of the Assassins in Syria was swift and decisive. Power struggles within the Mameluke Empire had ended with the murder of the Sultan Kutuz and the rise of his killer and successor, Baibars, in 1260. This leader was a tough and thorough man who quickly defeated his Muslim rivals and spread the recently formed Mameluke Empire across the Holy Land by defeating the Crusaders and driving them out for good. The Sultan Baibars governed his territories from Egypt and his conquests began to form the basis of a new Islamic Empire. There was no place in this empire for the cult of Assassins tucked away in the mountains of Syria. The might of Baibars can be judged by the fact that he soundly defeated the Mongol army of Hulegu, who had just utterly destroyed the Assassin population in Persia. How could such a tiny cult effectively defend itself against such a ruler? The answer was plain. It could not, and Baibars tested the Assassins' resolve by first taking away land that was theirs and then demanding taxes from them. In the early 1270s Sultan Baibars occupied several Assassin castles, and by 1273 he had conquered all of their strongholds, including Kahf, one of the most indomitable of them all.

Sultan Baibars had demolished what was left of one of the most widely respected and feared organizations of medieval times. The Knights Templar, too, fell to the Sultan, and so the two sects that seemed to have so many similarities were destroyed by a single Muslim general. In that same year, the Venetian explorer Marco Polo visited Alamut and saw the mighty citadel exactly as the plundering

Mongols had left it seventeen years earlier. He took away with him several stories of how the Assassins had operated in times past, including the account of the Garden of Paradise.

The organization of the Assassins could not have survived past the end of the thirteenth century, but its memory certainly did. The modern-day Ismaili leader the Aga Khan claims a direct bloodline to Buzurgumid, via the last Alamut Grand Master Khwurshah, whose heir was supposedly spirited away during the siege of Alamut. In this way the memory of the bloodthirsty Assassins lives on in the present decade. As we have seen, the tactics of the cult have also found supporters in later times. Although no direct connections exist, it is a strange coincidence that modern-day Shiite fanatics craving Paradise have been dispatched from Iran (the Persia of medieval times) to carry out suicidal executions in other countries. The infamous suicide car bombs, packed with explosives and driven into a target by faithful Shiites, made headlines in the early 1980s. The young bombers, both men and women, first made relaxed video-tapes of themselves before they carried out the mass murders. In them they proclaimed their devotion to God and their hatred of the enemy. One of the most spectacular results of these suicidal attacks was the destruction of the US Marine barracks in Beirut on 23 October 1983, in which 241 soldiers were killed. Assassin doctrine, it seems, has been re-created by the people who invented it to begin with.

CHAPTER 5
The Thugs –
India's Dark Angels

When the Europeans took up residence in India and began the task of administration and governorship, they little knew that below the surface of Indian society lay a murderous cult that took thousands of innocent lives each year. The pilgrimage season was a time of travel for many, and the Thugs preyed upon these pilgrims along the roads of India. Unlike many grisly cults and organizations that engage in murder on a large scale and in a secretive manner, the Thugs had no obvious purpose. The religious nature of the huge cult meant that wealth and political power were rare by-products of this unwholesome group, not its prime motivation. They killed for their goddess. The fact that thuggee was a religious practice partly explains why the group's motives were so unfathomable. But as a religion it was one of the most bloodthirsty in human history.

The terrible crimes of the Indian Thugs were so seemingly random, so pointless and so well camouflaged, that few Indians knew of their existence. Those who did know kept the secret well guarded, as was in their best interests. It took the extraordinary skills of deduction and methodical investigation of one Briton, William Henry Sleeman, to bring the cult into the open and there extinguish it – killers, accomplices and instigators all.

Sleeman worked for the East India Company in the first half of the nineteenth century, a time when the Company was the only real representative of British rule on the Indian subcontinent. As a local magistrate working in Jubbulpore, he first came face to face with Thug killers, about whom, so far, he had heard only rumours. Scant documentation by earlier European travellers had fuelled his imagination and he very much wanted to learn more. At his posting in Jubbulpore in the early 1820s, a large group of travellers carrying suspected stolen items had been detained. Since no one would come forward to claim any of the items, they were allowed to be on their way. But one of the group lingered to talk with Sleeman. By bluff, Sleeman tricked the guilt-ridden Indian into admitting that, indeed, the men were robbers. More than that, he said that they were Thugs.

For his own safety this first turncoat, called Kalyan Singh, was locked away, and Sleeman rode off in pursuit with a column of troopers. The travellers were soon surrounded and false claims of brigandage were put before them. It was gambled that they would co-operate to prove their innocence and they gladly returned to Jubbulpore. Once there, they were accused of thuggee and locked away. Kalyan Singh's brother, Moti, was also a member of the gang and freely joined Kalyan in giving Sleeman the evidence he needed to convict the murderers. This evidence was abundant – and shocking. Moti led Sleeman and his soldiers to a well-concealed grave among a grove of mango trees. There the freshly buried bodies of three men and a boy were uncovered. All had broken necks. Many more corpses were to be unearthed . . .

Among the killers who were hanged was a police officer and even a government courier. It seemed that the cult stretched into all parts of society. In fact, thuggee was much like a sinister web of silence that had trapped the rich and poor, important and not-so-important. Sleeman had twenty-eight of the gang hanged and seventy imprisoned. From this first incident he had created a starting point in his investigation; he had exposed a tiny branch of this vast cult and it could lead him further into the secret world of thuggee. His two informants (or 'approvers') would be the first of many, and they would be the key to exposing the cult and whoever controlled it at the organization's centre. When England learned of these bizarre yet murderous gangs, the word 'thug' gained a permanent place in the language.

The Practice of Thuggee

In the 1820s very little had been heard of the Thugs. European travellers in India knew full well that robbers (dacoits) infested the roads and travel was always dangerous because of them. It was only when the British expanded into India that the society of assassins was exposed. Even then, the early investigators had no inkling that the stranglers they heard about were part of a vast organization operating across India. Only one or two writers had mentioned such a deadly secret society before Sleeman. Perhaps the earliest was a Frenchman named Thevenot, who visited India in the seventeenth century. He recorded that the most cunning robbers in the world could be found on the road from Delhi to Agra. They would sometimes use a beautiful woman as bait, who would, once up on a traveller's horse behind them, either strangle him or knock him down for the rest to murder. These robbers were expert stranglers, employing improvised garrottes of knotted scarves.

A British account had also been made of a sect of killers called Phansigars. Dr Richard Sherwood was a surgeon at Fort St George in Madras and had written the document in 1816. His study of the cult, which strangled its victims, was lengthy and quite accurate. He had discovered several names for the assassins, including Thugs,

Phansigars, Ari Tulukar, Tanta Kalleru and Warlu Wahndlu – all words that denoted death by strangulation. The first encounter with Thugs may have taken place, according to Sherwood, in 1799. A gang of about 100 killers was arrested near Bangalore, but there were accounts of the crimes of these stranglers from across the land. Also included in the doctor's notes were several Thug words, part of a secret language that Sleeman termed Ramasi. With his aptitude for languages, Sleeman mastered Ramasi, helped by Sherwood's notes and Moti's guidance. He even printed a Ramasi booklet for the use of his officers in their work against the cult.

When this evil secret society of assassins was brought to the attention of the East India Company, the official response was one of non-intervention. The Thugs boasted a religious calling and were devoted to a Hindu goddess called Kali. Despite the atrocities committed, the Company did not want to be seen to be persecuting one of India's many religious groups. Sleeman remained at odds with this opinion and was able to convince the Company to act only when the sheer scale of the cult at last came to light.

Because the Thugs were killing to please their goddess and to carry out a sacred act, there was always a pattern to their murders. Rituals and ceremonies dominated almost every aspect of this grisly trade and each person had his own part to play in the murders.

Usually a small group of Thugs out in front would meet a party of pilgrims or other travellers. These deceivers (*sotha*) would try to endear themselves to the travellers with conversation, song and even music. Often these scouts would ask if they might travel alongside the pilgrims for mutual protection. Once the suspicions of the group had been allayed, secret signs would be left for the rest of the Thugs to let them know that a party of victims had been infiltrated. These Thugs would then join the travellers with the same requests for protection. The stranglers had the patience to wait many days until the entire Thug gang had joined the group. At this point there were usually more Thugs than victims! When a suitable opportunity arose, two of the Thugs called *beles*, or grave-diggers, would walk ahead of the main party and select the location for the killings. Nearby they would dig the graves with magical pickaxes. Soon the pilgrims and their Thug companions would arrive and set up camp for the night. Beds would be made, food cooked and fires lit. As the travellers relaxed and were entertained by the *sothas*, the Thugs got into position for the mass murder, three to a traveller if there were enough. Suddenly the leader gave the *jhirni*, the death call, and the Thugs were upon their victims.

The strangler (*bhartote*) whipped his yellow scarf, or *rumal*, around the victim's neck and strangled him. Helping him was a second Thug, the *chamolhi*, who grabbed the victim's legs and forced him on to his face. A third tried to incapacitate him in any way he could, by kicking him between the legs, seizing his hands or sitting on him. The scarf was knotted at either end and would not slip from the *bhartote*'s fingers. Across the camp site every traveller was being similarly dealt with. Within seconds it was over.

When the intended victims were in postures that made it difficult for the *bhartotes* to carry out their work, the *sothas* had to get them to bare their necks. Most often they would encourage a sing-song and when the travellers were in full flow with heads thrown back, the stranglers attacked. Most *sothas* were skilled in the use of musical instruments and knew many songs for just this situation. If the pilgrims were all asleep or lying down, then one of the *sothas* would scream that he had seen a snake or scorpion. The reaction of most of the sleepy-headed victims was to jump up out of bed – and into the *rumals* of waiting *bhartotes*.

Once the murders had been committed, the bodies had to be disposed of. It was only then that the gang could pray to Kali and offer up the human victims as a sacrifice. Occasionally the preparations for burial would be interrupted by other travellers. In this case sheets were thrown over the recently strangled bodies and the thugs claimed they were companions who had just died from disease. This hopefully dissuaded the newcomers from getting too close! Thugs took as much care with the burial of their victims as they did with their selection and murder. It was the meticulous way in which they covered up their crimes that allowed the Thugs to continue to strangle year after year without being discovered. When ritual graves (or *beles*) were located by Sleeman and his approvers, they sometimes contained more than 100 bodies, going back centuries. When the British began travelling the land, Thugs were never tempted to strangle them. All Europeans were traceable and were important enough to warrant an investigation should they go missing. To attack such targets was anathema to Kali's Thugs.

Usually the dead littering the ground after a kill would be dismembered by ritual butchers (*lughas*); if time was pressing, then the legs only would be hacked off, or the victims would just be doubled up. The corpses were often mutilated beyond recognition to prevent later identification. This would also undoubtedly speed up the rate at which the bodies decomposed. Repeated stabbing of the corpses was carried out to stop them from swelling and disturbing the topsoil. The possessions would be pilfered from the victims and their bodies would then be carefully placed into the grave dug earlier by the *beles*. Once covered with earth and vegetation, the morning sun would dry the soil. Camping over the *bele* further destroyed any traces of freshly dug ground. It was at this camp over the grave that Kali was venerated in a ritual feast.

118

This feast was the Tuponee, the climax of the divine mission the gang had undertaken. Inside a tent the Thugs spread out a cloth and sat upon it, gathered around their leader. The younger initiates sat outside this circle. The gang's consecrated pickaxe (*kussee*) was placed on the cloth before the leader. With it was a piece of silver (an offering to Kali) and a special communion sugar (*goor*) held in reverence by the Thugs. The gang leader then dug a small hole in the ground and as he prayed to Kali he poured in some of the *goor*. Holy water was then sprinkled into the hole and over the sacred axe as the gang joined in the prayer to the goddess. All who had killed that day were allowed to taste the *goor*. If by chance a young untested Thug tasted it, he had to leave the camp and strangle someone.

Was the *goor* drugged? The Thugs believed that a man who had eaten the *goor* had given his soul to Kali and that she owned him. He was a Thug for life; indeed, the *goor* gave men the overwhelming desire to strangle and brought them closer to their gang. It banished remorse, human compassion and guilt. The taking of the *goor* became a communion, with all participants revelling in their grisly profession. The Grand Master of all Thugs, Feringheea, told Sleeman: 'If I were to live a thousand years I should never be able to follow any other trade.' Thuggee was, at once, a religious calling, a career and a pastime.

The magic pickaxe used by the *beles* to dig the graves and by the leader during the Tuponee had supernatural powers. It was imbued with all the mystery of the Crucifix and was worshipped every seventh day. Experienced Thugs were reputed to be able to call the pickaxe and at once cause it to fly into their hand. Such fantasies could lend credence to the theory of the *goor* as a drug.

To join a Thug expedition and murder innocent travellers a cult member did not first have to reject all the principles of virtue, moral correctness and justice. It was the paradox of the religion that Thugs believed themselves to be honest and pious men. They were convinced that all benefited from their evil deeds: their victims were sacrificed to Kali and went straight to Paradise; Kali herself benefited from the sacrifice; and the Thugs had the patronage of the goddess and would go to Paradise. This aspect of the Thug mentality again made the detection of cult members difficult. When the pilgrimage season ended after the winter, the Thugs melted back into everyday life. Most retired to a peaceful existence, sometimes with great status or responsibility. Policemen, government agents, doctors and even nurses to white families were Thugs. Their religious nature meant they were trustworthy and honest. The word '*thug*' (properly pronounced 't'ug') actually means deceiver, a reference to their veil of integrity. Most gang members spent their summer months at regular jobs, or lived off the spoils in unemployment. To cover their tracks further when the East India Company started to take an interest, the Thugs had to take up cover jobs as farmers, either for themselves or on the land of a sympathetic noble willing to take a bribe.

Before a Thug gang set off for its annual season's killing, it paid its respects to Kali and asked for good luck. A multitude of omens were observed before, and during, the Thug's hunt for human prey. The severed head of a sheep was examined; how the mouth and nostrils twitched when liquid was poured over them determined what kind of fortune the gang would enjoy. The theft of this sheep's head by a dog meant bad fortune for many years to come. Other signs from nature told the gang how they would fare. The sounds and actions of lizards and birds along the intended route were important; so were donkeys and jackals. Bad omens meant that the road was unlucky. The omens were then read on others until an auspicious path was found. Numbering anywhere from ten to fifty-plus men, the gang set off to locate travellers for sacrifice to Kali. Every man hid his true nature and the gang masqueraded as pilgrims or other travellers with elaborate stories and identities.

Kali told the gang not only which road to follow but also which victims to select. The gangs merely carried out her wishes. Some bands of pilgrims would remain unmolested by Thugs because one of their members was seen as a bad omen. Women were not to be strangled because Kali was female, although the Hindustani Thugs (thought of as violators of many of the cult's taboos) would kill men *and* women. Cripples, lepers and blindmen would not be touched, nor would craftsmen such as metalworkers, masons, potters, carpenters, laundrymen and shoemakers. Indians of the Kamala caste would be allowed to live and so would anyone driving a cow or female goat. Many people must have unwittingly escaped almost certain death as a result of having one of these 'charmed' individuals travelling with them. By the time Sleeman had begun his crusade against thuggee, many of these taboos were being regularly broken, and the Thugs attributed his victories to this.

The killing of a tiger by a Thug was taboo. The tiger was thought to be of special significance to the cult, and members considered themselves tigers, preying on men as the great cat does. Fate and the universe impelled both creatures to hunt humans. It is the way of nature; the victims of thuggee had their own death 'written on their foreheads'. Killing a tiger inevitably brought death to the Thug.

Sleeman's greatest weapons against thuggee were the turncoat Thug, gaoled and threatened with the gallows, and the ordinary Indian who came forward with evidence. Such witnesses were very rare initially, as no one wanted to face reprisals from freed Thugs or to have to travel across India to give evidence. Thug gangs rarely carried out their religious duties close to home, journeying at least 100 miles from home so that the killings would not be connected with them and there was no chance that the victim's relatives would recognize them. To combat these fears, Sleeman arranged for written evidence to be used in court and made association with thuggee punishable by either life imprisonment or death. But he also had to contend with a conspiracy of complicity. Rich landowners and rajas sanctioned local Thugs, as long as the gangs hunted elsewhere and returned with enough loot to buy their silence. This patronage of the cult had kept it sheltered and hidden for 500 years. All Sleeman could do was pay informers to identify these rich patrons.

There is little evidence that Thugs killed only for the treasures it brought them, but it cannot be denied that the wealth of a particular caravan or party would have made it especially attractive. It must have been very frustrating to see one of these rich groups go on its way because it contained a woman or a carpenter. Greed may have resulted in the breaking of age-old taboos, and been indirectly responsible for the cult's downfall. The hasty murder of rich and prominent people may have made the gangs clumsy. In one such incident, a Thug gang was able to trick a group of travellers into leaving a larger party to travel with them (for lower cost). The grove they camped in that night was all ready for the murders to follow. But the group included women and children. All but the two children were strangled to death. These young survivors were instantly adopted by two of the Thugs, but one continued to cry for his mother. To shut him up, this boy was grabbed by the legs and had his head smashed against a rock. His body lay undisturbed till morning, but was then found by the local landowner, who organized an armed pursuit of the careless Thugs. Catching up with the gang, his riflemen forced the Thugs to flee, leaving behind their spoils.

The second boy was raised as a Thug strangler. Usually, the sons and nephews of Thug members were initiated into the cult at an early age. At first they were groomed for membership and assessed to see if they could follow the holy trade and keep it a secret. They would be trusted only to keep watch and carry messages, not watching their first killing until the gang could be sure that they would agree to join the stranglers. On reaching his eighteenth birthday a novice Thug was able to take the *goor* and murder in the name of Kali.

It was not just rich and powerful landlords who kept thuggee a secret. The nature of Indian society meant that travel for many was time-consuming and dangerous. Wild or poisonous animals, disease and traditional robbery were ever-present threats; relatives rarely investigated the disappearance of a family member for this reason. Victims of thuggee would not be reported missing for weeks or months, due to the slow speed of travel in medieval India. The peace and security that the British brought to the country, along with new roads, was a double-edged sword. More people ventured out in the pilgrimage season, providing the Thugs with many more opportunities for murder. It must be remembered, too, that the secret society went out of its way to conceal its murders. The idea of using a *rumal* was to prevent bloodshed, and no other weapon was used, except for the swords sometimes carried by the Thug sentries who guarded the edge of the killing area. These would cut down any fleeing victims 'lucky' enough to escape death by strangulation.

The Thug gangs did not avoid rich travellers; neither did they favour them particularly. Any marked for death by Kali were simply killed. But rich victims were especially desired and a gang would go to some lengths to see that a wealthy traveller fell victim to the charms of the *sothas*. When the omens of the goddess favoured a party of poor travellers, the Hindustani Thugs would let it pass and use the good luck to trap a richer group. The Deccan Thugs disagreed with this reasoning, believing that once pilgrims had been marked by Kali, they must die. To do otherwise was to court the anger of the goddess of destruction.

One gang displayed particular ingenuity and determination in the pursuit of a Muslim nobleman, or Mogul. The Mogul was travelling on horseback, accompanied by several servants, and was well armed. Although he seemed to have little to fear on India's open roads, he refused the request of a group of Hindus to travel with him. He had heard of Thugs and was well enough armed not to need the protection of other travellers. These Hindus were in fact members of a Thug gang and no amount of persuasion would allow them to join the Mogul's party. They had no choice but to let this rich nobleman pass. But they did not give in so easily, and arranged for several of their number to meet up with the Mogul the following morning. These Thugs were Muslims who again asked for the Mogul's protection, especially since they shared the same faith. But again the noble refused and threatened the Thugs with violence, and again the Thugs had to let the Mogul continue his journey.

Still undeterred, the Thugs arranged for members of their gang to lodge for the night at the same roadside inn (*sarai*) as the Mogul. Rather than approach him again, they engaged his servants in conversation and became friends. When the sun rose, the Thugs left the inn and set out on the road. Later that morning the Mogul's party overtook these clever Thugs and the Deceivers again struck up conversation with his servants in an attempt to join them. When their lord ordered the Thugs away, his own servants spoke in their favour and asked for the Mogul to grant them his protection. But the Mogul insisted, driving the Thugs away yet again. It seemed that this rich prize was to slip through the Thugs' fingers, but they had one last ruse to try.

Five more Thugs, dressed as Muslim sepoys, set out ahead of the Mogul and on an open plain in the wilderness got ready to meet the Mogul's party. They had strangled a lone traveller and sat weeping over his body as if he were a dear friend who had succumbed to exhaustion. When the Mogul came across this scene, he enquired about the dead man and was told by the Thugs that they were poor, uneducated men who knew little of the Koran, and thus could not bury their comrade with the proper funerary rites. They appealed to the Mogul to carry out this religious service for them and, being a good Muslim, he agreed. Readying himself for the burial, he dismounted from his horse, removed his sword, pistols, bow and arrows, for he could not carry out this holy ritual with them on. After washing, he began the solemn rites. Two of the sepoys flanked him, the others stood among his servants. In a flash the Thugs strangled the Mogul and his servants! The five stranglers were efficient and quickly had the bodies ready for burial in the grave they had prepared for their 'comrade'.

There are practically no other groups in history that have carried out systematic murder using the highways of the land as both a place to select their victims and their killing ground. Only the irregular warfare of the Vietnam conflict can provide a comparison. Project Delta, devoted to in-the-field patrols that penetrated deep into the heart of Communist territory, organized specialized 'Roadrunner' teams. These were staffed by indigenous Vietnamese soldiers who disguised themselves as Viet Cong guerrillas and travelled up and down the trails and tracks in the hope of coming across an enemy unit. Once the Roadrunners had successfully infiltrated a Communist unit they would stay with them, eating at rice stations, moving through villages and avoiding American troops. Their mission was to either leave the guerrillas after as much intelligence as possible could be gathered or lead the Communists into a fatal American or South Vietnamese ambush. Such a strategy called for agents with great cool and an ability to pass themselves off convincingly as regular Viet Cong, but for the worshippers of Kali there may have been no feelings of guilt or fear of discovery. Their actions were divinely inspired, the natural methods of worship for the savage cult.

Origins of the Cult

The great mystery of thuggee is not how it remained virtually undetected for 500 years, but how it first began. What were its origins? With no written Thug evidence, the beginnings of the secret cult are obscure. Perhaps the most bizarre fact is that Kali is a Hindu goddess, yet the Thugs were mainly Muslims. Kali is not mentioned anywhere in the Koran, but the cult may have identified her with Fatima, the murdered daughter of Muhammad. Some Thugs believed that Fatima taught the cult members how to use the scarf as a murder weapon. The mixing of religion in the formation of the Thugs is noteworthy in a land where religious intolerance raged between Hindus and Muslims. The Islamic conquest of India put large parts of the country under domination and began the long-running enmity. Thuggee was a cross-breed religion, where Muslims recognized the Hindu gods and rituals. However, they paid little heed to the Hindu taboos that are part of that worship.

Kali is the Hindu goddess of death and is the wife of Siva. She is also known as Kali Ma, the Black Mother, Bhowani or Devi. The goddess was responsible for the defeat of Raktavija, the demon-king. As he led his demon army against the gods, he realized that they would be defeated. Raktavija attacked Kali himself and almost overcame her, since every drop of blood that spilled from his body became 1,000 giants who joined the fight. In a frenzied attack, Kali drank Raktavija's blood, killing him and preventing the birth of further giants. Her dance of victory was ecstatic, causing earthquakes across the earth and her husband, Siva, attempted to calm her, but in her frenzied state she threw him down and trampled him to death. Only later did she realize her crime.

The goddess of the Thugs is depicted as a black-skinned woman with four arms. In the first hand she carries a sword, in the second Raktavija's severed head, while her third hand is raised in a gesture of peace. The remaining hand is grasping for power. This echoes the two sides to the worship of Kali: her right side as mother and saviour, and her left as uncontrollable monster. The left hand has always signified ill-fortune and bad luck. She dances through space on the body of Siva, her tongue hanging out of her mouth and her eyes blood-red. Kali's jewellery is indeed grisly: a necklace of severed heads adorns her neck, while her girdle is composed of a row of hands. Each skull in her necklace represents a letter of the Sanskrit alphabet, which Kali had invented. Both of Kali's earrings are human corpses. It is plain to see why the Thugs chose her as their divine figurehead. She seems to have been an early Hindu war goddess with an appetite for blood, terror and disorder.

Why the Thugs believed that they honoured Kali by slaughtering innocent travellers is unclear. There is no established origin legend for their hideous practice, but Kali does feature in some Thug mythology. One tradition has her as the Thugs' protector, devouring the corpses of the victims they have murdered to obliterate any trace of them. A young Thug looked around one day to see the terrible goddess eating a body they had left for her. From that moment, she let the cult members dispose of their own dead bodies, but she first presented them with tools with which to carry out their murders. One of her teeth became the magical pickaxe (*kussee*), one of her ribs became a dagger and the hem of her garment became the *rumal* used to strangle travellers. Since white and yellow were Kali's colours, the *rumal* was always either white or yellow.

Another Thug legend has it that, as Kali paused during her struggle with Raktavija, she brushed the sweat from her arms and created two men from it. To these she gave the *rumal* and ordered them to begin killing Raktavija's demons. After they had done so, they brought back the strangling cloth but the goddess insisted that they keep it, using it in the future to kill all strangers who crossed their path. The noose as a killing weapon is known in early Hindu mythology as the *naga-pasa* ('dragon noose'). It was used by demons as they fought with the Hindu gods.

The historical origins of this murderous cult are just as obscure and riddled with conflicting theories. Most writers do, however, agree that thuggee is very old and dates back at least 500 years. The earliest mention of Thugs in Indian literature is in Zia-ud-Barni's history of Firoz Shah. This records that 1,000 Thugs were captured at Delhi in 1290 and the Sultan in power refused to let them be executed. The gang was given its freedom in Lakhnamut in Bengal and Sleeman thought this might have accounted for the trouble with Thugs that this area had in the future. Zia-ud-Barni's work was written in 1356 and it was not until the late sixteenth century that thuggee was mentioned again. Some 500 Thugs were captured in the Etawah district during the reign of Akbar, which lasted from 1556 to 1605.

Earlier references have also been discovered, but these may or may not refer to thuggee. One connects the stranglers with an ancient tribe called the Sagartians. These Persians were nomadic and were forced to give a levy of 8,000 cavalry to the army of King Xerxes. Herodotus mentions that they carried no weapons of bronze or iron except daggers; the special weapon upon which they relied was a lasso made of plaited strips of hide. This they used to strangle their enemies. The descendants of the Sagartians may have come to India with an Islamic invader and settled around Delhi. If indeed these are the first Thugs, then the cult dates back to at least 500 BC, a history some 2,200 years long!

The village of Ellora in north-east Bombay province may also hold clues to the age of the Thug sect. Great temples there point to the village being a site of special religious significance; there are Jain, Buddhist and Hindu temples in the area. Ancient caves near Ellora are decorated with eighth-century carvings, and some Thugs believe that every ritual and activity of their profession is recorded accurately there. They also believe that the carvings were made divinely, since no Thug would ever depict his crimes for all to see, or instruct a mason to do so either. In his book *Things Indian*, written in 1901, Crooke describes one of the Ellora carvings: 'We have a Thug represented strangling a Brahman who is worshipping the emblem of Siva, whereupon the God comes to his rescue and kicks down the Thug.' Whether or not the Ellora caves depict Thugs is a matter of conjecture. Feringheea told Sleeman that no Indian outside the cult ever recognized that Thugs were depicted in the carvings, but every Thug who visits Ellora sees his own trade recorded there. Many went to satisfy their curiosity; the Ellora caves were never a place or worship for the sect. Perhaps Ellora should be taken as another piece of Thug mythology, especially since only one of their number could actually identify the Thug representations.

If the first Thugs *were* immigrant Muslims, could they have been connected with Hasan's refugee Assassins? Some writers believe there is a connection. Members of both were almost exclusively Islamic and both groups dedicated themselves to the practice, and perfection, of assassination. Since major Islamic conquests took place after AD 1000, it is likely that refugee Assassins did indeed enter central India at about this time. Delhi was captured by Muhammad of Ghur in 1192 and Thugs are mentioned in the age of Firoz Shah, a century later. Ismailis, fleeing their homeland following the fall of Alamut, may have arrived in India and discovered the Hindu worshippers of Kali carrying out their terrible rites. The penetration of the Kali cult by ex-Assassins would certainly go some way towards explaining the worship of a Hindu deity by Muslims. In fact, we can suggest that the worship of Kali may have been entirely respectable until the domination of the Assassins. Such a small but widely spread cult would have made a good cover for their operations. What exactly the Assassins could gain from the ritual murder of travellers and the dedication of those murders to a Hindu goddess is beyond speculation. However, as Chapter 4 has indicated, the Assassin community at Alamut never enjoyed a permanent religion, but had to adapt and alter their beliefs according to the philosophy of the Grand Master at the time. Was the Hindu Kali just another stage in the development of the Assassin religious psyche?

Historians will never know for sure how thuggee began or who began it – Sagartian mercenaries, resettled Assassins or native Indians with a taste for blood. Like the bloodline of a people, the answer is probably a mix of each, the combination of ritual, custom, intent and accident making up the first Thug murders.

Tracing the origin of the cult is made more difficult by the existence of other secret gangs of murderers. These generally had no connection with the Thugs, but followed their own horrible agendas on the roads of India. One sect operating in the Burdwan district was, however, a branch of thuggee that had taken to water. The Pungus worshipped Kali and had the same beliefs and rituals as their land-based cousins. Rather than haunt the roads for their victims, they took to the many boats that carried cargo and passengers along the rivers. One of the gang kept a careful look-out for the all-clear and then gave the *jhirni* by striking the boat's deck three times. At this signal the crew and passengers would be strangled and their bodies thrown overboard. If blood was seen in the water coming from the bodies, then the Pungus had a tradition that they must return the way they had come and carry out another floating murder. They also differed from the usual Thugs in their Ramasi language, which was very unlike the one Sleeman had learned.

An Irishman called Creagh was the founder of one robber gang that turned to secret murders. The Tasma-Baz began as a gambling outfit at Cawnpore, with Creagh and a few Indians taking bets on a Hindu version of the shell game, Tasma-Bazi. The game used a folded leather strap and soon became a lucrative source of income. His followers started up Tasma-Baz gangs of their own and began paying off local policemen to keep away from their scams. With a growing underworld presence, the Tasma-Baz turned to murder and robbery. There were no religious overtones to these gangs. Members were outlaws and rogues and liked to kill with drugged sweetmeats given freely to players. The drug most used was taken from the datura plant and usually knocked out the victim. It was more commonly used in less lethal quantities smoked in the traditional hookah.

Datura was also used by the killers known as Daturias, who travelled India poisoning for profit. They fed people the drug in other foods and, when the victims lay unconscious, were free to murder and rob. The lucky few who recovered from the drug were sometimes able to help the authorities track down the gangs.

Resembling the Thugs most in their methods were the Megpunnites. These gangs lived from the sale of children to the slave trade, and were forced to kill many parents to get to them. Megpunnaism is an Anglo-Indian word formed from *mekh* (a peg) and *phansa* (to hang). Like the Thugs, these gangs employed nooses to strangle their victims. Once they had murdered the adults, they stole the surviving children and either used them for sex or sold them on. Girls were obviously the most popular and many stayed with the gang, and, in some cases, even going as far as to help other members in their murders.

It seems incredible that these secret societies knew nothing of each other's existence. But their disguises and clandestine behaviour meant that few Indians were aware of any of them until they were exposed and crushed. As was the case with the Thugs.

The Destruction of the Cult

William Sleeman's first collected notes and reports were to form the basis of a system for the destruction of the evil Thug cult. Methodical investigation and careful cross-referencing was to lead to the exposure of cult members and gangs. It was Sleeman who began these investigations, at first as a pastime or hobby, but later in an official capacity, charged by the East India Company with the cult's destruction.

Beginning slowly, with interviews of the first Thugs he had caught, he began his records. Included in them were names and dates, the locations of gang villages and well-used *beles*. He expanded his system as his work grew, and found himself mapping out some vast family tree of interconnected Thug gangs and gang members.

The search for an end to the terrible activities of the gangs became an official duty for Sleeman in 1826. The East India Company had shifted its position and decided to back the suppression of thuggee. By 1830 he had free rein to investigate the ritual murders over the whole of central India. Already, in the four years prior to his official position as chief investigator, Sleeman had convicted hundreds of gang members. The East India Company could not brush aside such gains and had little choice but to back him. The size of the problem was too vast to ignore.

Equally, Sleeman was now becoming too important and troublesome to the gangs for them to ignore. Several assassination attempts were made on his life, but all failed.

The captain had suspicions that some master Thug, an arch-criminal of great power and villainous intent, lay at the centre of the family tree he was slowly creating. But no proof could be found. His diligent researchers hinted at the existence of some shadowy kingpin, and in the process earned Sleeman his nickname of 'Thuggee', for his single-minded obsession. His trees were of immense value in connecting one Thug to another and one gang to another. Differences in the cult from region to region were noted, as were new words of Ramasi, hunting grounds, *beles* and collaborating nobles. This tree of linkages grew larger each year and was accompanied by a map showing areas of historical Thug activity. Sleeman hoped (and was eventually able) to predict the attacks of gangs, their size and possible base of operations, as well as suggest the names of prominent members or leaders. These family trees were mainly created using the testimony of ex-Thug approvers, who also helped him catch fellow stranglers or local gangs. Only

Witches dance widdershins *(counterclock-wise) around the Devil who, in the form of a goat, is being kissed on the buttocks by a witch. This medieval myth derives largely from earlier Roman and Greek witch cults.* (The Bodleian Library)

Vase detail showing a frenzied worshipper of the Greek cult of Dionysus tearing apart an animal. (Mansell Collection)

Relief of a wheatsheaf from Eleusis. Wheat and barley were sacred to the Greek goddess Demeter and feature regularly in depictions of the Eleusian Mysteries. (Sonia Halliday Photographs)

Bacchanalian festivities were often depicted as shown in this relief, accompanied by a dancing satyr and ecstatic Maenad. The god Bacchus held sway over the emotions of his cultists and whipped them into an orgastic frenzy. (Mansell Collection)

Right: *Modern-day Druids celebrate the summer solstice at Stonehenge. This monument pre-dates the original Druids by over a thousand years, but Roman desecration of Stonehenge suggests that the cult may have held its rituals on the site.* (Hulton Deutsch)

Left: *Statuette of the Celtic deity Taranis, whom the Romans associated with Jupiter. He holds a wheel and a thunderbolt, and the Druids may have sacrificed to him by burning human victims alive.*

Statue of Mithras, the popular but mysterious Roman god, slaying the cosmic bull in order to benefit mankind. An ear of corn, symbolizing life-from-death, springs from the wound, while Ahriman's servitors, Scorpion and Snake attempt to poison the dying animal. (Mansell Collection)

Bust of Commodus, the Roman emperor who identified himself with the demi-god Hercules. Here he is dressed in the Nemean lion-skin, clutching Hercules' club. (Mansell Collection)

A medieval manuscript depicting the fiery execution of Jacques de Molay, the last Master of the Knights Templar, and one of his lieutenants. (The British Library)

Left: *One of many seals used by the Knights Templar, the order that depended on a reliable and efficient system of communication. (The British Library)*

Right: *The Assassin castle of Masyaf, near Hama in modern-day Syria, the western headquarters of that infamous cult. (David Nicolle)*

Thug carpet weavers. These rehabilitated Thug killers had previously joined other members of the cult in terrorizing nineteenth-century India. Their carpets later became much valued. (The British Library)

Caught completely by surprise, a traveller is dragged from his horse by eager Thugs. Within hours his body, his belongings and even his horse would have vanished without trace. Such was the fate that welcomed the unwary. (The British Library)

Left: *Book illustration which depicts an intruder being stabbed through a wall. The Japanese shogun Tokugawa Ieyasu employed ninja warriors as his palace guards. As this picture shows, they were as skilled in defence as they were at attack.* (Japan Archive)

Below: *An accurate and atmospheric photograph of a ninja clan member at work.* (Japan Archive)

Attacking without warning, from behind his victim, this ninja shows why members of the cult were experts at assassination. (Japan Archive)

Book illustration of an agile ninja penetrating the outer defences of Fushimi Castle. All the hallmarks of a classic ninja mission are here: the solitary agent in black garb, using stealth and cunning to enter a building. Note his sheathed sword and abundance of equipment. (Japan Archive)

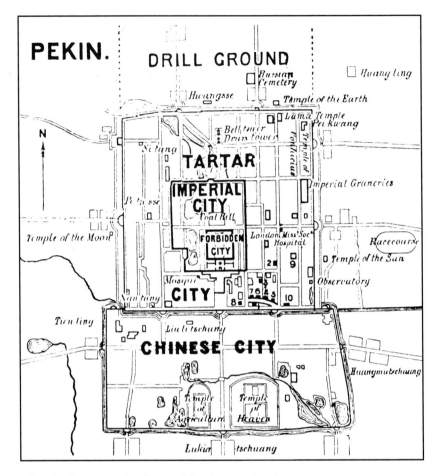

Plan of Peking, 1900, battleground for the Boxer Uprising.

1 German Legation, 2 Belgian Legation, 3 British Legation, 4 French Legation, 5 Italian Legation, 6 Japanese Legation, 7 Spanish Legation, 8 United States Legation, 9 Tsungli Yamen, 10 American Mission (Hulton Deutsch)

Illustration of allied troops coming under attack from Boxer cultists during the siege of the British legation. Peking, 1900. (Hulton Deutsch)

Above: *Mao Tse-tung before the fear-crazed years of the Cultural Revolution. His revolutionary thinking harkened back to the Boxer Uprising.* (Robert Hunt Library)

Following the relief of the Peking legations came the reprisals. Here a captured member of the Boxer cult has met his end at a formal execution. (Hulton Deutsch)

"Lest We Forget". A corner of the British legation in Peking is being visited by Chinese officials following the Boxer Uprising. (Hulton Deutsch)

when the maps and family trees were distributed to other officers working to bring down the Thug conspiracy would enough information be amassed to bring down the entire organization.

That it was a single organization (a single 'tree'), Sleeman was convinced. Occasionally references to the head of the murderous secret society would be encountered, but they were never complete enough to act upon. Once he was able to act, he knew that the cult would not last long. Eliminating the master Thug would be analogous to beheading a dangerous snake; it would die soon after the fatal blow was inflicted. His identity continued to remain an enigmatic secret, but Sleeman's ever-growing and carefully kept records would sooner or later pinpoint him.

Each morning began with an update of the latest information and Sleeman matched new data with old to try to piece together the identity of the Thug's master strangler. On one unforgettable morning, Sleeman believed he had this leader's name: Feringheea. Born of noble blood, Feringheea was handsome and bold, charming and persuasive, intelligent and cunning. He had been born during the siege of his father's estate by government troops and survived the destruction of his father's property. Writing the name on a piece of paper was far removed from actually capturing the man himself, however, but now the campaign had a focus and a definite goal. Capture the Thug Feringheea and the five-century cult of mass murder would dissolve around him.

The mountain of records was of great value to Sleeman and his officers. Many times they were instrumental in the capture of gangs. One of Sleeman's men, Captain Borthwick, was able to correctly pick out a gang of Thugs from his records based on the location of several murders and eyewitness testimony. The murders had been committed in 1829 in Rutlam State by what at first appeared to be Bhil aboriginal tribesmen. When he examined the remains, Borthwick was convinced that Thugs were responsible, not Bhils. The locals gave him a description of a large group of travellers who had come that way recently. They were apparently returning from a pilgrimage to a holy place in Gujarat. Using his records, Borthwick was able to guess which gang was responsible and told the Rutlam police chief to pursue them, accompanied by only three horsemen! When the chief caught up with the pilgrims, he had to convince them to return with him to Bhulwara. Cleverly he pretended to be an opium inspector. The government monopoly of opium trafficking meant that it had troops posted along the roads to apprehend smugglers. With the threat of pursuit by these troops, the chief persuaded the pilgrims to turn back. The Thugs hiding among the travellers were happy to go along with the policeman; they knew full well they were innocent and it would do them no harm to be given the all-clear by the government! At Bhulwara, Borthwick's records identified a Thug who, once confronted, became an approver. He turned in his entire gang to Borthwick and owned up to participating in the strangulation of eighty people so far that year.

The time was not far off when the king of Thugs himself, Feringheea, would turn to approving to save his own life. In 1830 Sleeman seemed to be getting closer to this leader, but Feringheea kept slipping from his grasp. His investigations in southern India were proving fruitless, even though a large part of Sleeman's resources were directed at this one aim. The use of approvers, as spies and deceivers, would be the weapon used to catch the arch Thug. It was ironic that thuggee fell due to the subterfuge of these double-agents; the cult had trained its members well.

Feringheea had wandered into the centre of Sleeman's territory. At a village near Jubbulpore the cult leader organized a meeting to discuss the next season's activities. It was at this village that the government struck, capturing Feringheea's family but failing to take the leader. Sleeman moved them to Saugor, hoping to use them to catch Feringheea. A second attempt also failed, and the head of the Thugs escaped alone. The remnants of his gang joined up but were now so few and so dispirited that Feringheea abandoned them in favour of a new group of Thugs. These he would recruit at the village of Kisrai. Unknown to the leader, two approvers at Kisrai were ready to turn him in. He was caught there in December 1830.

The meeting between Sleeman and Feringheea took place the following month. The Thug was given just one minute in which to switch sides and become an approver. Rather than face a fitting execution by hanging, Feringheea chose to inform on his own organization. This act of clemency was not a popular one. To let the orchestrator of this abominable cult live while countless thousands had died seemed too much. The injustice was compounded by Feringheea's admission that his gang had strangled 100 men and five women on their last expedition. Sleeman saw, however, that a willing general can disband his troops. This general proved very willing indeed; if he had regrets or loyalties to Thugs still practising their trade, he did not show them. Feringheea was pardoned and be began the task of locating the *beles* full of dismembered travellers that had been used by his gang. Close by, the local village had been a sanctuary for Thugs, under the protection of a conniving landowner. A second alarming revelation was that one of the cult's greatest burial places was located right under Sleeman's nose in Narsinghpore, where he had been a magistrate in the 1820s. Sizeable bands of Thugs from all across India used the nearby groves as meeting places and stopping points during their campaigns.

With the head of the evil cult behind bars, the days of thuggee were numbered. Feringheea told Sleeman every secret of the religion, including beliefs, techniques, past activities, present members, Thug bases and other information. Anything the weary investigator wished to know was explained to him by his eager approver.

Convicted Thugs or those awaiting trial were placed in a specially built prison at Saugor. Those found guilty of thuggee were hanged and their cells given to the fresh inmates arriving daily. Others associated with the cult but not themselves murderers were sometimes deported or gaoled for life. The executions numbered in the thousands and the Thugs died without remorse or guilt, many throwing themselves from the gallows. They believed that Kali had assured them a place in Paradise and were eager to join her. Doubtless, too, they disdained execution at the hands of a *chamar* (skin-curer), who was of the lowest caste.

By the middle of the nineteenth century the cult of thuggee was almost non-existent. Sleeman saw the destruction of the evil society through to the very end. He was made General-Superintendent for the Suppression of Thuggee and brought many more of the stranglers to trial. By 1840 3,689 Thugs had so far been tried, with only 466 of those executed. Over 1,100 were imprisoned (usually for life), and ninety-seven were acquitted. Many Thugs were transported for life or died before verdicts could be passed. Approvers who helped to expose the cult and its members numbered fifty-six. Between 1840 and 1850 another 531 Thugs were brought to trial, the last of their kind. Untold thousands of Thugs, safe in anonymity, never came to trial, or even under suspicion.

The cult reappeared briefly in the Punjab throughout 1853 but was quickly and easily suppressed by Captain James Sleeman (William's nephew). Murders in the name of thuggee were also reported as late as the 1940s, but it is doubtful that any real links existed. From Jubbulpore Sleeman directed his men in the last operations against the surviving Thug gangs, and from this town he attempted to re-educate the sons of Thugs. His aim was to give them a trade to follow, and in this he was highly successful. His craft schools taught would-be stranglers the arts of weaving, building, brick-making and, most famously, carpet-weaving. Thug carpets were renowned in Victorian England, the Queen herself ordering one. It was delivered to Windsor Castle for display in the Waterloo Chamber. Huge and seamless, the carpet measured 24 by 12 metres and weighed around 2 tons. This gift can be seen as the end of the campaign against the cult. The carpet was almost a peace-offering by the sons of Thugs as reparation for the sins of their fathers. No Thug would, of course, view it like this. According to Thug philosophy, all those Thugs who were put to death by the East India Company now dwelt in Paradise.

Estimates have put the total death toll at the *rumals* of Thug stranglers at somewhere near 12 million! This very rough figure is based on 40,000 murders each year across India for 300 years. Who knows how many dismembered corpses lie under Indian soil even today? Not even the Thugs themselves could guess the age of their profession, and no gang was foolhardy enough to keep written records of its murders. As a guide to numbers, one gang of twenty Thugs caught by the East India Company boasted an average of 256 murders *each* during their lives as Thugs!

The true horror of thuggee lay in its inherent amorality. Its adherents truly believed they were righteous devotees of a goddess who promised Heaven in return for human sacrifice. Their actions were ultimately evil, though such a term is very subjective. No Thug considered his actions anything but pious. The existence and prosperity of the cult is a testament to the dark, fanatical side of religion. It is possible that Thug gang members considered themselves the moral arbiters of God's judgement, India's 'dark angels'.

CHAPTER 6
Ninja and Ninjutsu –
Japan's Secret Warrior Cult

In the minds of modern media audiences, the ninja are superheroes. *Are* superheroes, because to the average person the ninja never went away. Countless movies depict the modern ninja as a deadly black-clad practitioner of an arcane but effective oriental martial art. Operating alone, the ninja is a masked hero, a righter of wrong and settler of scores. As if to reinforce this view of the ninja as a modern phenomenon, exponents of the ninjutsu martial art in Japan and the USA today claim direct descent from the ancient Japanese ninja *ryu*, or schools. Their teachings hinge on the idea of the ninja as hero and spiritual guru, as if to vindicate the existence of a cult of assassins in the modern world. For this is truly what the ninja were: a hereditary cult of murder, arson and deceit. Like the Assassins, most ninja clans were mercenary groups killing generals and aristocrats for money.

Even children in Japan and most of the western world are familiar with the ninja, especially since the explosive popularity of the *Teenage Mutant Ninja Turtle* cult at the start of the 1990s. Now ninja turn up regularly at fancy-dress parties, in toyshops and comics. They have gone the way of the western gunfighter, the Druids and Robin Hood. All have been mythologized to such an extent that any 'bad' elements associated with these characters have been eclipsed by their more heroic and commendable qualities (for example, the gunfighters robbed and murdered, and the Druids carried out human sacrifice). This process began some time ago, around the start of the seventeenth century, when depictions of the ninja in Japanese books began to feature black-clad men of mystery able to kill someone without being detected. The ninja was already becoming endowed with the formidable and magical powers that would later turn the character into a superhero. This transformation from assassin to warrior-magician coincided with the decline of the ninja as a fighting force in Japanese warfare and politics. As memory of the real-world ninja faded, their skills of stealth and trickery were elevated and transformed into magical powers and the ninja himself became a folk-hero.

The role of the faithful and honourable Japanese warrior – the samurai – also fell into decline. Samurai were roughly equivalent to the knights of Western medieval history, operating in a feudal society and owing allegiance to their master (the *daimyo*). Not only were the samurai deadly battlefield fighters, heavily armed and armoured, but they dedicated their lives to the pursuit of their master's goals. If disgraced, the ritual suicide of *seppuku* (more commonly known as *harakiri*) would be performed. Even samurai wives would follow their husbands to the grave in this manner. Obligation, honour, loyalty, face – all were the cornerstones of the feudal society in Japan from early medieval times. And in the shadows lurked the ninja, flourishing in this noble climate even though the ninja ignored such codes of conduct. He was a state terrorist, a guerrilla fighter and a spy. Ethical considerations played no part in the ninja mind-set; there was never any such thing as a 'fair fight' with the ninja. No ninja, for example, would ever allow an opponent to retrieve a dropped sword, as a samurai would automatically do. So, who would have use of such men? Why were they allowed to exist at all?

In the strictly defined nature of samurai warfare and society certain options were just not available, and sometimes these options were sorely needed. Modern military strategy countenances such techniques as assassination, surprise commando raids, the targeting of specific command posts, intercepting messages and the use of misinformation. But no *daimyo* could ask his honourable samurai to perform these deceptive and underhand deeds. Instead, he made use of the unconventional mercenary warriors, the ninja, who occupied this niche. Only when Japan settled into a long period of peace did the use of ninja decline, but for most of Japanese history warfare and the interminable feuding of rival *daimyo* racked the islands. Both the Japanese emperor and the supreme war-leader, the *shogun*, were mostly figureheads, especially during the chaotic civil wars between 1450 and 1615.

The First Ninja
The concept of unconventional warfare was probably introduced to Japan from China. The Chinese general Sun Tzu, one of ancient history's greatest military minds, compiled *The Art of War* some time between the sixth and fourth centuries BC. Much of his book stressed that war was the final card to be played during a political struggle, and that other methods should also be used to defeat an opponent; physical force was only one of many techniques. His thirteenth chapter addresses the use of espionage to achieve one's objectives, and is considered by many to have inspired the growth of ninja in Japan during later centuries. Sun Tzu countenances the use of spies whenever possible, explaining that foreknowledge of the enemy's situation will ultimately bring victory. He identifies several categories of spy, including double-agents and suicide-

agents, but he praises most of all the spies who penetrate enemy encampments or castles and return with up-to-date intelligence. To the Japanese of later times, these were ninja.

Shonshi was the Japanese name for Sun Tzu, and a Japanese text called *Shonshi Nihongi* quotes Sun Tzu many times. It is thought that *The Art of War* reached Japan around AD 700 and the book was readily accepted and figured prominently in the development of warfare in the islands. By AD 800 the tactics that would later become associated with the ninja appeared in Japanese warfare with the start of the Heian period, and the establishment in the islands of a new sect of Buddhism called Shingon. Both were to have a profound influence on the development of the ninja cult.

The Heian period (AD 794–1192) saw the emergence of a great series of splendid and powerful families that dominated politics and society. Families such as the Minamoto, Sugawara and Taira fought each other for the highest positions in the land. With much to gain (and much to lose), the great families began to resort to the underhand methods of Sun Tzu, sending out the first ninja against each other. Now, one antagonist could strike at another without a fully fledged war in progress: a cold war. At the centre of these devious operations was the tiny mountain province of Iga, close to the imperial capital of Kyoto. During the Heian period this province came under the sway of the Hattori family, who hired out their highly unconventional warriors to feuding families. These 'men of Iga' were saboteurs, spies and assassins – in short, the first of a long tradition of ninjas.

The tumultuous Heian period saw the growth of the secret Shingon sect, which had its origins in Chinese Buddhism. It is thought to have been introduced in AD 806 by the monk Kukai and, unlike traditional Buddhism, which opened its temples to all people, it initiated members and refused entry to those it thought unsuitable. As a defence against established Buddhism, the cult made its home in the Japanese mountains, specifically Mount Koya and the mountains of Iga. This new sect was also known as *mikkyo*, the 'secret knowledge' or the 'true word', and this mysterious aspect gave the initiates of the Shingon cult the status of mystics. Through their secret devotion, it was believed that each initiate would be able to achieve Buddhahood. Adept Shingon members were magicians of some skill, using finger magic (called *kuji-kuri*), examples of which are commonly found on Buddhist statues today. Different signs could be created by twisting the fingers together in different combinations, and the Shingon initiates used these finger signs to enhance the power of their ritual words. One Shingon book lists almost 300 different signs! Legendary exploits featuring Shingon magicians were often coloured by their use of many different *types* of magic, and initiates seemed to specialize, so there are examples of fire magic, toad magic and spider magic. Other types, too, will have been practised.

Coinciding with the influx of Shingon Buddhists into the Iga area was the arrival of Chinese warrior-monks and warlords with the remnants of their armies, following the collapse of the T'ang dynasty. The warrior-monks (or *yamabushi*) settled in the region, and journeyed regularly on hard pilgrimages from shrine to shrine through the mountains. *Yamabushi* were later associated with the ninja, perhaps because the latter often disguised themselves as the warrior-monks and were able to roam the region freely. Both were fighters; indeed, the *yamabushi* were involved in the guerrilla struggles of early Japanese history, when both Buddhism and Shintoism vied for imperial favour. Like members of the mystical Shingon cult, the *yamabushi* were also known for the magical abilities that they acquired through the suffering and hardships that their travels brought them.

No doubt the ninja clans were deeply influenced by the independent nature of both *yamabushi* and practitioners of Shingon. The *kuji-kuri* finger magic of the Shingon wizards also impressed itself on the culture of the Iga families, and was later used by ninja. This magical association cloaked the ninja profession with an aura of mystery, and to many the practitioners of the ninja art were at once cunning warriors and subtle magic-users. Just as Shingon wizards had mastered magical themes such as fire and spiders, the ninja may have practised a form of stealth or warrior magic, inherited directly from the Buddhist sect.

In the early years, what would later fall to the ninja to carry out on the battlefield was undertaken by a small number of exceptional samurai. During the Gempei War (1180–85) two powerful families fought each other, and two samurai brothers, Kawara Jiro and Kawara Taro, performed a night-time raid against the Minamoto in true ninja style. In the end, however, it was this latter noble clan that claimed victory, and it did so with ninja activity of its own.

As individuals, ninja warriors are mostly unknown to us, unlike their glory-seeking opposites, the samurai. Only occasionally were names recorded: for example, when the military leader Yoshitsune fled across Japan from his brother Yoritomo, he was accompanied by several loyal companions, among whom was Ise Saburo Yoshimori, a ninja from the province of Kozuke. What's more, the group at one point travelled as *yamabushi*, a common disguise for ninja. Other ninja 'heroes' infrequently break the surface of obscurity, often to meet a horrible fate by being boiled in oil by the authorities. No wonder, then, that the ninja were reluctant to advertise their achievements!

Although the ninja clans operated all over Japan, the strongest concentration of families was in the province of Iga and the Koga region of Omi province, south of the imperial capital, Kyoto. This mountainous area provided both a training ground for the clans and a safe haven from the forces of the *daimyos* who they might anger in their work. Such security meant that the Iga/Koga clans could operate in isolation as mercenaries. The virtual impossibility of successfully attacking the ninja clans rendered them politically neutral, in much the same way that Switzerland was neutral during the Second World War (indeed, the Swiss were also noted for their mercenary armies in earlier times). The Japanese clans living in Iga and Koga formed the ninja 'cult' that through loyalty and military excellence survived the wrath of powerful *daimyos*. Eventually it was a long and relatively undisturbed era of peace that was to signal the end of the cult, but until then the ninja held on to their freedom tenaciously.

Dominating the ninja organizations in Iga were the families of the Hattori and Oe, but there seems to have been little direct rivalry between them, since the clans co-operated in a way unique in feudal Japanese society. Various schools or traditions of ninjutsu (the art of the ninja) developed in the Iga/Koga regions, and one estimate has put the number of clans following the Koga school at around fifty. These schools flourished during the power plays of the Kamakura period (1192–1333), hiring out their special guerrilla methods to first one lord and then another. One family in particular, the Wada, who were in possession of a whole string of hilltop forts, were so powerful that they were able to provide a bolt hole for the *shogun*-to-be, Yoshiaki, in the late sixteenth century. And yet the Kawai Aki-no-kami family had fought *for* a *shogun* a century earlier during the chaotic civil wars of that period. For centuries the sheer invulnerability of the ninja clans seemed assured, and ninjutsu reached its height during the so-called *sengoku-jidai*, or 'Age of the Country at War', which ran from 1450 to 1615. But a harsh warning was to sound in the year 1579, when the great warlord Oda Nobunaga sent his forces into Iga to crush the ninja once and for all.

The Shadow Art
Although the clans did not follow the honourable and chivalrous codes of conduct that the samurai clans had universally adopted, they were not uncivilized and lawless. A ninja clan organized itself in much the same way as a samurai family, with a web of obligations and loyalties, but it cloaked itself in secrecy and mystery. Not only were the identities of the main clan members secret, but the very skills and traditions of ninjutsu were equally shrouded in mystery. These skills were grouped into schools, or *ryu*, that systematized the

clan techniques and formalized the training of young members. A *ryu* had its own combat methods and philosophy, and differed in weaponry, the types of mission that it undertook and the favoured equipment or techniques that it employed. Some writers claim that at least one ninja clan had high-minded ideals and accepted only defensive or punitive commissions, but if so, it must have been the exception.

Ninja in different geographical regions established their own *ryu*, so that there was the Iga *ryu*, the Koga *ryu* and so on, as well as schools named after their founders, such as the Nakagawa *ryu* of Nakagawa Shoshunjin. The secrets of each were closely guarded and the special techniques passed down from father to son or from a ninja master to his pupil. When the ninja of the Nakagawa *ryu* practised in one corner of the castle where they trained, no one was allowed near them for fear they would see the secret techniques of the cult. *Daimyo* Tsugaru benefited from the *ryu* during the mid-seventeenth century, since its founder, Nakagawa Shoshunjin, was one of his own samurai. All aspects of their training, according to the writer Watatani, were highly secret, and only the *daimyo* himself could order the ninja agents into the field. Anyone who disseminated ninja techniques to others was immediately executed by the clan, but this did not stop writers of the period committing the art of ninjutsu to paper. During the years of the ninja decline, books that listed some of the amazing techniques previously employed by the stealthy assassins became popular as curiosities. The most authoritative of these surviving works is the *Bansen Shukai*, a handbook of ninjutsu written by Fujibayashi Yasutake in 1676.

At the head of a ninja clan sat the *jonin*. He was the overall leader and directed political policy and strategy, approving commissions and directing the clan towards certain goals. Usually the *jonin* had a cover that hid his real identity from even his own staff. Some *jonin* were able to support two or more separate families in the course of their hidden life, without one knowing of the other's existence. Below the *jonin* were the *chunin*, or clan middlemen, who oversaw the day-to-day running of the clan. These officers were responsible for training the actual field agents (the *genin*), setting up contracts and missions and supervising the clan's affairs. Most would be retired *genin* or even ninja who were now unfit for fieldwork (through accident or combat), which meant that they added their own experience of ninjutsu to the corpus of secret knowledge passed down to the students. The lowest rank in the ninja organization was *genin*, or ninja proper. *Genin* conducted operations and carried out the hazardous missions that earned them their fearsome reputation.

Trained in the use of weaponry, unarmed combat, and survival and infiltration techniques, the ninja *genin* were espionage agents and commandos well ahead of their time. Ninjutsu, the science of ninja, became codified by each practising *ryu*: techniques proved to work were retained, while others were discarded. Today these techniques are practised by only the élite fighting forces of the world, skilled in cross-border infiltration as well as counter-terrorism. When SAS troops stormed the Iranian embassy in London in 1980, the parallels that could have been made with the ninja were numerous. Black-clad experts, with faces continually hidden, entering the building via windows, using high-tech flash-bang grenades to stun and disorientate, and wielding the best weapons available with considerable skill. SWAT teams, special forces and counter-terrorist units are all the true descendants of the ninja cult, although they have internationalized and updated both techniques and approach.

The great modern misconception about ninjutsu is that every mission involved the agent dressing up in black, penetrating a castle or other building, committing his murder and then making off without ever having been detected. But there are several accounts of different approaches. In the first instance, the ninja often operated in teams, and secondly they would attempt to mimic the uniforms of the defenders if it were at all possible. When Tokugawa Ieyasu hired over eighty ninja in 1562 to carry out a night-time raid on the castle Kaminojo, the deadly agents dressed as the castle guards and, once inside, pretended to be traitors, which caused confusion and chaos within the walls. At this point they set fire to the buildings and made their escape. These ninja were from Koga and were led by Tomo Yoshichiro Sukesada. Ieyasu was greatly impressed with their abilities. When he later became *shogun*, he hired both Koga and Iga ninja as his palace guard, a role similar to that of the mercenary Swiss Guard at the Vatican.

Kaminojo was not an isolated episode, and similar ninja attacks were commonplace. In 1560 the rebellious Dodo, vassal of the *daimyo* Rokkaku Yoshitaka, found himself under siege from his lord. Unable to take the castle, Yoshitaka hired the services of ninja from Iga. By penetrating the castle on his own, the leader of the ninja band was able to steal a *chochin*, or paper lantern, that bore the *mon* (heraldic badge) of Dodo's forces. With this in their possession the crafty ninja fabricated more of them and, dressing as the defenders, walked up to the castle gates and were simply allowed in. Once inside, they used their standard tactic of setting fire to buildings. This caused confusion, destroyed property and tied up the defenders with fire-fighting duties, allowing the ninja to make their escape or carry out their assassination.

Rokkaku Yoshitaka also found himself the *target* of ninja from Iga, this time hired by another of his opponents, the Asai family. This gives some indication of the truly mercenary nature of the ninja. Three ninja chiefs from Iga were hired by the *daimyo* Asai Nagamasa to infiltrate the castle of Futo, held by the Rokkaku samurai clan. In this instance, the ninja force was a raiding party, with the objective of starting fires within a castle as a signal for the rest of the Asai army to attack. Again, the combination of the confusion caused and the drain on manpower, with people needed simultaneously to put out the fire *and* man the defences, must have been an effective one.

Training for a ninja began early, perhaps as young as five or six, and the regimen was almost impossibly tough. The children concentrated on co-ordination and flexibility, only learning the basics of weaponry when they had reached the age of twelve. Exactly which weapon and fighting styles were taught depended on the individual *ryu*, and as the trainees mastered the martial arts day in and day out, they also built up their strength and stamina. Long runs were made and physically demanding exercises, such as hanging for extended periods from the branches of trees, were carried out. Stamina, patience and strength were all valued by the ninja *ryu*. Some ninja were even reputed to be able to travel up to 160 kilometres in one day!

Some *ryu* specialized in supplying female ninja agents for missions. Called *kunoichi*, these seductive women would seem unlikely candidates as spies, which enhanced their effectiveness. Men would let down their guard more easily in front of a woman and, with a poison-tipped hairpin in the *kunoichi*'s elaborate coiffure, this might prove a fatal mistake . . .

Not all exponents of ninjutsu were born to it, however. Some were warriors from a very traditional background who had joined the ninja cult. One such man was Tsukahara Bokuden, the son of an expert swordsman who joined the Iga ninja when his family was ruined by the machinations of Oda Nobunaga. Another samurai-turned-ninja was Yagu Jube'e Mitsuyoshi. The famous Ishikawa Goemon, who was more outlaw than ninja, became a folk-hero in his lifetime; he began his career by robbing his master and then murdering the men sent to arrest him. Goemon, who was reputed to have studied ninjutsu with the Iga *ryu*, could not evade the authorities for ever and was eventually captured and executed in 1595. Like all robbers (and many ninja), Goemon was put to death by the nightmarish method of being boiled slowly in oil.

Many ninja techniques seem questionable, although several modern ninja profess their authenticity. As with other cults in this book, it is almost impossible to verify a statement about a particular cult, since by their very nature cults are secretive. This is especially so with the ninja, since membership of a ninja clan would bring almost inevitable death if that membership were to be revealed to the authorities. Seemingly impossible or magical feats credited to the ninja could only enhance their reputation and create an atmosphere of awe and superstition, thus helping to ensure their survival.

Central to the ninja philosophy (if there truly was such a thing) was the concept of disguise. For the purposes of travelling incognito through the countryside or in populated areas, a ninja could adopt a variety of disguises, known as *shichi ho do*, the 'Seven Ways of Going'. Most ninja (like the *jonin* who supervised the clan operations) lived under a *nom de plume* for much of their lives, and the Seven Ways of Going provided a number of distinct and very useful false identities for the *genin*. The seven were:

Sarugaku actor or entertainer
Ronin masterless samurai, wandering warrior
Shukke Buddhist monk
Komuso wandering priest
Yamabushi mountain warrior-monk
Akindo merchant
Hokashi musician

Some of these disguises were useful in that they allowed a concealed weapon to be carried, ready for immediate action. A musician's flute could be weighted and used as an effective club, the *yamabushi* could carry a staff with a concealed blade, and both the *ronin* and the *yamabushi* could wield a sword openly. Any ninja traveller could carry a staff that was specially fashioned to hold a secret chain weapon. Against an unarmoured or surprised foe, any of these weapons would be highly effective, and surprise was almost guaranteed if the ninja could play out his adopted role well enough. The night-time commando missions usually required a copy of the costume that the soldiers guarding the target castle were wearing. Or, more infamously, the ninja would don a head-to-toe black garment that rendered him almost invisible. Such a costume included a hood that left only the eyes uncovered. It is said that ninja even had access to white versions of this suit for concealment in snow, and a camouflage version for woods and forests. There is some evidence that agents wore a light chainmail suit under their forbidding black costume, or, more intriguingly, chainmail sleeves with which a desperate ninja could attempt to parry the sword blows of an opponent.

Use of disguise was just one aspect of the ninja art, but illustrates its main emphasis: that it was better never to have to deal with an enemy than to face him. Everything possible was to be done to avoid encountering guards, soldiers, servants or whoever. Deception and invisibility were the primary weapons of the cult; swords and other martial tools were considered a back-up. Young ninja were taught different methods of deception, called *kyojutsu ten-kan-ho*, which included such simple tricks as throwing a stone into a moat or leaving a door ajar to trick the enemy into thinking the ninja had fled in a certain direction. A brave agent could even approach a guard directly and attempt to bluff his way past with a tall tale. Perhaps the most enduring feature of the ninja's medieval reputation was his ability to become invisible; stories were circulated of successful political assassinations, but no intruder was ever seen and no method of infiltration was discovered. Again, special attention was paid to the art of moving silently and invisibly during training, since the agent's survival often depended on never being detected. *Nuki-ashi* was one technique of walking silently, but frightened nobles and warlords devised many ways of trying to catch the dark agents out. A simple string of bells might signal the ninja's presence, as might a loose board; in fact, this latter notion was successfully developed into 'nightingale flooring', specially constructed so that however one stood on it, it squeaked loudly and alerted palace guards to the ninja's presence. A working example of a nightingale floor still exists in Nijo castle at Kyoto, installed for Tokugawa Ieyasu in 1600. It is a modern-day memorial to ninjutsu.

The grounds of a palace or castle had often to be negotiated first before a ninja could enter the buildings and commit his crime. Whether he was to carry out murder, arson, theft or just reconnaissance, the agent had to negotiate grounds that were usually well guarded. But here also the ninja came prepared. Training was given in camouflage and concealment among vegetation or rocks, and in the shallow waters of moats or ponds the ninja was able to hide while he breathed through a snorkel – a hollow piece of bamboo could be used for this, as could a specially made hollow scabbard. This technique could even be attempted under soil!

To gain entrance to a building, lockpicks or small crowbars were sometimes carried, along with a bewildering array of other gadgets. Again, how many of these instruments were used by the practitioners of ninjutsu is impossible to decide. Some items (such as a Ferris-wheel machine for launching an army of ninja over a wall) are of recent invention, and others (such as the two dummy heads strapped to a ninja's shoulders) are probably derived from ancient Japanese myths. A variety of collapsible ladders were known to have been used to scale castle walls, and so too were ropes and grappling irons. Exceptional physical skill was needed for the climbing of walls, battlements and roofs, and early training was invaluable here. Not only were agility and balance taught to young ninja, but also the ability to dislocate one's own joints. If a ninja was bound and left unattended, the dislocation of a shoulder may have allowed him to wriggle free (the same technique was used by Harry

Houdini, the famous American escapologist). Such control over the body required an iron will and a mastery of pain. One trap was proving impossible for a ninja to master; he had caught his foot while he prowled the corridors of an enemy castle and now discovery by guards was becoming an increasing danger. The man decided to cut off his foot and make good his escape, thus saving his life.

During his escape from buildings he had penetrated, the ninja ran an increasing risk of detection. The evidence of his unlawful entry, whether a fire, a dead body, a stolen document or whatever, would quickly be discovered. Exfiltration is the technical term for an agent's escape from an enemy area, and the *ryu* paid as much attention to this aspect of the mission during training as they did to all the others. Sometimes pursuit by guards was almost inevitable, and to distract them or hinder their chase small multipronged spikes called *tetsu-bishi* could be thrown on to the ground. Common footwear, even for samurai guards, was straw sandals that were easily pierced by these nasty devices. More bizarre pieces of equipment are also reputed to have been in use, including 'blinding powder' cast into a pursuer's eyes from a blowpipe, and 'flash bombs', made up of reactive chemicals inside an egg or fragile pot. Both could give a ninja vital seconds in which to make his escape, or alternatively to conceal himself within the castle or palace grounds.

Hiding in the moat or the grounds was one thing, but sometimes closets, chests and false ceilings would become impromptu hiding places. A very effective tactic was to *remain* at the scene of a crime, knowing that the samurai would probably search just about everywhere else! Ice-cool nerve was required, but such nerve more than once enabled a ninja to remain in the very room, near the freshly dead corpse, where he had carried out the murder. The supple and agile ninja was even able to squeeze himself up into the corner of a room over a doorway, remaining invisible to someone checking the room from the door. But secreting oneself in the rooms of the target had its dangers, as the ninja Yamoto found out in 1478. His mission was to kill the high-ranking samurai Herrito; he planned to remain hidden in the roof beams of his victim's bedroom and then drop down into the room to murder the sleeping man, but the plan went awry. Herrito entered the room in the company of two companions, and the men sat down to play a game of *go* only 3 metres from Yamoto! For five hours the three men played their game and the ninja was forced to stay silent and motionless so as not to be discovered and executed. Eventually the samurai climbed into bed, and within an hour Yamoto had crept down from the rafters and murdered him. The murder of a sleeping victim might not go as planned if he were only feigning sleep, so the *Bansen Shukai* explores at length the different types of snores that exist, and details the differences between light and deep sleep, the snores of men and women, and whether or not a sleeper was faking a snore. Such a person would probably be killed by the ninja immediately.

The Fighting Art

Although the ninja spent years training to avoid detection and consciously went out of their way to avoid combat in the field, they have gained the reputation as master-warriors and martial-art experts. No doubt the ninja benefited from superior and prolonged training, but it is doubtful that a typical ninja could match the martial excellence of a skilled samurai. Why else would agents such as Yamoto go to such excruciating lengths to avoid combat? Samurai armour was of excellent quality; the twin samurai swords, the long *katana* and the short *wakizashi*, were sharp, durable and expensive. The samurai, from an early age, received constant instruction in hand-to-hand combat, swordfighting and archery. No ninja could hope to stand up to a samurai in a fair fight . . . which is why the ninja never fought fairly.

Their martial art was ju-jutsu, which was adopted by all Japanese warriors of the day. It was a system of self-defence with 'no holds barred'. Useful in offensive and defensive situations, the art used the maximum force to achieve its ends and was less a systematized martial school than a label for a broad range of armed and unarmed Japanese fighting styles. By the late nineteenth century, classical (or traditional) ju-jutsu was little practised outside the underworld. Peace may have settled over Japan, but the Yakuza gangsters still resorted to violence to achieve their ends, and ju-jutsu was the fighting style that they used. Debt-collectors, minders in brothels and the fighters in fairground-style challenges all kept the ancient samurai and ninja fighting art alive. Today ju-jutsu has been revived as a sport following the abandonment of its less savoury techniques. Some of the more violent techniques were honed and refined by different ninja *ryu*. The Iga and Koga *ryu* incorporated martial techniques called the muscle-and-organ-tearing method (*koshijutsu*) and the bone-breaking method (*koppojutsu*).

While the Assassins of the Middle East, founded and perfected by Hasan-i-Sabbah, were content to rely on the dagger and the scimitar to carry out their suicidal murders, the ninja are well known for the wide array of weapons they had available. Most of ninjutsu's extraordinary variety of deadly implements often had a dual use, reducing the amount of equipment that the ninja had to carry with him. Most agents would carry the ninja sword, or *ninjato*. This sword was shorter than the samurai's *katana* (roughly 60 centimetres, as opposed to the *katana*'s 70–90), and not only that, but it was also of much poorer quality, far below the standards of workmanship that a samurai expected of his blade. Partly this was the result of infrequent use, but it was also because the sword was made blunt enough to be grasped and used to pull a man up a wall, using the guard as a hook. Alternatively, the *ninjato* could be jammed into the ground and used as a step-up, and an attached cord enabled the ninja to pull up the sword after him. As already mentioned, the scabbard could be made with a hole at the end, permitting its use as an emergency snorkel or an improvised blowpipe.

Few weapons were actively discarded by the ninja clans: everything had a use at some point, from daggers and spears to bows, blowpipes, *bo* staffs and even early examples of the arquebus (a primitive hand cannon). Compare this with the modern-day armouries of the élite commandos, complete with silenced sub-machine-guns, handguns, night-vision goggles, stun grenades, tear gas, sniper rifles and laser sights. Special equipment combined with intensive training produced a warrior with a highly specialized mission: infiltration, murder and sabotage. His weapons reflected this role. The *bo* staff was commonly about 1.5 metres in length, and when made of bamboo was able to conceal a long knife or weighted chain. A *bo* with attached chain was referred to as a *shinobi-zue*, and since most holy men carried a staff as a matter of course, a ninja disguised as such could carry a very effective weapon around with him. Another chain weapon was the *kusarigama*, a long chain attached at one end to a sickle. Either the chain or the sickle could be used offensively on their own, or they could be combined, the sickle to attack an opponent while the chain tripped and entangled him. Alternatively, a dagger could be attached to the chain's end and the weapon would become a *kyoketsu-shogei*, to be employed in a similar fashion to the *kusarigama*. The *manriki-gusari* dispensed with an attached weapon and was simply a metre-long chain weighted at either end. It had the advantage that it could be concealed and was both a flexible club and a method of entanglement. The *jo* stick was a heavy club just over half a metre in length and was useful both in defence and in attack. Combining the concept of chain weapon and club was the infamous *nunchaku*, composed of two small but heavy rods connected by a short length of rope or chain; the chain was supposed to give power and speed to the blows of the *nunchaku*.

Perhaps the most frightful weapons in use by some of the ninja clans were the *shuko*, or 'tiger claws'. These were metal bands that strapped over the hands and mounted iron claws on the palmside. These had obvious uses in combat, but also served as valuable aids in climbing; they made trees, posts and wooden walls far easier to

145

climb, as well as stone walls with discernible cracks. A version for the feet was also known of, called *ashiko*.

More popularly associated with ninjutsu are *shuriken*, small iron throwing stars that were never really designed to kill but could injure severely if thrown in the face or else distract a guard. The small stars were thrown either overhand or Frisbee-fashion and may have been given enhanced potency by the addition of a contact poison. Poisons were also sometimes smeared on the *testu-bishi* already mentioned.

Poison suited the ninja way of fighting. Its use was never considered an honourable method of killing someone by the samurai, but the ninja did not recognize a fair fight anyway. One of the most effective blade poisons that was both cheap and in ready supply was human excrement. As a poison, this would not kill a victim outright but would aggravate any wound, causing infection, perhaps gangrene and death. It was a tactic never forgotten in the Orient. The Viet Minh nationalists used similar tactics in Vietnam against the Japanese invaders during the Second World War, smearing sharpened *punji* sticks with human excrement and then lining a concealed pit-trap with them. Both the French and US forces who later occupied Vietnam discovered the use of this poison the hard way, losing many men because of it.

Murder by more traditional poisons was also carried out by the practitioners of ninjutsu, and the range of natural poisons from which they could choose was wide. Cyanide was manufactured from the seeds of apples, apricots, almonds, cherries and plums, although huge amounts of seeds were first required. Even the leaves of some seemingly innocuous plants, including tomato and rhubarb, are poisonous and under the right supervision become powerful poisons. By far the two most lethal poisons were taken from the deadly death-cap mushroom and the even deadlier blowfish. This latter is, even today in Japan, considered a great delicacy, but if it is not prepared correctly it is fatal, since the fish's gall-bladder contains a lethal poison. Now and then in Japan, diners are accidentally killed as a result of eating blowfish. No wonder, then, that it was a very popular poison with the ninja clans! A tiny piece of the blowfish gall-bladder needed only to be slipped into the food of a victim and the chances of its being detected were remote. Death would have followed soon after.

Ninja were reputed to be able to heal as well as kill and were equipped with some sort of first-aid kit. In the field, this would be used for the treatment of wounds, snakebites and suchlike. There were herbal concoctions used to banish hunger and thirst while a ninja was out on a mission, and also lightweight preparations of food that could be carried without unduly encumbering the agent.

146

Like their modern-day special forces descendants, ninja were taught a whole range of wilderness survival skills, including the ability to cook rice without a pot of any kind. The rice was soaked in water, wrapped in cloth and buried in a shallow pit. A fire, lit over the rice, would cook it. Less useful skills were also passed on, and these add to the bizarre lore of ninjutsu that was more superstition than science. For example, it was believed that the analysis of tree rings gave an accurate indication of the points of the compass, and, just as bizarre, that the changing eyes of a cat were held to tell the time.

One interesting survival technique for cold Japanese nights was the use of a *doka*, a small iron box in which a burning coal was kept. This kept the agent himself warm, thawed his chilly fingers before conducting delicate operations such as lockpicking and could be used to light a fuse.

The *Bansen Shukai* gives an account of ninja techniques of water travel that seems rather far-fetched. One is the use of wooden 'water-shoes' for walking across water, and another variant substitutes large airtight pots called *ukidara*, which were supposed to serve the same purpose. An inflatable skin was put to use in crossing moats and lakes, and this would have been more than a buoyancy aid, since it would also keep the ninja's equipment dry for the mission ahead. A sophisticated and very modern concept in marine operations was embodied in the *shinobi-bune*, a prefabricated little scout boat that could be carried into the field within a large box and then unpacked to be used by a single ninja.

Triumphs and Tribulations of Ninjutsu

Not all ninja were from Iga and Koga; neither were all ninja mercenaries. Outside these two provinces, there were ninja who acted as an adjunct (albeit a secret adjunct) to the established military forces of several *daimyo*. These agents were in effect the élite force of the army, performing hazardous castle-raiding operations during wartime. These loyal ninja forces were first recorded in the 1540s, during the fierce war between the samurai families of the Amako and the Mori. The war outlasted several *daimyo* and as the Mori fought for territory, the Amako were slowly destroyed. Ninja entered the field of battle during the fight for Yoshida no Koriyama in 1540, acting as a military raiding party.

Thirty-five years later, the Hojo family, who would soon rise to prominence on the Kanto Plain (upon which sits modern Tokyo), would also suffer the ravages of covert ninja operations. The family's dangerous rival, the Satake, did not just send the traditional ninja against the Hojo, but developed an interesting new tactic. Mounted scouts as well as ninja foot patrols were a danger to any commander, since they were able to report the size and position of his camp back

147

to the enemy. What the Satake did was to send out *kusa* ('grass' agents) into the surrounding area. As Hojo scouts approached, the *kusa* would ambush them and prevent the family from discovering the strength of the Satake. The *kusa* were less ninja than anti-ninja ninja!

In 1580 the Hojo family was in a position to use its own ninja against a new foe, the Takeda clan, and the raids they made were classic ninja operations. When the leaders of the two samurai families, Hojo Ujinao and Takeda Katsuyori, came together to do battle, Ujinao had at his command a unit of ninja called the *rappa*, who were commanded by the fearsome Fuma Kotaro. During the battle, the *rappa* made repeated night-time raids on the Takeda camp, creating havoc and serious damage by setting fires and even kidnapping people. By imitating the Takeda war-cry during these attacks, the enemy became confused and dispirited, and as each night fell on Katsuyori's camp his men quaked in fear of what the darkness would bring. They knew what ninja were capable of, for, like most samurai families, the Takeda had ninja of its own.

Although feared and respected, occasionally these shadow warriors performed more humble tasks. In 1566, when the Takeda military commander, Iidomo Hyobu, marched to war at the battle of Wari-ga-toge, he inadvertently forgot the Takeda battle standards, which would not only prove demoralizing for his own forces but would make it almost impossible to control the various elements of the Takeda army. Fortunately, a young Takeda ninja named Kumawaka volunteered to make his way back to the Takeda fortress and return with the standards. But although he arrived at the castle in good time, he found it on full alert and impregnable, fearful of attack. As a skilled and crafty ninja, Kumawaka did not let this minor inconvenience delay his mission and was able to penetrate the Takeda defences using his training. The standards were retrieved and sent hurriedly back to an anxious Iidomo Hyobi.

If the dark agents were most useful as élite siege commandos, they were most feared as invisible assassins, and it is this aspect of their profession that has left the longest-lasting impression of the ninja. Every *daimyo* feared silent death at the hands of these expert killers. Many high-ranking officials, *daimyos* and others, would go to extreme lengths to avoid this danger. Fugasiti, a *daimyo* living in Iga province, was ever alert to the threat of murder and was always accompanied by a guard of samurai. His castle was well constructed, with a wide moat and easily defended and patrolled halls. Samurai guarded every possible entrance and one warrior was even left to guard Fugasiti's bedroom at night. All to no avail, for the *daimyo* was found dead one morning with his throat slit. The lone samurai guarding him had been similarly dealt with, yet no one at the castle had reported any signs of an intruder.

As the Assassins of Syria had already discovered, perhaps the most effective way to murder a well-guarded notable was to infiltrate his staff and personal bodyguard. When the victim felt safe and secure, and when his guard was down, then the infiltrator would strike; but the Assassin was assured of his own instant death. The ninja never performed assassinations by this method, preferring to subtly penetrate the many layers of defence that the frightened samurai lords wrapped around themselves. In fact, the co-opting of enemy guards on to the ninja side was an almost impossible task, given the strict obedience and profound loyalty owed by even the lowest samurai to his *daimyo*.

Oda Nobunaga, Takeda Shingen, Uesugi Kenshin and Toyotomi Hideyoshi, some of Japanese history's greatest leaders, all survived ninja assassination attempts. With wealth and power came the elaborate methods of protection needed to stay alive to enjoy them. *Daimyo* began carrying personal weapons, and many of them had vast numbers of bodyguards in tow. Takeda Shingen had over 6,000 household warriors for defensive purposes, but even these were no guarantee against attempts on his life. He was the target of a lone ninja dispatched to murder him by Oda Nobunaga, but the assassin fouled up and was pursued by Takeda soldiers to a nearby wood. There the ninja concealed himself in a pre-dug hole in the ground and successfully evaded the *daimyo*'s troops.

Hideyoshi became a bitter enemy of Tokugawa Ieyasu, and sent a ninja into his palace, whereupon the agent skilfully hid himself under the floor, waiting for an opportunity to emerge and kill Hideyoshi. But the ninja was somehow detected and skewered through the floor by a guard's spear. To finish him off, a ninja was brought in to try and smoke the would-be killer out with an early type of flame-thrower. The most remarkable demise of a Japanese *daimyo* is attributed to the aforementioned Uesugi Kenshin, who took such precautions against assassination that he could be killed only when a ninja concealed himself in the sewage pit of the *daimyo*'s lavatory. As Kenshin seated himself there, the ninja is said to have impaled him through the anus with a spear. He did not die immediately, but staggered out to die in silent agony several days later. Controversy and speculation still surround Kenshin's ignominious demise, and it is now generally thought that he did in fact suffer a stroke while at his toilet.

Oda Nobunaga was fully aware of the power of the ninja. Like many a *daimyo* before him, he not only employed ninja against his rivals but had them sent against him. One is reminded of the adage, 'He who lives by the sword, dies by the sword.' Nobunaga did not die at the hands of enemy ninja, however, although several concerted attempts *were* made. One agent of ninjutsu, called Sugitani Zenjubo, ambushed the warlord as he rode with his retinue through the Chigusa Pass. Unusually, he attempted the assassination from a distance, using two readied hand-cannons (the medieval arquebus) with whose use he was highly skilled. Zenjubo hit the *daimyo* with both shots, but fortunately for Nobunaga his body-armour saved his life. Unfortunately for Zenjubo, although he escaped the wrath of the *daimyo*'s guards, he was arrested several years later and executed for the crime.

In 1573, two years later, an attempt was made to stab the *daimyo* to death in his castle, but the intruder, sent by his rival, Manabe Rokuro, and unlikely to have been a ninja, was captured and committed suicide. The penultimate assassination attempt on Nobunaga (the last, by one of his generals, succeeded) was again carried out with firearms. Three ninja fired a large cannon at Nobunaga and his staff during a visit to Iga province, which Nobunaga had recently invaded and despoiled. The *daimyo* again evaded death, but seven of his staff were killed in the indiscriminate murder attempt.

Nobunaga had become one of the foremost warlords of his time and vied for supreme control of the whole of Japan. As part of his conquests, the *daimyo* declared war on the tiny province of Iga, the heartland of ninjutsu. Its neighbour, Ise, had been captured by the *daimyo* and his son had been installed as commander. The defeated samurai family, the Kitabatake, fled from Ise to the mountainous safety of Iga and called on one of Nobunaga's greatest rivals for help. Once these renegade samurai had been identified by Nobunaga as a continued threat, the *daimyo*'s son, Oda Nobuo, was charged with the destruction of the Kitabatake rebels, as well as the formidable Iga ninja who sheltered them.

Never before had the Iga clans been forced to defend their homeland from an enemy marauder, and in 1579 what was to become known as the Iga Revolt was to be a supreme test of the clans' military skill. The initial battle for Iga was won by the ninja in the unconventional style typical of ninjutsu. The Oda general, Takigawa Saburohei, had rebuilt an old fort in Iga called Maruyama, with the aim of using it as a jumping-off point for further raids. He had his own ninja scout out the local terrain and establish the size of the enemy forces, but the ninja of Iga, not to be outdone, infiltrated their own agents into the workforce charged with the castle's reconstruction. With this advantage, the Iga clans decided to move against the fort and were eminently successful, driving out Saburohei to a nearby village. After Maruyama had been captured by the men of Iga, it was destroyed, thus depriving Oda Nobuo's armies of its use in any follow-up campaigns.

A second attack on Iga would be launched by Nobuo from neighbouring Ise, but as the army entered the mountains of Iga it became the target of ninja ambushes and was forced to retreat. The guerrilla tactics employed against it were favoured by the mountainous terrain, enabling the ninja to achieve total surprise and conceal themselves in local settlements once the battle was over. It is a form of warfare that has troubled generals for millennia, from the Hittites in Asia Minor to the Roman legions in Scotland and the Soviet Union in Afghanistan. Wisely, Nobunaga suggested that Nobuo should use ninja himself in the execution of his military raids on Iga.

In 1581 a renewed offensive on the ninja heartland was aided by the use of traitors, and quickly Nobuo, at the head of six large and independent armies, marched inexorably into Iga. As they moved, the armies carried out a 'scorched earth' policy, destroying farms, crops, villages and towns in an attempt to stifle the ninja's support and deny them safety and resupply. Military leaders through the ages have learned that such a tactic is one of the only effective ways to defeat guerrilla armies. Forced to fight on the enemy's terms, the ninja families retreated to isolated fortresses and were put under siege. Invariably these sieges ended in disaster for the men of Iga, even though classic anti-siege operations were occasionally carried out by them.

Finally, the outcome of the Iga Revolt rested on a single siege, at Hijiyama. Many ninja survivors had retreated from Oda Nobuo's forces until, at Hijiyama, they were left with nowhere else to run. A powerful ninja family, the Hattori, were in command at the castle and organized a last stand of the refugee Iga warriors, but the massed troops of the attackers proved too much for the wily ninja and Hijiyama fell. From Iga, the ninja who survived the military decimation by the Oda forces fled to other parts of Japan, many establishing ninja *ryu* of their own. Iga would no longer be the centre of ninjutsu; its day was done.

It is thought that most (but not all) of the ninja *ryu* established in Japan were created by refugee ninja from Iga following the Iga Revolt. This theory not only emphasizes a continuity of tradition and learning but also explains why Iga ninja turn up, for instance, as Tokugawa Ieyasu's palace guard twenty years later. His province of Mikawa provided a haven for many Iga ninja fleeing Oda Nobuo's deadly armies, probably because the *daimyo* already had firsthand knowledge of the ninja's usefulness in eliminating rivals.

Ieyasu had sent a ninja (unsuccessfully) to kill his rival Toyotomi Hideyoshi. A further link existed, since Hattori Hanzo, one of his 'Sixteen Generals', originated from Iga province. These links, being tentatively formed in 1581 as refugee ninja were being accepted into Mikawa, would save the *daimyo*'s life in the year that followed. Ieyasu had allied himself with Oda Nobunaga, but the old *daimyo* was murdered by Akechi Mitsuhide, one of his generals. Tokugawa Ieyasu, cut off from his home province and without substantial forces, felt vulnerable and threatened by the general. From Sakai, the *daimyo* travelled overland and took the unorthodox route through the mountainous terrain of Iga, recently devastated by Nobunaga's son. Bandits and the elements could have wiped out his small force, but locals assisted Ieyasu with guides to accompany him through the province. The families in Iga who had seen relatives flee to Mikawa were grateful to the *daimyo* and showed their gratitude by helping him avoid the robber gangs.

Perhaps because of this episode, Tokugawa Ieyasu later took 300 men permanently into his castle guard, and in this way ensured the continued loyalty of the Iga and Koga ninja. By employing a large contingent of the region's ninja and by securing the loyalty of others, Ieyasu deftly neutralized the danger from this formidable corps of assassins. No rival could now benefit from their deadly skills, and Ieyasu could monopolize ninja tactics and expertise. From this point onwards, the cult of ninjutsu was inextricably linked with the rising fortunes of the Tokugawa family. With the number of *daimyos* in competition for Japan's ultimate position of power dwindling away, leaving fewer, more powerful contenders, Ieyasu would find his household ninja army of considerable use.

With the death by murder of Oda Nobunaga at the hands of one of his generals, one of the Nobunaga family supporters rose to prominence. This great war leader was Toyotomi Hideyoshi, who was able, in a relatively short period, to become the master of Japan. Hideyoshi had become Japan's military dictator (or *kwampaku*), since he lacked connections to the Minamoto family line and could therefore not become *shogun*. From 1583 Hideyoshi began a campaign of reprisals against those nobles who had plotted against his late lord. Among his more influential allies was the wise Tokugawa Ieyasu, who became ever more powerful in the new political climate. Ieyasu stayed at home during Hideyoshi's extravagant scheme for the conquest of Korea and China. In 1592 the warlord's vast army crossed to the mainland and began the invasion of Korea. Along with the massed ranks of cavalry, infantry and samurai élite was a unit of ninja, hired specially for the occasion. It is likely that Hideyoshi was able to hire ninja who still roamed free, ninja who had not been absorbed into the Tokugawa family military and who continued to offer their services. The castle Chiguju, at the great city of Seoul, was put under siege by Hideyoshi's forces and the ninja were able to infiltrate the fortress and start fires, causing confusion and panic in classic ninja style. A second invasion of Korea, begun in 1597, ended in disaster for the Japanese forces when Hideyoshi was killed the following year.

The way, it would seem, was now wide open for Tokugawa Ieyasu, with his ninja force, to take complete command of Japan. But Hideyoshi had left an infant heir, the young Toyotomi Hideyori, who acted as a rallying point for opposition forces determined not to allow Ieyasu to seize power. At the battle of Sekigahara in 1600, the fortunes of Japan were decided. Ieyasu defeated his enemies and was proclaimed *shogun* three years later. In this last decisive armed confrontation between rival claimants for command of the country, ninja played no part, which is significant, since it also initiated a period of decline for the Assassins, culminating in their disappearance.

They did appear briefly on the battlefield against Toyotomi Hideyori, when the lord, now grown to maturity, rallied every renegade samurai in the land who would fight against the *shogun*. Masterless samurai (many of them survivors of Sekigahara) flocked to Hideyori's banner and the massive Osaka castle became their base of operations. Although the rebel army made no move against Ieyasu, the growing power within the walls of the fortress could not be ignored for ever. In 1614 the castle was put under siege and Tokugawa employed his contingent of ninja (from both Iga and Koga) very successfully. A band of his ninja did enter Osaka castle on a mission to destabilize relations between the different rebel factions, but the outcome of this attempt is not known. Was it mere coincidence, however, that one of the rebel generals took his own life at around this time?

Perhaps the very last use of Tokugawa ninja in Japan was during the Shimabara Rebellion of 1638. Tokugawa Iemitsu was the reigning *shogun* at the time and he was forced to step in and break up the revolt when local forces failed to suppress the revolutionaries. Initially just the angry protests of oppressed farmers, the Shimabara Rebellion exploded into a full-scale military conflict when the Christians (at that time severely persecuted) became involved and used the revolt as a means to fight back. Christianity had entered Japan from the mid-sixteenth century onwards but had always been a secret religion. On the island of Kyushu the Christians had taken up arms to defend their faith and their lives. But however cruel and oppressive the local Kyushu *daimyo* had been, such overt displays of defiance to Japanese authority could not be tolerated. To dislodge the rebels from their fortress on the Shimabara peninsula, a force of samurai troops was dispatched, along with a unit of ninja.

Members of the Tokugawa ninja unit carried out scouting missions around the castle and each night made daring raids inside the castle's perimeter. Because the defenders' food supplies were at such a low level, attempts were made by the ninja teams to smuggle out food from the castle. A variety of useful intelligence was gathered by the shadow warriors, including a layout of the fort, the strength of the enemy force and the special passwords used by guards and officials. To gain entry on one occasion the technique of deception strategy, or *kyojutsu ten-kan-ho*, was used: friendly troops opened fire on defenders with their arquebuses and in doing so forced them to extinguish their lights. In the fear-filled darkness that followed, the ninja were able to sneak undetected into the castle grounds. On one mission into the castle the ninja captured a rebel banner in an attempt to lower the defenders' morale – a tactic that had been used effectively by ninja in the past. Eventually the Shimabara Rebellion came to an end as the defenders' provisions ran out and parts of the castle defences fell to the *shogun*'s ninja. As a result of the rebellion, the sporadic persecution of Christians in Japan turned into nothing less than a total ban of Christian practice in Japan.

From 1640 until the end of Japanese feudal society proper in 1868, the role of the ninja declined rapidly, as did that of their gallant antithesis, the samurai. With no opposition and therefore no warfare, the *shogun*'s need for highly trained warriors and élite assassins faded. Today, martial arts *ryu* purporting to practise and teach the skills and the fighting arts of ninjutsu have little direct connection with the ninja schools of old. Skills and techniques may well be inherited from authentic ninja teachings, but the essential reason for the existence of these groups has radically changed. Gone is the mercenary attitude, the adaptation of the latest weaponry and the employment of murder, terror and arson to further political careers. Modern ninja seem to find the history of the cult distasteful and a little embarrassing, and have left the real-life legacy of ninjutsu to the twentieth-century commandos and SWAT troops. Around the world, these modern-day shadow warriors employ all the cunning and adaptability of their medieval Japanese ancestors, and enjoy a similar aura of mystique, admiration and fear.

CHAPTER 7
The Boxers –
The Fists of Righteous Harmony

For many people, the Communist Revolution in China that resulted in the accession to power of Mao Tse-tung in 1949 was the country's only great revolution, and certainly its most famous. But this great land, vast in both size and population, has been rocked by a long series of revolutions that will doubtless continue into the future. Perhaps it is something about the nature of the Chinese people, or the construction of their monumental government structures, that invites such frequent change. There is little evidence to show that China has given up the preoccupation with social change. The pro-democracy supporters who perished in Tiananmen Square during the summer of 1989 were martyrs to a cause that has continued to flourish despite persecution. Any future revolution in China will surely centre on the defiant and covert pro-democracy activists who remain.

Such is the obsession with revolution and rebellion that these activities have even become intertwined, at times, with Chinese government policy. In 1966 Mao Tse-tung instituted the Cultural Revolution, a political concept as bizarre as it was frightening. It involved the formation of an 'army' of supporters across the whole of China who were loyal to Mao Tse-tung alone. Mao had increasingly found himself isolated in Chinese politics, revered as a wise statesman but practically ignored in the running of the country. His enemy, the Chinese Communist Party, had become dominated by university graduates and Communist revisionists under Mao's successor, Liu Shao-ch'i. Supporters of Mao, called 'Red Guards', were encouraged to attack the government, as well as all the established institutions. Intellectuals, members of the middle classes and landowners were often dragged into the streets, publicly humiliated and even killed. Youths denounced their parents and their teachers, and for over three years the nation was paralysed by fear and hatred. Soon, the Red Guards were fighting each other in the name of Mao and no one was sure which group of Red Guards truly represented the Communist leader. In truth, none did, since Mao had lost control of his fanatics soon after their formation.

The revolution had taken a popular and violent hold, and the principal targets of Mao's Red Guards – his rivals in the universities, the Politburo and local government – were systematically removed. Chaos and anarchy reigned until Mao, disturbed by the extent of the destruction that he had unleashed, began the movement's suppression in 1968. Fading away by the summer of 1969, the Cultural Revolution had had nothing to do with art and literature, but everything to do with political survival and unbridled revenge. It had been a runaway revolution, resulting in perhaps 400,000 deaths, established by the head of state while being directed *at the state itself.*

Chinese history is replete with similar political movements with equally violent results. One such movement is known in the West as the Boxer Uprising or Boxer Rebellion, which took place in 1900. Almost forgotten now by modern Westerners, the uprising involved most of the important European powers, a secret and war-like magical cult, and an empress dowager reigning on behalf of her nephew.

Like Mao Tse-tung, the empress dowager who ruled China at the close of the nineteenth century commanded fanatical loyalty. Her name was Tsu Hai, and she had become the sole ruler of the sprawling Chinese Empire in 1898 by deposing the legitimate ruler, Emperor Kuang Hsu. This stubborn and determined matriarch had already ruled China from behind the scenes for forty years. She had been the concubine of a previous emperor and had had the tenacity to hang on to power ever since. Unlike Mao Tse-tung, the empress dowager had no immediate rivals, either equals jealous of her position or underlings eager to see her toppled. But there did exist in China enemies ready to eat away at her power and crush her authority. These enemies had forced their way unwanted into the country as traders and missionaries. To the Chinese they were *gweilos*, 'white ghosts', but these representatives of the great industrial powers were all too real.

Along with the European traders came Christians, and resentment against these zealous missionaries soon erupted. Roman Catholic churches preached without respect for local Chinese traditions or customs. Unwilling to offend the foreigners, the government had also granted concessions to missionaries, giving the clergy substantial authority. This, coupled with the fact that local people blamed the coming of the foreigners, especially the Christians, for many of their ills, meant that anti-Western feeling was running high. Mao Tse-tung had created his Red Guard organization, but the empress dowager was able to co-opt an already existing secret society to do her bidding, the I Ho Ch'uan, known in English as the Fists of Righteous Harmony, or 'Boxers'. Throughout 1899 and 1900 the Boxers rose up against anything that symbolized Western society. Churches, trading posts, railways and telegraph poles were destroyed; ministers, Chinese Christians, members of the European legations and Western sympathizers were murdered. The Boxer Uprising was a wholehearted attempt to kick the Europeans out of China.

Where did the Fists of Righteous Harmony originate? This question, though difficult to answer, is important, because the cult seemed to emerge suddenly from the shadows and then fade away just as spectacularly in 1900. The Boxers did not exist in isolation; a complex tapestry of secret cults and sects has existed throughout the history of China, many dedicated to the revolutionary mission of overthrowing the established government. What made the Boxers so unique was that the empress dowager, like Mao Tse-tung after her, was able to redirect this anti-government zeal against a personal enemy, in her case the representatives of the invasive Western powers. But it was not to be Mao's artificial Red Guard that became the direct descendant of the Boxers and its related secret societies, but the globe-spanning criminal conspiracy known today as the Triads. Now infamous as one of the world's most ruthless and impenetrable criminal syndicates, the Triads feature prominently in the story of China, the Boxer Uprising, and the 2,000-year revolution to overthrow the Chinese emperor. The story of these shadowy societies features political manoeuvring and rebellion across one of the largest empires in the ancient world.

A Mandate from Heaven

The Chinese imperial throne was founded in 221 BC with the establishment of the Ch'in dynasty. China had by this time become a centralized and unified state, composed of many large provinces often located far from the imperial capital. Administering these provinces could not be done by the divine emperor himself, and so each province had its own government, that was forced to act almost independently of the imperial throne. The emperor's position as ruler of China (known as the 'Middle Kingdom' by those who dwelt there) and Son of Heaven was as much religious as it was political. He had the Mandate of Heaven through his compassion, moral strength and righteousness, and this gave him absolute authority over every Chinese subject. But if the emperor were to overstep the Mandate of Heaven and act in a way unfitting for the ruler of the Middle Kingdom, then he no longer had the right to rule. Heaven itself was the judge of the emperor's conduct and would occasionally give a sign that change was required. A comet, earthquake, flood or famine often signalled to the masses that the emperor had fallen out of favour with Heaven. At such a time an uprising against imperial authority would place on the Dragon Throne a new emperor.

Revolution, then, seems to have played a great part in the psychology of the Chinese right to rule since the nation's inception over 2,000 years ago. The secret societies that sprang up all across China during the early years of Chinese history provided a stable community-within-a-community and a protection against harsh provincial governments. Secrecy was paramount when confronted by a government that would resort to torture and death to suppress its enemies. This need for subterfuge meant that members were required to remain loyal to the secret society on pain of death, and the mechanism used to enforce this loyalty was ritual initiation. Mixing Confucian and Taoist thought with Buddhist theology, the initiation became a religious ceremony. Cult members were bound by the sacred oaths that they made at their initiations. They pledged loyalty to their brothers and promised to keep secret the mysteries of the society. In return for their devotion to the cult, members received its protection against the oppressive forces of the Chinese Empire.

Each society had originally provided a local service that benefited the community in some way. Many were trade guilds protecting markets, or guilds of craftsmen or farmers. These early beginnings formed the basic foundation upon which the later Triad societies were built. When the provincial governments carried out their corrupt and harsh practices against the local Chinese, it forced the local societies to fight back, using secrecy and subversion to protect their interests. Retaliating, the local administration outlawed the offending society, which in turn resorted to deeper levels of secrecy and more aggression in its opposition to the government. As a secret society grew in size and power, it would begin to challenge not just the provincial government, acting on behalf of the Chinese emperor, but the emperor himself. Thus each of these proscribed sects became a government-in-waiting. Some writers consider them to have been groups ready and waiting to pay heed to the omens and unseat the current emperor at Heaven's call.

The first emperor to wage war against a secret society engaged in insurgency was the military leader Wang Mang, who had trouble with the rebellious Red Eyebrows sect. The peculiar name of the cult was derived from its members' practice of painting their eyebrows red when in battle. They played a part in the uprisings during the emperor's reign, but were not responsible for his eventual death by assassination in AD 23. Succeeding Wang Mang was the highly successful Eastern Han Dynasty (AD 25–250), and the Red Eyebrows now had no further role to play since their revolutionary mission had been successful. Their reward for playing an active part in the power struggle would be annihilation. The new dynasty had no use for rebels who had since turned to robbery to sustain themselves and troops were sent against them. Such an effective guerrilla force was too dangerous to remain alive. By an ingenious ruse of painting their own eyebrows red, the government troops infiltrated the cult and caused chaos wherever they struck. The Red Eyebrows were thus successfully eradicated.

The Han Empire reached a cultural peak in the second century AD. It traded silk with the Roman Empire and spread its authority even further into Asia. Many more secret societies were ready to take up the struggle against the newly established Han dynasty, however. Problems of succession provided ample opportunity for the groups to foment revolt. Among the sects were the Iron Shins and the Copper Horses, the Green Groves and the Big Spears. Robber-heroes like these became legendary figures, valiantly fighting corruption and oppression on behalf of the Chinese people.

The greatest threat to the stability of the Eastern Han dynasty was the society known as the Yellow Turbans. For ten years the mystic leader, Chang Chueh, plotted and organized his secret cult and, by AD 184, he had a substantial following of loyal revolutionaries. Chang taught the Yellow Turbans his own brand of Taoist magic, called *t'ai p'ing-tao*, and this included the power of healing through the practice of penitence. Sickness was attributable by the Yellow Turbans to sin, and penitent members would publicly confess their wrongdoings and wash in the cult's magical waters to cleanse themselves. A greater vision was pursued by Chang: namely, the replacement of the Azure Heaven that gave the emperor his mandate with a Yellow Heaven. This belief accounts for the origin of the society's ritual colour.

To guard against the evil influence of demons on cult members, magical Taoist amulets were worn by the cult, a practice that was echoed fifteen centuries later by the White Lotus sect, who wore amulets to protect themselves against the more up-to-date danger of bullets! But the Yellow Turbans were more than just a religious cult; they were organized, military-style, into thirty-six *fang*, a great *fang* being 10,000 men and a lesser *fang* consisting of 6–7,000 men. Each was led by a general who took his troops into battle, and with this magical army the cult succeeded in taking large areas of northern China.

These gains transformed the Yellow Turbans from a revolutionary and magical secret society opposed to imperial rule to a provincial government in its own right. But Chang Chueh (or his generals) mismanaged the new-found territories, rewarding the loyal Yellow Turban members at the expense of those not initiated into the cult. Eventually the society was crushed by the armies of the emperor and the gains made were all lost. Despite the defeat of the Yellow Turbans, however, the Han Empire collapsed and split into several smaller kingdoms. Three great generals (out of the thirty-six) may have survived the Yellow Turbans to establish themselves as powerful rebel leaders. One of the surviving warlords, Liu Pei, became emperor of the kingdom of Shu, and he, like his compatriots Kwan Yu and Chang Fei, entered the halls of Chinese legend. The trio had sworn a blood oath in a peach garden, an act that folk-legend and secret-society tradition would never forget. The significance of the peach garden and the taking of an oath would later figure in cult initiations. So too would Kwan Yu, who was later deified as the god Kwan Ti, after being murdered by an enemy of Liu Pei. Kwan Ti was the god of literature, warfare and also of the blood-oaths taken by secret societies.

Centuries of division and reunification followed the fall of the Han Empire, until a vibrant and rich civilization established itself. The T'ang (AD 618–907) was one of China's greatest dynasties, and the era was significant for secret societies, because although the Buddhist religion increasingly influenced art and literature, it was also periodically suppressed. When this occurred, its adherents went underground and joined with the secret societies for survival, passing on elements of Buddhist worship, symbolism and ritual. Modern Triad societies can trace their Buddhist rituals back to this point in history, when Taoist and Confucian sects became infused with Buddhist ceremony.

The White Lotus Society

Perhaps one of the most influential of China's historical secret societies was the White Lotus Society. Like others, it was forced from time to time to change its name in order to conceal its identity. Government authorities of the Sung dynasty (AD 960–1279), which came to power some time after the fall of the T'ang, were never well disposed towards the cult. Both Confucian and Buddhist authorities had banned it and would have destroyed it if they could. It became the White Lily Society, the White Yang Society and also the Incense-Smellers. This very powerful new sect was associated with other prominent societies at the time, especially the Eight Trigrams Society, the Heaven and Earth Society and the Nine Mansions Society.

Religion played a large part in the society's life, and some Chinese writers have detected a strong influence of Manichaeism in the White Lotus. This is of some interest, since Manichaeism was a Christian sect established by a Persian mystic in about AD 240. As previously mentioned, Mani had absorbed the Gnostic teachings of his father and created a fusion of Christian and Persian ideas. The new cult was heavily influenced by Persian Zoroastrianism and a religion we have already met: Mithraism. As previously discussed, the cult of this dualistic god influenced several medieval Christian heresies, including the Cathars and the Knights Templar. The mystic taught that faith should be replaced by personal illumination, and that light and darkness were in eternal conflict for the human soul. Mani was executed in AD 276, skinned and beheaded, but his cult survived and spread west across Europe to the south of France, and to China in the east. Such a broad appeal may be traced to Mani's declaration that he was the successor of the teachings of Jesus, Buddha and the Persian holy man Zarathustra.

The Buddhists were opposed to Manichaeism, perhaps on the grounds that it claimed to supersede their own faith. It was not until the Sung period that the sect received strong attention from the government. With persecution its followers went underground to practise their faith covertly and in smaller, unconnected groups. The White Lotus Society in the north of China began as one of these Manichaean sects, and it flourished to become a revolutionary group of great importance. Of course, the original beliefs brought eastwards by the first Manichaeans were gradually reinterpreted or replaced with current Chinese thought, particularly in regard to Taoism and Buddhism. Although proscribed by the Sung emperors, the White Lotus played a part in the rebellion against their successors, the Mongols, who had toppled the Sung and established their own Yuan dynasty (1279–1368). For a time the White Lotus Society became known as the Red Turbans and its leader, Han Shan-tung, fought determinedly against the Mongol administration. This and other uprisings eventually helped to destabilize the occupying Yuan government, and the Mongols were driven from China. Han Shan-tung claimed to descend from the rightful Sung dynasty, but both he and his son died before a new dynasty could be founded to replace that of the Mongols. His place as head of the White Lotus Society and rightful emperor of the succeeding dynasty was instead taken by Han's fellow rebel and Buddhist monk Chu Yuan-chang. This man assumed full imperial powers in 1368 under the title of Hung Wu ('Extensive and Martial').

The emperor Hung Wu was, according to the writer Jerome Ch'ên, a Manichaean, and this is a likely proposition considering the role played by the White Lotus in helping him to power. Later secret societies revered Hung Wu above all other historical figures and pledged their allegiance to the Ming dynasty that he founded centuries after its demise. The veneration of Hung Wu may have been due to this link with Manichaeism. In fact, the sect believed that darkness stole some of the cosmic light and hid it within the human soul, establishing the 'divine spark', or 'luminous self', as it was called; perhaps this was one reason why Hung Wu named his dynasty the Ming ('Bright'). Mani himself played on the connection of light with power, goodness and truth, calling himself the Illuminator and his cult's inner circle the 'illuminated elect'. A separate tradition states that the White Lotus Society gave the Ming dynasty its name because of its belief that there were two prophets sent to earth by Buddha on a mission of peace; both of these prophets were called Ming Wang.

It was the pure Chinese blood of Hung Wu, together with his achievement of expelling foreigners from China, that the secret societies respected, for as a ruler he was more feared than revered. Terror and despotism were refined by the Ming dynasty, and torture as an instrument of government practice was commonly employed. For three centuries, certain secret societies (among them the White Lotus) played no part in dynastic history, although they were proscribed in 1394 and their members threatened with execution. This was their reward for supporting a successful rebellion and it was a pattern repeated time and again, from the era of the Red Eyebrows onwards.

When rebellion did eventually break out in the Ming Empire during the 1620s, the White Lotus Society was involved and active. This decline accelerated when the last Ming emperor abolished the imperial postal service in 1629. As communication with parts of the empire broke down, rebels and bandits in northern China, led by the unemployed postal couriers, began to seize territory. In the wars that followed, the Manchu people to the north-east, who had menaced the Chinese Empire for decades, sought to exploit the chaotic situation. A Manchu army marched into China in 1644 and entered Peking that summer. Once more a foreign people had claimed the Dragon Throne, but the Manchus would be far more successful than the Mongols, and their rule would remain unbroken up until the early years of the twentieth century.

'Overthrow the Ch'ing and restore the Ming!'

From the establishment of the Manchu dynasty, known as the Ch'ing, the secret societies were united in a common purpose. Every effort would be expended on overthrowing the Ch'ing emperor and replacing him with one of Ming lineage. Hung Wu became a heroic symbol and reminder of what could be achieved through revolution. He had defeated the foreign Mongols and founded a truly Chinese dynasty. Now the secret societies aimed to repeat his victories. The second Ch'ing emperor, the tough K'ang Hsi, made firm attempts to suppress the revolutionaries, as well as both Taoists and Buddhists. Proscriptions began in 1662 and targeted by name such sects as the White Lotus, the White Lily, the Origin of Chaos, the Incense-Smellers, the Origin of the Dragon and the Hung Society. This last sect seems to have assimilated elements of the White Lotus Society, a sect that is heard of less and less following the edict of 1662.

The societies shifted their attentions south, where Ming sympathies were strongest and the Ch'ing hold was weakest. Fukien and Kwantung, China's two most southerly provinces, became the revolutionary heartland for these groups, and for the Hung Society in particular. Like the White Lotus that had influenced it, the Hung Society used a variety of aliases, including the Heaven and Earth Society and the Three United Society, under the latter of which it became more popularly known in English as the Triad Society. Since the Triad Society has managed to survive into the present day, much is known of its inner rituals and organization that is mere speculation with many of the other historical cults. It is known, for example, that Kwan Ti, the god of secret oaths, was recognized by the Triad Society as a patron deity, and his worship was taken up by the other secret societies. Religious belief and mysticism played a great part in all of the cults, mainly due to the influence of Taoism and Buddhism in their practices.

Many offices within the Triad societies (there are now many autonomous Triad groups, sometimes with their own sub-branches or lodges) possessed ritual names, such as Dragon Head, Incense Master and White Paper Fan. The hierarchy of each Triad headquarters was always rigidly defined and ritualistic, being headed by the society's overall leader, the Shan Chu. Acting as deputy and stand-in for the Shan Chu was the Fu Shan Chu, a position that still carried considerable power, as did the ceremonial offices of Heung Chu (Incense Master) and Sin Fung (Vanguard). These latter members were responsible for the ritual and religious practices of the cult, organizing initiations and being able to demand punishments for wrongdoers. A council of department heads came next in the hierarchy and these various officers dealt with day-to-day, mundane activities of the criminal organization, such as discipline, education of the young, intersociety diplomacy, propaganda, recruitment, finance and the welfare of the current membership.

Other positions of note were the Pak Tsz Sin (White Paper Fan), Cho Hai (Messenger), Hung Kwan (Red Pole), Chu Chi (Lodge Leader), and the fairly infrequent Cha So (Treasurer). Similar to the Mafia *consigliere*, the White Paper Fan was an educated man and a trusted Triad adviser, discussing tactics and policy with the Shan Chu. Members of the office often moved up into the Incense Master's position, since the White Paper Fan seems to have been more of a specialization than a formal rank.

This is also true of the Messenger, who liaised between the various lodges of the society (if any existed). He would, in addition, act as the cult's link with the outside world, and be responsible for the collection of money owed to the Triad. Perhaps the most sinister rank in the Triad cult was the Red Pole, holders of which were often department heads. Red Poles were the enforcers, the disciplinarians and hit men of the Triad Society. Often skilled in the martial arts (traditionally Ta'i Chi Ch'uan, but today including pistols and sub-machine-guns), the Red Pole planned and led attacks on rival societies, the government or victims of the society's criminal enterprises. At one time the Red Poles led up to fifty armed Triads on crime raids, but today numbers are smaller. In a similar position to the Triad leader (the Shan Chu) were the leaders of other Triad lodges affiliated to the main organization. Known as the Chu Chi, they usually had their own deputies, called Fu Chu Chi. At the very bottom of the Triad organization was the Sze Kau, the initiated rank-and-file.

Numerology, the magical significance of certain combinations of numbers, was certainly held in high regard by these early societies and is an essential element in Triad ritual, even today. Obviously the number 3 is of great significance to the Triad Society, denoting Heaven, Earth and Man; Creation is mystically associated with the number 3, and everyone has three souls. Number symbolism (and in particular the number 3) was applied to the Triad rank structure, so that each position within the organization had a ritual number).

The Shan Chu was known as the 489, or 21 (since 4+8+9 is 21, as is 3 x 7; the number 3 is Creation, the number 7 is both Luck and Death). Other mystical connections abounded, though many have now been lost. The Deputy Leader, Incense Master and Vanguard were all equal in rank and all 438s, the White Paper Fan was a 415, the Messenger a 432 and the Red Pole a 426. The ordinary Sze Kau was a 49.

Initiation was often a long and complex process, lasting in its entirety for three days, and it took place within the society's headquarters. Candidates for membership were required first to procure a sponsor already within the organization, to whom was paid a fee. A further payment was made to the society's coffers. To guard against infiltrators, both the Incense Master and Vanguard checked the initiate's credentials.

Each Triad hall was set out to symbolize the mythical Triad city of Muk Yeung (the City of Willows) with a symbolic 'gate' on each of the four walls. The initiation ritual took place within this hall and involved the drinking of blood taken from all the prospective initiates, followed by a long series of questions and answers, and the crucial swearing of the thirty-six oaths. Headbands and ceremonial costumes in a Buddhist style were worn by all, and there were several symbolic acts of death and murder, as an illustration of the fate that awaited traitors. All the officers of the Triad attended these initiations, giving the ceremony an air of authority and tradition.

Constant references to the Triad values of obedience, loyalty and secrecy were made, often in the form of vague (or not so vague) threats. Much of this traditional initiation ceremony has now been abandoned by the societies and the three-day initiation rite can now be rushed through in just one hour.

The emphasis is still on the swearing of oaths, however, and the maintenance of absolute secrecy. Part of this Triad secrecy involved the learning and use of covert hand-signals, similar to those used by the Freemasons or the ninja. The way in which a man held his chopsticks or offered money to a stranger contained identifying signals that another Triad member would immediately recognize.

Regional differences between the northern and southern societies existed but were mainly the result of differing cultures and language. While the White Lotus in the north evolved into new sects, such as the Eight Trigrams, the Torch-Bearers and the Red Fists, in the south it became assimilated primarily with the Hung (or Triad) Society. Because secret societies have a habit of cloaking both their operations and their origins in mystery, not much is known about the foundation of the Triad Society. What is certain about the early Hung Society was the power of their slogan, 'Overthrow the Ch'ing and restore the Ming!' It gave the society a physical enemy, a reason for existence and a method whereby it could begin to unite anti-government feeling throughout southern China. Whether or not the Hung Society existed before the rise of the Manchu dynasty, it certainly received its greatest impetus after that point. Modern Triad members claim that their brotherhood came into existence during the siege of a semi-legendary monastery called Shao Lin.

Every culture has its great martyrdom, a point in space and time where brave ancestors struggled heroically against an evil force intent on their destruction. Great Britain's little Expeditionary Force was almost wiped out on the beaches of Dunkirk, the Texans fought desperately against the Mexicans at the Alamo, and the ancient Spartans always remembered how 300 of their number died to save the rest of Greece. To the Triad Society, the attack on the monks of Shao Lin is of equal importance, and part of a pattern of resistance that swept through south and west China from 1673 to 1681. A general uprising of Ming supporters against the Ch'ing had begun, but could not stand against the Manchu armies. Hundreds of thousands of people were killed in the fighting or were executed.

Among the patriots were 120 warrior-monks well versed in the arts of war, from strategy to the deadly T'ai Chi Ch'uan martial art known today as kung fu. Legend has it that their monastery of Shao Lin, somewhere in the mountains of Fukien, became a rallying point for anti-Ch'ing forces. Such a thorn in the side of the Empire could not be left unchecked, and in 1674 a great army was sent against it.

For three weeks the warrior-monks defended the monastery against Ch'ing attacks, but a traitor in their midst allowed a few of the troops to enter, disguised as coolies. From within, the soldiers' task was made much easier; the monastery was set alight and the monks, caught by surprise, were massacred. The legend maintains that only eighteen of the original 128 monks from Shao Lin escaped the blazing monastery. Of these, only five survived the ensuing hunt that the Manchu forces embarked upon, and these five are known in Triad lore as the First Five Ancestors of the society.

Every detail of the Five Ancestors' wanderings and their founding of the society is remembered in the elaborate rituals of the Triad Society. Events have special significance and lessons to teach the initiate and help explain why the cult operates as it does. For example, each Triad lodge was laid out as a representation of the mythical City of Willows. It was there that the Five Ancestors first began recruiting society members, and where they made their headquarters at the Yee Hop Tim fruit stall in the city's Taiping market. Initiates for centuries after would pass through the 'entry of the fruit-seller' during their enrolment into the society. This was probably an attempt to link the first initiations with those taking place years later.

A fiery and desperate beginning to the cult helped establish the Triad Society as a revolutionary group dedicated to battling the Ch'ing dynasty at every turn. Members pledged their loyalty to the Triads and that loyalty superseded any other; even death in the service of the society was expected to be given if asked for. Rebellions against the Ch'ing always involved the cult, prompting the ruling dynasty to proscribe it. Among the rural peasantry, especially in the south, the rebel society achieved a heroic status somewhat similar to that of the French Maquis fighting against the occupying German forces during the Second World War.

An enduring fame and almost mythical reputation were heaped on the rebellious Triad members in the eighteenth-century novel *Shui Hu Chuan*. Better known to the West as *The Water Margins*, the book was banned by the Ch'ing as subversive in 1799. It featured a large force of bandits and fugitives from government justice who lived in a marshy wilderness away from civilization and waged guerrilla war against provincial despots. The novel must have had some basis in fact. Ch'ing policy had been to match every Chinese official in the vast government bureaucracy with a Manchu overseer, totally undermining any feeling of responsibility the Chinese people had for their own destiny. The resulting corruption, coupled with injustice, drove a deep rift between the people and their rulers. It was said that during the rule of the Ch'ing, the army protected the emperor while the secret societies protected the people. Of course, the inference was that the people required protecting from the emperor.

As the gap between the Ch'ing and the peasantry grew, the Triad Society expanded to fill it. Where the Manchu administration was often unreliable or even antagonistic to its citizens, the cult became a shadow government, meting out justice, resolving disputes and, one assumes, collecting taxes. Consolidating these gains meant that the time for a national uprising to overthrow the Ch'ing was approaching ever nearer, and as time passed several attempts were made. From 1787 up until the middle of the nineteenth century several revolutions were launched, but all met with failure. Many survivors of these abortive attacks fled to parts of South-East Asia, Australia and the west coast of America. What was needed was a nationwide mobilization of anti-Manchu forces that could assault government troops on all fronts.

An opportunity presented itself in 1850, when a fanatical holy man attempted just such a strategy with his Society of God-Worshippers. China was plunged into civil war for fourteen years while the unbalanced Hung Hsiu-chuan proclaimed himself the brother of Jesus Christ and emperor of China. How deeply the Triads were connected with this uprising, known as the Taiping Rebellion, is not known. That the legendary Triad market Taiping is mentioned by name points to some involvement, as does the instigator's name, Hung being both the name of the first Ming emperor *and* the alternative title of the Triad Society. This peculiar man originally entered the examinations for the imperial civil service and, on failing, began his holy war against the Ch'ing bureaucracy. Much of his theology was a poor reworking of the Christian doctrine that he had already encountered, but it was illogically amalgamated with elements of Taoism and Buddhism. During the cult's ceremonies Hung would read aloud from the Bible and then make food offerings at family ancestor shrines in the Taoist way, but he (conversely) believed in the Eighteen Hells of Buddhism. However mixed up Hung Hsiu-chuan's theology was, it attracted a great number of avid followers and instilled a fanaticism that engendered the destruction of temples and shrines, and the murder of holy men of whatever theological persuasion. Perhaps if the movement had spent less energy attacking Buddhist and Taoist religious institutions it might have made greater political gains. As it was, the Taiping Rebellion shook the Chinese Empire to its core. In only one year Hung was strong enough to proclaim a Taiping state (Kingdom of Great Social Harmony). Other military success followed with the capture of a series of cities and in 1853 Nanking was seized, becoming the Taiping capital of Tianjing (Celestial Capital).

Anti-Buddhist behaviour must have only alienated the majority of Triad Society members from participating fully in the Taiping Rebellion, since the Triad was most influenced by Buddhism in its hidden rituals and beliefs. But this did not stop it exploiting the anarchic situation in southern China, or stop individual Triad members joining the ranks of the God-Worshippers. Ming supporters may have welcomed the opportunity to throw off Ch'ing overlordship, but the established Triad organization seems to have played little or no part in helping the Taiping Rebellion achieve this goal. Had the Triad Society given up its avowed mission of 'overthrowing the Ch'ing and restoring the Ming'? The lack of substantial gains over the past 200 years had pushed the society into criminal activities as a method of economic survival, and the simple fact that the Triad was so vast meant it had become the *only* underworld culture. In this way it resembled the equally patriotically motivated Irish Republican Army of modern-day Northern Ireland. The IRA has in the past indulged in armed robberies to bolster its finances, and it has found drugs just as easy to smuggle into the Province as explosives or firearms. Additional revenue has been forced out of Ulster businesses, both large and small, in a very effective system of extortion, and IRA activists have also been known to dispense summary justice to wrongdoers in the community, particularly in the form of 'kneecapping' both informers and such apoliticals as young car thieves. Triad sources of revenue most commonly revolved around prostitution, gambling, protection money and the cultivation and sale of opium; all were considered immoral and illegal by the God-Worshippers.

However unimpressed the Triad was with Hung and his cult, the secret society took advantage of the fact that imperial troops were thoroughly engaged across China. Rebellions on a much more cautious scale were carried out throughout 1853, the first of which saw the Triad assume the name of the Small Knife Society during the capture of the port of Amoy. Some 2,000 Triad members held the city for three months, spurring the society on to greater successes. Later that year Shanghai was captured by Triads from Fukien and Kwantung and held for a year and a half. When the cult was eventually forced out of the city, the Manchu troops sacked and despoiled it, just as the Triads had done before them. Other successes were achieved, most notably at Canton (where the Triad took the name of the Red Turbans) and the profitable trade route of the Pearl River; both came under Triad influence for some time. Such gains were not fully exploited, however, for although together they were considerable, there seems to have been little overall control surrounding the Triad revolt.

As the Taiping Rebellion foundered, the Triads lost any advantage they might have gained. Hung Hsiu-chuan committed suicide, while his followers were rounded up and executed. Communist Chinese today look on the rebellion as an abortive attempt at a social revolution that was directed against the upper classes, but in reality it resembled a religious uprising, with the Manchu rulers forming part of the religious establishment. By the end of 1864 something like 20 million lives had been lost through the monumental folly of the Taiping Rebellion. More were to die at the hands of the vengeful Manchu authorities, and horrible tortures and death awaited the rebellious Triad members who had pointlessly risen up in the south. Over 1 million captured Triad members were executed in Kwantung province alone, either by decapitation, live burial, whippings of 1,000 lashes or agonizingly slow strangulation. Such a massive retaliation forced many members of the society to flee the country. Hong Kong became a popular refuge for Triads, as did the goldfields of California.

New secret societies were established in central China, perhaps encouraged by some of the successes of the Taiping Rebellion. Two of the most important of these Triad splinters were the Green Group and the Red Group. One other sect, the Elder Brother Society, was composed of veterans from the Manchu armies, and it established itself during the years of the Taiping unrest. There are no details of the society's goals or beliefs, but there were contemporary reports that the sect was intent on revolution. The Elder Brothers spread all over central and western China and came to government notice in 1870. A further attempt at revolution in 1891 amounted to nothing when the leader of the veterans' society was arrested, along with a British citizen, C.W. Mason, a customs official in Shanghai, who had smuggled in firearms and explosives for the conspirators.

What remained of the rest of the Triad Society after the Taiping Rebellion was still an active force in the southern provinces. Indeed, the Sunning area of China, to the south-west of the Pearl River, rose up in rebellion at the instigation of the secret society in 1892. Like previous Triad attempts, the gain proved ephemeral. It seemed that the Triad revolution, kept alive and simmering for two centuries, would never come to fruition.

A major social upheaval and numerous sporadic coups had not been exploited by the society. The increasing reliance on criminal activities for a sense of purpose may have had something to do with this state of affairs, and so too might the slow but steady exodus of members from China to the safe havens of Hong Kong and South-East Asia. The mainland, even in the south, had become a dangerous place for cult members, since there seemed little sign of Ch'ing weakness. The spectacular victory of the emperor's forces against the massed armies of Hung Hsiu-chuan can only have served to demoralize the Triad Society and its associate cults. In the north, however, the story was a different one.

Great Swords and Righteous Fists

North of the Yangtze River, the White Lotus Society had been in its heyday strongly connected with the Eight Trigrams Society. With the waning of the former, the Eight Trigrams had blossomed and by 1786 had eventually grown to become probably the greatest secret society in northern China. This year marked the eruption of a Trigram-backed rebellion during which thousands of cult members ran amok, until they were suppressed two years later. A measure of the danger that they presented to the Manchu dynasty can be gauged by the 1788 government decree that ordered the total extermination of the Eight Trigrams. It is clear that the imperial authorities considered this sect highly dangerous, mixed as it was with remnants of the White Lotus Society. Other cult connections later became apparent, but of particular importance was the one that existed with the Fists of Righteous Harmony (known to Europeans at the end of the nineteenth century as the 'Boxers').

This branch of the White Lotus was to do what the Taiping Rebellion failed to achieve: namely, successfully unseat the Manchu government. But in doing so, the Fists of Righteous Harmony were destroyed themselves during the uprising in 1900, and it was left to other secret societies, in particular the Triad Society, to exploit the situation that had been created.

How the Eight Trigrams Society came to develop into the Fists of Righteous Harmony is unclear. There is little direct evidence to link the two, but a great deal of similarity. Perhaps the most conclusive indication of a connection between these two sects is the fact that the Eight Trigrams is mentioned in the famous and most ancient Chinese divinatory text, the *I Ching* (*Book of Changes*). There the Trigrams are divisions of the universe in relation to eight cardinal points. Each division is known as a *kung* or mansion, and the eight are arranged around a ninth, central area. These nine mansions provide the society with its alternative name, the Religion of the Nine Mansions. In accordance with its origins, the Eight Trigrams Society was organized into eight groupings, each representing a mansion and commanded by a cult leader. One of these mansion chiefs assumed the leadership of the entire religious society. Much the same organization was used by the later Fists of Righteous Harmony, although only three mansions were mentioned by name during the uprising of the society in 1900: Heaven (Ch'ien), Water (K'an) and Earth (K'un).

The basic subdivision of a *kung* in the Boxer organization was a *t'uan*, which was responsible for the spiritual and physical welfare of its members. Each rural *t'uan* controlled a single village from its central temple, and was led by a Boxer official called the Ta Shuai. Boxers in the cities rallied around a headquarters temple that probably controlled part of the city, as a gang would today. Altars, religious statues and tablets often adorned the insides of these temples, and many possessed an adjacent boxing ground. Beneath the Ta Shuai was an official responsible for basic administration and another for the induction and training of new Boxer recruits. The leaders of the Fists of Righteous Harmony were not strong, able commanders of efficient local fighting forces but prominent Boxers who survived the early skirmishes. One such leader who rose from obscurity to fame was Li Wên-ch'ing, who took the name of an earlier Chinese revolutionary and was also known as Red Lantern Chu. The lantern in his title may refer to the symbolic 'Lamp of Ten Thousand Years' which features in Taoist magic.

Where the two cults overlapped in organization, they also overlapped in geographical location. The primary region of the Eight Trigrams was the area north of the Yellow River that encompassed the provinces of Shantung, Chihli and north-east Honan. In 1774, 1786 and then again in 1813 the Eight Trigrams rose up in rebellion against the authorities. In 1899 and 1900 the Fists of Righteous Harmony also began their rebellion in this region. A further point of connection between the two societies existed. Under the name of the Religion of the Pattern of Heaven, the Eight Trigrams' rebellion of 1813 was led by the aforementioned Li Wên-ch'ing and it ended in abject failure. Almost eighty-five years later, the Boxer Uprising was led by another Li Wên-ch'ing. Was this later society an independent group in some way related to the Eight Trigrams or a direct descendant? Indeed, was it the same organization after a simple name change?

The complex network of intermingling cults and sects in imperial China makes such assertions unworkable. There is no practical way to prove conclusively whether groups were related and contiguous or just adopting aliases designed to confound the authorities. The best that can be done is to compare customs, rituals and organization. In this respect, and with the supporting evidence of the same locality and replication of the leader's name, it seems likely that the Boxers who fought against Christians in northern China in 1900 were the same as the Eight Trigrams of well over a century before. Two Boxer leaders, Wu Hsiu and Ta Kuei, captured by government forces at different locations, both admitted belonging to the Eight Trigrams Society; some of the lower-ranking Boxers also declared themselves members of both.

The Chinese writer Lao Nai-hsuan, who lived through this chaotic period, regarded the Boxers as part of, or closely related to, the Eight Trigrams sect, the Red Fists and the previously mentioned White Lotus Society. His study, called *I Ho Chu'an Chiao Men Yüan Liu K'ao (The Historical Origins of the Fists of Righteous Harmony)*, appeared in print in 1899. The Fists of Righteous Harmony were specifically mentioned by name in the year 1727 within a government edict that accused them of instigating riotous behaviour among the uneducated masses. Also mentioned was their strange art of mystical boxing. Further government reports in 1818 make a similar assertion, and also chart the spread of the cult into Shantung and Chihli. Members were usually executed when the authorities discovered them, an indication that the cult harboured serious opposition to the Manchu establishment. Criminal activities typical of most Chinese secret societies also characterized the Fists of Righteous Harmony in the early years of the nineteenth century. Protection rackets, and an involvement in gambling dens and prostitution, caused government concern. What may have caused even more concern was the complicity of local officials with the society, and Lao Nai-hsuan asserted that members performed a kind of local police service, giving them the power to carry out their criminal activities almost unhindered. Such a situation could not continue unchallenged, and although the society was not eradicated, it was made significantly more law-abiding.

The crucial aspect to the survival of the cult was its practice of T'ai Chi Ch'uan, or Supreme Ultimate Boxing. Also known as Shên Ch'uan, or Spirit Boxing, the practice kept the society alive throughout the nineteenth century, when government pressure had forced it to adopt a lower criminal tone. This martial art followed a tradition that went back at least as far as the First Five Ancestors and the monks of the Shao Lin monastery. There is some incongruity here, with Buddhist monks practising a fighting art, but the Japanese Buddhists had long countenanced the existence of the *sohei*, or warrior-monk, dedicated to defending Buddhism by force of arms. In fact, H. A. Giles, writing before the First World War, argued that the Japanese ju-jitsu fighting art (ju-jitsu is the modern rendition of the original ju-jutsu) that found employ among the samurai and ninja on the battlefields of Japan was derived from the T'ai Chi Ch'uan of the Boxers, Eight Trigrams and Shao Lin monks. The Japanese imported several aspects of warfare from China – the basis for ninjutsu, we have seen, can be traced back to the works of China's greatest general, Sun Tzu. The T'ai Chi Ch'uan of the Boxers was first a martial art, but it survives up to the present day as a system of exercises designed to improve the body. In the nineteenth century it was also capable of endowing the practitioner with magical abilities. What these abilities might have been can be deduced from the alternative title for the art: Spirit Boxing.

One of the most remarkable claims of the Boxers was that they could render themselves impenetrable to bullets. This was achieved by the use of T'ai Chi Ch'uan during a special ceremony that was conducted on the boxing ground adjacent to most Boxer lodges. A specific incantation was taught to the potential warrior which might take just a day to learn correctly or it might take many months. He would then go to the boxing ground at an appointed time and begin his special exercises. While he did so, he recited the spell of invulnerability three times, and hoped by this method to summon a spirit to possess his mortal body. If all went well, the man would enter a fit-like state, frothing at the mouth, twitching and rolling his eyes, and by this witnesses would observe his possession, shouting out, 'God descends!' From that moment on, the cult member was thought to be invulnerable to sword blows and bullets. (A similar magical cult also appeared briefly on the plains of North America as Native Americans fought with primitive weapons against the US army.)

When it became only too obvious to the Boxers that members *were* being seriously injured or killed while supposedly invulnerable, the individual was deemed to be an infiltrator of the cult who had got what he deserved, or it was thought that the ritual had not been performed correctly. As the magic began to fail more times than it worked, the Boxers, like the Thugs of India, blamed the lax attitude of many cult members to the strict rules laid down by the society. Strangely, though, the Europeans who faced the Boxer warriors were often disconcerted to find them hard to kill. Sublieutenant M. E. Cochrane of HMS *Centurion* wrote:

They work themselves into an extreme state of hypnotism and certainly do not for the moment feel body wounds. We have all learned that they take a tremendous lot of killing and I myself put four man-stopping revolver bullets into one man before he dropped.

The Fists of Righteous Harmony were not the only Chinese secret society to boast indestructibility through the use of magic. During the White Lotus rebellions of the eighteenth century one cult leader was found dead on the battlefield with a small mirror worn as an amulet next to his heart. The man's intention was that the magical mirror should deflect the bullets, arrows and sword blows of the government troops. Contemporary with the Boxers was the Great Sword Society, which also practised martial arts and rituals of invulnerability. When the Boxer Uprising gathered pace, most of the Great Sword members joined either the Fists, the militia or the Chinese army in the fight against the foreigners.

Ch'ing edicts warned of the dangers of the Boxer sect on their re-emergence into the open in 1898, highlighting its involvement in gambling, riotous behaviour, extortion, swindling and the public demonstration of martial arts. New members were being recruited, initially as *yen fa*, which was the lowest rank of the cult, but a second level (*shang fa*) also existed for those Boxers who came 'under the spell'. Women were also welcomed as participating members of the sect, and they had their own mysterious society called the Red Lanterns, as well as the more mundane Cooking-Pot Lanterns, which performed the services of commissary. Again, the Taoist lantern symbol featured as a title of the cult. The distinctive feature of the Fists of Righteous Harmony was the colour red; socks, sashes, turbans and caps could be this colour, and often the battle-ready Boxer decorated his sword or spear with scarlet ribbons.

At first initiation into the Boxers was very strict. The name of a candidate was written on a piece of paper and the paper was then burnt. If the candidate's name could afterwards still be read among the ashes, then he became a Boxer. As the uprising gained strength, this rite was abandoned to allow as many young men as possible to be recruited. This may have been difficult (especially during the early years of the Boxers' existence), since the cult laid down strict rules of behaviour for its members, including total abstinence from sex, tea and meat. No moral laws were to be broken and the Boxer had to embrace austerity. It is doubtful if such measures were upheld during the height of the Boxer Uprising, since the veteran Boxers familiar with the ritual and history of the cult would have been outnumbered by newly initiated farmers with a grievance and an opportunity to display that grievance.

Ruling China at the end of the nineteenth century was the Manchu dynasty, dominated by the emperor's aunt Tsu Hai, the empress dowager. She had ruled the country from behind the scenes for forty years and was not about to hand it all over to 'barbarians'. Although she knew of their great power, the empress dowager cannot have fully understood the size and potentially overwhelming force of the European nations. China had already been humiliated in the Opium Wars and the ceding of Hong Kong to Britain, and was now being mapped out for commercial conquest by foreign powers, with separate 'spheres of interest' all clearly delineated. But Britain's colonial problems with the Boer farmers in South Africa, for instance, may have suggested to the Chinese that the great powers *could* be successfully threatened. On this basis, some vague strategy may have been concocted by the empress dowager and her staff at the beginning of 1900. It would seem that naked force was not considered an option in forcing foreign powers out of China; perhaps violent retribution was both expected and feared.

The Fists of Righteous Harmony Society had originally espoused the slogan, 'Overthrow the Ch'ing and destroy the foreigner!' By virtue of the pacts and treaties that both parties were signatory to, the foreign powers were as iniquitous in the eyes of the cult as the Manchus, and were part of the establishment. For some reason in

1899, the direction of the Boxers' anger changed; now the slogan was, 'Support the Ch'ing and destroy the foreigner!' This switch from an anti-dynastic to a pro-dynastic policy is impossible to explain. Perhaps the Boxers changed the cult's direction of their own accord, deciding to attack a target that they actually had a chance of defeating (remember that the Manchu dynasty had been securely in power for two and a half centuries). But the more intriguing possibility exists that the empress dowager was somehow able to reverse the cult's orientation, and turn an enemy into a friend. This was part of a sophisticated 'anti-foreigner' programme that she had initiated, and the support of the Boxers was to be if not the ultimate goal, then the result. Her reasons were obvious. The Boxers were not connected to the Chinese government in any way and were 'deniable assets' in modern terminology, yet they could rid the land of the Europeans' profiteering, religion and industrialization.

Boxer activity first came to official notice in the province of Shantung during May 1898. The provincial governor, Li Ping-heng, sent a report to Peking concerning the cult's influence in riots and other disturbances that were breaking out between the local Chinese population and the Christians (both foreigners and Chinese Christian converts). In spring the following year, this governor was replaced by Yu Hsien, who approved of the Boxers to such an extent that activity in Shantung actually began to increase. More Christians were beaten and murdered, homes were burnt and the symbols of foreign powers, such as railways, mines and telegraph poles, were attacked. German representatives put pressure on the emperor dowager to remove Yu Hsien, and she obliged them, only to grant him the governorship of Shansi province. At his new posting it seems he had little need of Boxers to pursue his aims, executing forty-five Christian missionaries and their families in a single day!

When the new governor of Shantung began a campaign to suppress the Boxers, he was warned against it by the empress, and in early 1900, as the uprising began to gain definite momentum, she gave her public support to the Boxer cult. When the attacks increased in tempo and ferocity, the European powers petitioned the empress to suppress the cult, but she answered that she was unable to stop the depredations of the Boxers. She was, like others, captivated by the thought of a mystical army preparing to drive out the 'foreign devils'. The sinister and supernatural cult would be infinitely more effective than her own army and, more than that, it would cost the government nothing.

With such august support, the Boxers became ever more daring in their harassment of Christians and Europeans. Outlying communities were attacked and settlements razed to the ground;

churches, missions and farms were dealt with in a similar fashion. No resistance was offered, for these targets were the undefended homes of women, children and men of God. Whites were killed or savagely treated, white Catholics especially so, since their colonial regime seems to have been all the more authoritarian. The local Chinese converts to Christianity were likewise murdered. Torture often preceded death at the hands of the ferocious cultists. Hatred of the Christians spurred on the cult to greater atrocities, but the hatred was neither irrational nor misplaced. All of the colonial powers had carved out pieces of the empire for their own use and towns were taken by force on occasion. On a more personal scale, local disasters were often blamed on the Christians, often because their monstrous churches, chapels and cathedrals violated all the laws of *feng-shui*, the rituals that surrounded the location and design of buildings so as not to offend the all-powerful spirits of earth, wind and water. What action the government army took against the anti-foreign marauders was half-hearted and ineffective, and within only a short space of time the Boxers had turned their attentions to the northern provinces and the imperial capital, Peking.

The Boxer Catastrophe

The greatest concentration of white settlers lived around the city of Peking, where they could interact more freely with the great population there as well as with the imperial government. Apart from traders and missionaries, Peking was also home to the diplomats of foreign powers. These government representatives lived together in a single area of the city where their legations were located. There were eleven such legations: British, American, Japanese, German, French, Austrian, Russian, Spanish, Belgian, Dutch and Italian. The ministers, their official staff and all of their families felt increasingly threatened by the Boxers, and this fear was communicated to the outside world. The fanatical cult that had originated in Shantung had spread slowly over the months from village to village until it had reached the province of Chihli, at the centre of which was Peking. By the last week of May in 1900, the Fists of Righteous Harmony had reached the many gates of the imperial city.

The empress dowager's foreign office, the Tsungli Yamen, did little to protect the legations from danger, promising armed guards but not providing them in adequate numbers. Rather than have to depend on unreliable Chinese protection, the foreign powers began building up a small garrison of soldiers, much to the displeasure of the anti-foreign faction of the Chinese government. In addition, the allied naval fleet that was anchored at the mouth of the Pei Ho River in the Gulf of Chihli decided, after some prevarication, to send reinforcements to Peking. This 2,000-strong expedition was commanded by Admiral Seymour, and it left on 10 June by train. The first leg of the journey took it to the port of Tientsin, and as it rolled further north it had to garrison stations and settlements so as not to have its line of retreat cut off. But at Tang T'su, on the way to the capital, this was exactly what happened. Boxers made several fanatical attacks on the trains and succeeded in isolating the expedition by destroying rails, bridges and water-tanks. During their attacks the Boxers cut the throats of their wounded, hoping to deny the allies any prisoners. What had set off as a relief force now found itself faced with the prospect of having to fight its way back to Tientsin through Boxer-infested country. It eventually retreated southwards along the Pei Ho River and reached Tientsin by 26 June.

During the desperate retreat of the expedition, the allied fleet at the Taku Bar at the mouth of the river moved to attack the imposing Taku forts which guarded access to the river and could prevent the fleet moving upstream to Tientsin. Nine ships of the fleet approached the forts and, when their ultimatum to the Taku forts to surrender had almost expired, came under fire. Landing parties were able to take the Taku forts by 17 June, but the empress had managed to learn of the fighting there and mistakenly assumed that the victory was a Chinese one. Flushed with false success, she declared the whole of China at war with the foreign powers and summoned the Chinese army to join with the Boxers. China's Grand Army of the North was ordered to enter the legation area of Peking and slaughter every European it found, but the tough defenders were able to put up stout resistance.

Peking was experiencing panic: there were lootings, fires and other disturbances, murders were carried out on the streets, and several times guards from the barricaded legation quarter entered the streets to rescue endangered Christians. On 20 June the German minister, Klemens Graf von Kettler, was murdered on the streets of the imperial capital by a Chinese army corporal. Soon after this disturbing event, a mob of Boxer fanatics attacked the Austrian legation, but they were driven back by machine-gun fire. Trenches were hastily dug and barricades were built; the legation was now under siege. The tiny allied force within the confines of the legation area was hard-pressed, and it used ingenuity and skill in defending the other Europeans. Peking was now totally isolated from the rest of China, the allied fleet, the Seymour expedition and the allied garrison at Tientsin, which itself had come under attack from Boxer cult members. Everywhere Europeans and Christians were being attacked by the cult and now also by the Chinese army.

The foreigners at the port of Tientsin had to defend a five-mile perimeter from the massed attacks of the fanatics and the soldiers.

All kinds of merchandise were employed as material for barricades, including expensive bales of silk! A courageous mining engineer called Herbert Hoover was able to help in the construction of Tientsin's defences; this man would later become president of the United States. Being so close to the fleet off Taku, those besieged at Tientsin were the first to be relieved by the timely arrival of an allied army on 23 July. Once Tientsin had been secured, more troops were assembled in the shattered city for a second attempt to reach Peking and the foreign legations, from where no word had come since the beginning of June. No one knew whether the besieged were dead or still struggling valiantly against the Boxers. When the multinational force had collected, it began the journey to Peking on 4 August. Following the line of the river and the railway inland, it encountered pockets of Chinese resistance, usually from rogue elements of the army, since the Boxer cult members were now becoming a rarity. Either they were low in numbers from their fanatical attacks on allied positions or they were abandoning their cause to fade back into the population. From the start of August, the Boxers no longer feature in the uprising as a credible military force, but only as lone murderers and criminals to be hunted down.

In Peking the different foreign legations had pulled together in this desperate struggle for survival, sharing food and water and combining their tiny troop numbers in an attempt to defend the legation area. The head of the British legation, Sir Claude MacDonald, led the defence of the 3,000 civilians with only 389 men, seventy-five volunteers and twenty officers. By far the greatest military asset the legations possessed was Colonel Goro Shiba. Both the colonel and his twenty-five Japanese soldiers fought valiantly against a far greater number of Boxers and Chinese troops. All knew that a single lapse in the defence would bring about the certain death of everyone within the legation area, and this tense drama was the source of much heroism, tinged as it was by the lack of any information whatsoever about the state of the allies elsewhere. Had they fled China? Was a relief column just outside of the city? Did anyone know they were still alive? The siege of Peking was to last an agonizing fifty-five days.

The empress dowager and her close advisers within the Forbidden City palace complex at the heart of Peking had grown alarmed by the reports of the allied victory at Tientsin and so the Tsungli Yamen re-established contact with the beleaguered legations. Their tone was now one of desperation, and the legations were repeatedly offered safe passage to Tientsin. Guardedly, they declined to attempt the hazardous journey, fearing a trap. Further half-hearted attempts were made to resolve the awful siege. Flags of truce appeared one day, to enable the Chinese to bury their dead, who littered the streets surrounding the legations. Sir Claude MacDonald even met with one of the Chinese chiefs during another truce, and further communications resulted in a cart of fresh fruit being delivered to the thirsty and hungry defenders. But these sporadic overtures often ended as quickly as they had begun, the empress dowager being swayed sometimes by the moderate influence of Prince Ch'ing and at other times by the hardline anti-foreigner Prince Tuan.

One can imagine an old woman who, having placed her faith in the sinister forces of a secret cult, was forced to listen in shocked amazement to reports of the Boxers being cut down by gunfire just as easily as mortal men. Her hopes of expelling the 'foreign devils' by supernatural means had been dashed and she was now tentatively looking for some way to resolve the dangerous situation. The international consequences of annihilating the legations were too horrible to contemplate, and with well-trained and well-armed troops on their way to lay siege to Peking, some kind of compromise was necessary. Her army had modern rifles, a stock of machine-guns (which remained in their packing crates) and the massed manpower to easily overcome the legation defences in just a few concerted assaults. But still the siege dragged on.

Following a large battle to the south of Peking with government troops on 5 and 6 August, the international relief force marched on the city. It had already lost considerable numbers of men as battle casualties and, since they were low on water and blistered by heat, the severe hardships of the march had taken their toll. The polyglot army, including Russians, Japanese, French, Americans and British (mainly Indian levies), prepared to attack Peking, relieve the legations (if anyone were left alive there) and depose the empress dowager in the Forbidden City. As the armies assembled for the agreed start of the attack, it soon became clear that the Russians had sent in an advance party that had not only prematurely moved against Peking but also cut diagonally across the battlefield to attack the American objective, one of the massive gates. Whether the Russians had sent just a scouting party or actually desired the glory of breaching Peking's walls first is not known, but the planned assault on the city was abandoned and all of the armies moved into battle immediately. This combined effort, with each army charged with seizing different objectives, managed to throw back the Chinese defenders, and on the afternoon of 14 August the legations were relieved.

Little more than a mile from the legations stood the imposing edifice of the P'ei Tang Cathedral, which had been under siege for as long as the legations but was somehow overlooked during that first frantic day of liberation . . . and on the second. On 16 August a small force was dispatched to take the cathedral. In the tiny compound were 3,000

Chinese converts in desperate circumstances. They had suffered the horrors of Boxer raids and highly destructive mines that had been exploded underneath the compound. The defenders knew little of what was happening elsewhere, and the brave scouts that the forty French and Italian marines dispatched never returned, their heads and carefully flayed skins being displayed on poles by the Boxers. After an abortive assault on the main gates of the Forbidden City by the American contingent, Pe'i Tang Cathedral was eventually secured.

Ironically, during the cathedral's reconstruction by Chinese labourers following the siege, Bishop Favier was certain that most of the coolies had been active participants in the Boxer cult and were responsible for many of the horrors that he had witnessed during the days of the siege. But the bishop held no grudge. The first the defenders had seen of Boxer cult members was on 15 June, when a party of Boxers, all clad in red, assembled near the Pe'i Tang's south entrance. With ritual movements and magical signs, they began to advance on the cathedral slowly and ominously, brandishing burning torches and swords. The cultists then knelt to pray and, as they did so, the defenders opened fire on them, forcing them to flee.

Nothing could stop the allied armies now from despoiling Peking and taking their revenge on the Chinese who had caused all of them so much suffering. On 28 August the Imperial Palace within the Forbidden City was taken and during the following months the Russians occupied parts of Manchuria in northern China, while the German troops, led by Field-Marshal Waldersee, conducted sadistic and brutal revenge attacks on the peasantry around the capital. The empress dowager herself had fled after the fall of Peking, but she negotiated a surrender from the regional city of Sian on 26 December 1900. There was little that she could do now to prevent the foreign powers from taking whatever they desired and imposing upon the Chinese people and its government any measure, however unfair. In September 1901 the Boxer Protocol was signed, guaranteeing to the foreign powers very substantial reparations for the folly of the empress dowager's political adventure.

Old and wily, and a survivor until the end, the empress dowager died in mysterious circumstances on 15 November 1908, the day after the death of Emperor Kuang-Hsu himself. These two deaths are still unexplained, and highly suspicious, but they paved the way for the accession to the Manchu throne of the last emperor, two-year-old P'u-i, who reigned as Emperor Hsuan-t'ung until the revolution of 1911 brought to an end over 2,000 years of imperial rule.

The Triads Have Their Day
As it had done during the Taiping Rebellion, the Triad Society failed to exploit the anarchy that the Boxer Uprising created. This was

partly due to the political passivity of many southern provincial governors who did not take steps either to support or to hinder the Boxer movement. Thus the Triads did not participate in the weakening of the Manchu dynasty that had been a thorn in their side for a quarter of a millennium. But someone was active in Chinese politics who would change for ever the fortunes of the Triad Society; his name was Dr Sun Yat-sen. He would enable the secret society not just to attempt another coup but also to replace the hated Manchu dynasty with something *other* than a replacement emperor. Sun Yat-sen would break the mould of Chinese revolutions, and while he worked and studied overseas, he was constantly planning the structure of what would become China's first democratic republic.

At the Alice Memorial Hospital in Hong Kong, where he took up a position in 1887, Sun Yat-sen joined the Triad Society and held a variety of offices in several different Triad groups. One of these was the Hong Kong-based Chung Wo Tong Society, which helped to raise funds for and co-ordinate the activities of the Chinese Republican Party. Following a failed coup in 1895, Sun Yat-sen was forced to flee overseas, and travelled extensively among the Chinese communities in Hawaii, Hong Kong, mainland America and Europe. Expatriates across the globe rallied to his cause, from students and dissidents to businessmen and local Chinese leaders. Many lent their support to the Republican Party, and their assistance gave the movement a solid base of support, something earlier secret-society revolts had never really enjoyed. The Triad Society was to become both his strongest ally and his main political weapon in the forthcoming revolution.

With Triad support, Sun Yat-sen staged a successful revolution in the Chinese province of Canton, and this revolt spread quickly throughout the rest of the country, until the Manchu grip on China had been lost. The avowed purpose of the Triad Society had been fulfilled at last, and with the establishment of the Chinese Republic, the Triad found itself, just as other societies had before it, without an obvious purpose or objective. Previous secret societies, like the Red Eyebrows, found that the regime they had helped to establish considered their continued existence embarrassing, if not downright threatening. The Triad Society, on the other hand, was actually incorporated *into* the new government, becoming a semi-legal and recognized entity. Although Dr Sun Yat-sen dropped out very early on as China's president, he continued to urge the Triad Society to join the government as a legitimate organization, but he was flatly refused on the grounds that if the new-born Republic should fail for any reason, then the Triad would still be well placed to carry on the underground fight. Undoubtedly the real reason the Triad Society wanted to retain its secrecy and anonymity was to secure its criminal activities. While the Taiping and Boxer Rebellions had come and gone, the Triad Society had played only a minor role in the upheavals, and organized crime had instead provided a more reliable (and lucrative) way of life.

The greatest concentration of Triad members was now overseas. Continual harassment from the Manchu dynasty had forced tens of thousands of Triad members out of China and into Chinatowns from Australia to London, San Francisco to Singapore. Wherever Chinese people settled, the Triads would gain a foothold and exploit it. These settlements were initially familiar with the Triad and other secret societies as beneficial and quite legitimate local organizations, but revenues were gained increasingly by illegal methods, until by the end of the nineteenth century the Triad Society was a wholly criminal body devoted to the pursuit of wealth and its own survival. With the money raised abroad, the society in the past had been able to finance the secret struggle at home against the Manchus. As profits increased, it abandoned any political purpose and instead put all of its efforts into making money.

High-ranking Triad members featured prominently in China's new government, and for someone to achieve any sort of office within the civil service, connections with the Triad Society were essential. From 1911, it became less of a secret society and more of a society with secrets; it had become a powerful lobby group with influence. The cult now also had a free rein to extort, bribe and bully its favourites, while eliminating its rivals. Bankers, businessmen and even army generals made use of their Triad connections to further their own aims. Politicians in the new Republic often paid for Triad aid with rewards of exclusive rights to criminal activities within a particular locality, which further strengthened the society's hold on the criminal underworld.

From 1911 to the start of the Second World War, the Triad Society reached its greatest heights in China, but with the rise of Communism here was a force that could be neither forcibly subdued nor bought off. For some time General Chiang Kai-shek employed the Triad Society as his own irregular terror force in his war against the Communists, who were led by a political revolutionary called Mao Tse-tung.

At the close of the Second World War the bloody and bitter feud between the Triad Society and the flourishing Communist Party came to an inevitable head, and Chiang Kai-shek mobilized as many Triads as possible in his fight to save China from another revolution. Thousands were brought swiftly into the Triad army, but as the tide turned and Mao Tse-tung's troops took more and more ground, members old and new attempted to escape overseas, mainly to Hong Kong, Taiwan, Malaya, Laos and the soon-to-be divided Vietnam.

With the complete Communist takeover of China in 1949, the Triads became again a persecuted sect, and disappeared completely from Chinese politics soon after that date. Mao's seizure of all the country's opium-growing land by the start of the 1960s had totally cut off Triad drug revenue, shutting down the society in China for good.

However, as modern law-enforcement agencies around the world are aware, the Triad Society (or more specifically Triad *societies*, since the organization has splintered and divided) is not dead, but flourishes wherever Chinese people have settled and established communities. The days of the Triads as revolutionary groups are done, but the revolutionary spirit still smoulders among Chinese people. This spirit was cruelly but cunningly harnessed by an ageing Mao when he found his power waning before younger and more radical members of the Politburo; the result was the violent and destructive spasm of the Cultural Revolution.

Today the conspiratorial spirit is still embodied in the pro-democracy movement, whose members fight for the overthrow of the present totalitarian regime. Many of those demonstrating in 1989 wore headbands daubed with defiant slogans – a tangible link with the earliest secret Chinese societies, the Red and Yellow Turbans. Like the persecuted leaders of past revolutions, the prime movers have either gone into hiding or fled to sympathetic communities overseas. It seems that although both the Chinese government and the secret societies are forever changing, the two forces are locked in a struggle without end.

Further Reading

Readers may find material on some of the cults included in this book fairly difficult to locate. Included here is a general list of sources that have proved useful in researching *Warrior Cults*, together with other works that seem highly suitable as a stepping stone for more in-depth study. From the outset the intention of *Warrior Cults* was to collect together widely dispersed accounts of ancient cults and present them in a single volume. Naturally the reading list that follows will reflect this diverse approach.

Adams, A., *Ninja: The Invisible Assassins*, Burbank: Ohara, 1973.

Baigent, M., and Richard Leigh, *The Temple and the Lodge*, London: Cape, 1989.

Baigent, M., Richard Leigh and Henry Lincoln, *The Holy Blood and the Holy Grail*, London: Cape, 1982.

Barber, M., *The Trial of the Templars*, Cambridge: Cambridge University Press, 1978.

Booth, M., *Triads: The Chinese Criminal Fraternity*, London: Grafton, 1990.

Burman, E., *The Assassins*, Wellingborough: Crucible, 1987.

Campbell, G. A., *The Knights Templar: Their Rise and Fall*, London: Duckworth, 1937.

Cartledge, P. A., *Sparta and Laconia*, London: Routledge, 1979.

Cavendish, R., *The Magical Arts*, London: Arkana, 1984.

Chesnaux, J., *China from the Opium Wars to the 1911 Revolution*, New York: Random House, 1976.

Fleming, P., *The Siege at Peking*, London: Rupert Hart-Davies, 1959.

Frazer, J. G., *The Golden Bough*, London: Macmillan, 1959.

Goodwin, J., *Mystery Religions in the Ancient World*, London: Thames & Hudson, 1982.

Graves, R., *The White Goddess*, London: Faber, 1948.

Graves, R., *The Greek Myths* (two volumes), Harmondsworth: Penguin, 1955.

Hanzang, T., *Sun Tzu: The Art of War*, Ware: Wordsworth, 1993.

Hatsumi, M., and Stephen K. Hayes, *Ninja Secrets from the Grandmaster*, Chicago: Contemporary Books, 1987.

Hayes, S. K., *The Ninja and Their Secret Fighting Art*, New York: Charles E. Tuttle, 1981.

Howard, M., *The Occult Conspiracy*, London: Rider & Co., 1989.

Howarth, S., *Knights Templar*, London: Collins, 1982.

Idries Shah, S., *The Secret Lore of Magic*, London: Muller, 1957.

Jones, P. V. (ed.), *The World of Athens*, Cambridge: Cambridge University Press, 1984.

Keown-Boyd, H., *The Fists of Righteous Harmony*, London: Leo Cooper, 1991.

King, J., *The Celtic Druids' Year*, London: Blandford, 1994.

Lethbridge, T. C., *Witches: Investigating an Ancient Religion*, London: Routledge, 1962.

Lewis, B., *The Assassins: A Radical Sect in Islam*, London: Weidenfeld & Nicolson, 1967.

MacCulloch, J. A., *The Religion of the Ancient Celts*, London: T. & T. Clark, 1910.

Murray, M. A., *The Witch-Cult in Western Europe*, Oxford: Clarendon Press, 1921.

Posner, G. L., *Warlords of Crime: Chinese Secret Societies – The New Mafia*, London: Macdonald & Co., 1978.

Powell, C. A., *Classical Sparta: Techniques Behind Her Success*, London: Routledge, 1989.

Purcell, V., *The Boxer Uprising*, Cambridge: Cambridge University Press, 1963.

Rhodes, H. T. F., *The Satanic Mass*, London: Arrow, 1964.

Roberts, J. M., *The Mythology of the Secret Societies*, London: Secker & Warburg, 1972.

Robertson, F., *Triangle of Death: The Inside Story of the Triads*, London: Routledge, 1977.

Runciman, S., *A History of the Crusades* (three volumes), London: Peregrine, 1965.

Scullard, H. H., *From the Gracchi to Nero*, London: Routledge, 1988.

Sinclair, A., *The Sword and the Grail*, New York: Crown, 1992.

Spence, L., *The Mysteries of Britain*, London: Studio Editions, 1993.

Stark, F., *The Valley of the Assassins, and Other Persian Travels*, London: Murray, 1936.

Trevor-Roper, H. R., *The European Witch-Craze of the 16th and 17th Centuries*, Harmondsworth: Penguin, 1969.

Turnbull, S., *Ninja: The Story of Japan's Secret Warrior Cult*, Poole: Firebird Books, 1991.

Warry, J., *Warfare in the Classical World*, London: Salamander, 1980.

Webster, G., *The British Celts and Their Gods Under Rome*, London: Batsford, 1986.

Weiss, A., and Tom Philbin, *Ninja: Clan of Death*, London: W. H. Allen, 1981.

Willey, P., *The Castles of the Assassins*, London: Harrap, 1963.

Wilson, I., *Evidence of the Shroud*, London: Michael O'Mara Books, 1986.

Index